W9-BJK-917

DUBLIN

|CONDENSED|

(604)
764
0659

 emma miller

LONELY PLANET PUBLICATIONS
Melbourne • Oakland • London • Paris

contents

Dublin Condensed
1st edition – March 2002

Published by
Lonely Planet Publications Pty Ltd
ABN 36 005 607 983
90 Maribyrnong St, Footscray, Vic 3011, Australia
www.lonelyplanet.com or AOL keyword: lp

Lonely Planet offices
Australia Locked Bag 1, Footscray, Vic 3011
☎ 613 8379 8000 fax 613 8379 8111
e talk2us@lonelyplanet.com.au
USA   150 Linden St, Oakland, CA 94607
☎ 510 893 8555 Toll Free: 800 275 8555
fax 510 893 8572
e info@lonelyplanet.com
UK   10a Spring Place, London NW5 3BH
☎ 020 7428 4800 fax 020 7428 4828
e go@lonelyplanet.co.uk
France 1 rue du Dahomey, 75011 Paris
☎ 01 55 25 33 00 fax 01 55 25 33 01
e bip@lonelyplanet.fr
www.lonelyplanet.fr

Design Maria Vallianos, James Hardy, Andrew
Weatherill Maps Charles Rawlings-Wray Editing Lou
Callan, Bridget Blair, Gabrielle Green, Darren O'Connell,
George Dunford Cover Maria Vallianos, Daniel New
Publishing Manager Diana Saad Thanks to Kevin
O'Callaghan, Julie Mason, Alison Lyall, GIS Unit

Photographs
Many of the images in this guide are available for
licensing from Lonely Planet Images.
e lpi@lonelyplanet.com.au;
www.lonelyplanetimages.com

Front cover photographs
Top The Ha'penny bridge over the River Liffey
(Fionn Davenport)
Bottom Crown Alley near Temple Bar
(Richard Cummins)

ISBN 1 74059 269 7

how to use this book

SYMBOLS

- ✉ address
- ☎ telephone number
- 🚊 nearest DART station
- 🚌 nearest bus route
- ◷ opening hours
- ⓘ tourist information
- ⑤ cost, entry charge
- e email/website address
- ♿ wheelchair access
- ⚹ child-friendly
- ✗ on-site or nearby eatery
- V good vegetarian selection

COLOUR-CODING

Each chapter has a different colour code which is reflected on the maps for quick reference (eg all Highlights are bright yellow on the maps).

MAPS

The fold-out maps inside front and back covers are numbered from 1 to 6. All sights and venues in the text have map references which indicate where to find them on the maps; eg (4, K3) means Map 4, grid reference K3. Although each item is not pin-pointed on the maps, the street address is always indicated.

PRICES

Price gradings (eg €5.50/3-5/15) usually indicate adult/concession/family entry charges to a venue. Concession prices can include child, pensioner and/or student discounts. Where euro prices were not available at the time of writing a direct conversion from the former punt was made, hence there may be price variations.

AUTHOR AUTHOR !

Emma Miller

Born and bred in the Melbourne suburbs, Emma always knew there was a bigger and weirder world out there, thanks to her immigrant fore-bears from London's East End and the villages of Eastern Europe. After studying journalism and working as a reporter on Melbourne's *Herald Sun*, Emma joined Lonely Planet, where she honed her skills as a travel editor and writer. Journeys across Asia and Europe followed, and it was while visiting friends in Dublin that Emma discovered the creamy rich goodness of a Guinness pulled from a real Dublin pub tap. Now a freelance writer and editor, Emma has worked on *The Guardian's* travel website and has contributed regularly to the travel section of *The Times* in London.

READER FEEDBACK

Things change – prices go up, schedules change, good places go bad and bad places improve or go bankrupt. So, if you find things better or worse, recently opened or long since closed, please tell us and help make the next edition even more accurate. Send all correspondence to the Lonely Planet office closest to you (listed on p. 2) or visit www.lonelyplanet.com/feedback/.

facts about dublin

Riding the crest of a remarkable economic boom, Dublin's landscape has changed immeasurably over the past decade. The Irish Republic's capital and its heart, Dublin now ranks among the top tourist destinations in Europe.

Intense urban renewal has rejuvenated the once shady streets of the city centre, and many Dubliners have embraced the glitzy new shops, restaurants, clubs and bars with unadulterated glee. For the first time in its independent history, the city is strutting its stuff with the unshakeable confidence of a boy-made-good.

But as the new rich snap up inner-city lofts and Armani suits, Dublin's poorer areas continue to suffer high crime rates, drug abuse and the increased costs of living. Gentrification is taking its toll elsewhere, with historic buildings and pubs that were once intrinsic to the city's character being beautified beyond recognition.

As the city morphs into its new self, Dubliners are grappling with what it means to be Irish, what it means to be prosperous and what it means to be living in a place that, for once, is drawing back emigrants and attracting newcomers.

What remains special about the city today – as it always has – is the spirit of the people, who ensure that despite whirlwind changes, Dublin remains one of Europe's most down-to-earth, friendly and accessible cities.

Dublin's buildings are reflected in the River Liffey, which divides the city into northside and southside.

HISTORY
Early Inhabitants
The Celts, Iron Age warrior tribes from Eastern Europe, arrived in Dublin Bay around 700BC, adopting Christianity in the 5th century AD after St Patrick's mission to Ireland. Dublin's modern Irish name, Baile Átha Claith, meaning 'Town of the Hurdle Ford', derives from an early Celtic settlement on the Liffey's northern bank.

Dublin became a major centre when Viking invaders established a trading port on the southern bank of the Liffey, near a *dubh linn*, or black pool, in the early 9th century. In 1014 the Vikings were defeated by the Irish high king, Brian Ború, but it was the Normans, fresh from victory in England in 1066, who gained lasting control in the 12th century.

Medieval Dublin
Despite sustained growth, a series of misfortunes befell Dublin during medieval times. In 1316 the Scots tried to invade, then in 1348 Black Death devastated the population. Silken Thomas Fitzgerald launched a failed revolt against Henry VIII's garrison in Dublin in 1534. Three years later Henry dissolved the monasteries. But the establishment of Trinity College by Elizabeth I in 1592 ensured the city a shining educational tradition.

Dublin's Pale
The phrase 'beyond the pale' originated when Anglo-Norman control over Ireland was restricted to the narrow eastern coastal strip surrounding Dublin, known as the Pale. Outside this area – or 'Beyond the Pale' – Ireland remained a wild place, and fierce Irish warriors launched regular raids on English forces from their strongholds in the Wicklow Mountains.

Protestant Ascendancy
In 1649, Oliver Cromwell seized Dublin and distributed Ireland's best land among his soldiers. Ireland backed Catholic James II in 1690's Battle of the Boyne, but when he was defeated by the Protestant William of Orange, Catholics found themselves excluded from parliament and their basic rights denied by new penal laws. Even Irish culture and music were banned.

In the 18th century, the city boomed. Protestant Huguenot weavers fleeing persecution in France established a successful cloth industry in the city. Trade flourished, and for a time Dublin was the fifth-largest city in Europe. But as the rich built fine Georgian mansions around stately squares, Dublin's largely Catholic poor lived in teeming slums.

Disaster & Decline
The 19th century saw famine, attempted invasions, rebellions and unrest between Irish patriots and Britain. In 1801, England abolished the separate Irish Parliament. Failed revolts were launched by Wolfe Tone in 1796, Lord Edward Fitzgerald in 1798 and Robert Emmet in 1803. During the

first half of the 19th century, Daniel O'Connell had some success in his non-violent campaign to recover basic rights for Catholics, but his political influence was limited.

While Dublin escaped the worst effects of the Potato Famine (1845-51), when the staple crop was blighted by disease, its streets and squares became flooded with starving rural refugees.

Memorial to the Famine's tragic victims

Independence Struggles & Civil War

In 1882, the British chief secretary, Lord Cavendish, was assassinated in Phoenix Park, and in 1905, Sinn Féin ('We Ourselves'), a republican political movement, was formed. But despite the ongoing struggles of a dedicated few, there was still little support for full Irish independence.

Another ill-planned revolt, the 1916 Easter Rising, laid waste to much of Dublin. But when the British executed the protagonists at Kilmainham Gaol – including rebel leader Patrick Pearse – they succeeded in turning a band of rebels into martyrs. The tide of public opinion was turning.

After the Anglo-Irish War (1919-1921) there were months of negotiation, and the Anglo-Irish Treaty was signed in 1921, creating the Irish Free State. It was not a full republic as the IRA had hoped for, but still subservient to Britain on many important issues. Nationalist rifts developed over the treaty, and fighting erupted between Free State supporters (led by Michael Collins) and anti-Treaty IRA forces (led by Sinn Féin president Eamon de Valera). Dublin's Four Courts building was shelled and O'Connell St became a battleground.

The Republic

Peace, of sorts, came in May 1923, when de Valera ordered the IRA to lay down its arms. In 1932, de Valera and his new party, Fianna Fáil, came to power, dropping all the treaty clauses they had fought against 10 years earlier. By WWII, Ireland – now called Éire - was a republic in all but name. Ireland left the British Commonwealth in 1949 and in 1955 became a member of the United Nations.

Universal free secondary education was introduced in the 1960s and the Republic joined the European Economic Community in 1973.

Dublin's economic climate changed dramatically in the 1990s, as interest rates tumbled, business burgeoned and foreign investment injected finance and reduced unemployment. But while the so-called Celtic Tiger economy is still much in evidence in the startling redevelopment of Dublin, not all sectors of society are benefiting. With the economic miracle impossible to maintain indefinitely, Dublin's true test will come in the next few years.

ORIENTATION

Greater Dublin sprawls around Dublin Bay, bounded to the north by the Howth hills and to the south by the Dalkey headland. The city is split – physically and psychologically – by the River Liffey, which courses through the centre. Traditionally, the areas north of the river have been poorer and more run-down, while the south boasts well-kept squares, expensive shops, restaurants and bars. But some Dubliners insist the real divide is east-west, with the wealthiest suburbs found nearest the bay, and the poorest suburbs to the west.

Dublin's main suburban train line, the Dublin Area Rapid Transit (DART), runs along the coast, linking the seaside suburbs with the city centre. The rest of Dublin must rely on private cars, gridlocked buses, the very limited Suburban Rail service, or its own pedal or foot power.

Major transport hubs for inter-city travel are Connolly train station and Busáras, (the main bus terminal) in the north-east, and Heuston station on the southside.

Two canals – the Grand Canal in the south and the Royal Canal in the north – form semi-circular arcs around the centre.

Bussing About

Dublin's extensive bus network radiates from the city centre to the vast suburbs surrounding it. While it is easy to travel from almost anywhere in outer Dublin into the city centre, very few buses travel across town, necessitating a trip into town and then out again.

Buses terminate and depart around the city; the greatest number of stops are on O'Connell St. On the southside, the termini are dotted around the north-west corner of Trinity College, just east of Temple Bar. Several buses also depart from Aston Quay in the south and Abbey St and Eden Quay in the north.

In this book, we list specific bus routes for a destination where it is feasible to do so. For central areas such as Temple Bar, around Grafton St and O'Connell St we've simply said that all cross-city buses will get you there, meaning any city-centre bus that crosses the Liffey will pass within a few minutes' walk of your target.

Martin Moos

ENVIRONMENT

Though Dublin does not suffer the severe air pollution that chokes some other European cities, it has its share of environmental concerns. Worst among them is traffic congestion, which blights the city centre and particularly the Liffey quays. The Liffey itself is also dirty, largely due to irresponsible dumping upstream. The lack of restrictions on motor exhaust fumes adds to the problem.

Non-smokers might find Dublin's lax smoking laws difficult to bear. Most pubs are incredibly smoky, and few restaurants make adequate provisions for diners who would rather eat in a non-smoking area.

On the positive side, the city is blessed with many parks, gardens and squares. While recycling is slowly taking off, it is not yet part of the collective consciousness. Littering can be a problem, with cigarette butts and fast food wrappers too often making their way onto footpaths.

GOVERNMENT & POLITICS

The Republic of Ireland has a parliamentary system of government. Parliament's lower house, or house of representatives (Dáil Éireann, often shortened to Dáil), has 166 members elected by public ballot. Members of the upper house (Seanad) are nominated by the prime minister *(taoiseach)* or elected by university graduates and councillors. Both houses sit in Leinster House on Kildare St.

The president is the constitutional head of state, but has little real power.

The main political parties are Fianna Fáil, led by current prime minister Bertie Ahern, Fine Gael and the Labour Party. Of the remaining minor parties, Sinn Féin has the most support, garnering around 6% of the vote.

At local level, Dublin is governed by three elected bodies: Dublin Corporation supervises the city; a county council looks after Dublin County; and Dun Laoghaire & Rathdown Corporation administers the port town.

The current government is a coalition of Fianna Fáil and the Progressive Democrats. It seems unlikely they will be shifted from power in the next general election, scheduled to be held some time before June 2002.

ECONOMY

Ireland – and Dublin in particular – is in the throes (some say death throes) of its greatest period of economic success since independence. Signs of the so-called Celtic Tiger economy are everywhere, from the cranes dotting the skyline to the new Mercedes purring around town. The renaissance has prompted an explosion in tourism and a reversal of the age-old trend of emigration.

From 1993 to 1997 Ireland's economy grew by a whopping 40%, leading to record-low unemployment, higher standards of living and lower interest rates. But while growth continues today, it has levelled off significantly, and economists have expressed concern about rising inflation, interest rates and spiralling house prices.

Ireland's reliance on new technology and foreign investment is seen by some as proof of the economy's frailty. Any move by the EU to introduce a Europe-wide corporation tax could see foreign companies moving elsewhere. Wage disputes in the public sector have also been cause for concern.

Did You Know?

- Dublin city traffic snarls are worse than those in New York, Tokyo and London. A recent study found it takes a car an average of 57 minutes to travel 5km
- Property prices have increased by more than 150% since 1990
- The percentage of people living below the poverty line in Dublin rose by 7% between 1991 and 1998
- In 1992 just 80 people applied for asylum in Ireland, now the figure is 8,000 a month
- The average Dubliner earns £19,000 a year, giving £12 to charity and £162 in tips
- Around 9800 pints of beer are drunk each hour by Dubliners from Friday night to Monday morning

Doug McKinlay

ARTS

Literature

With their unique perspective on life, and their use of phrasing and expressions translated from Gaelic, Irish writers have made a phenomenal impact on English-language writing.

Jonathan Swift (1667-1745), the master satirist and author of *Gulliver's Travels*, was the greatest writer of the early Georgian period, closely followed by Oliver Goldsmith (1728-74, *The Vicar of Wakefield*) and poet Thomas Moore (1779-1852). Oscar Wilde (1854-1900), renowned for his legendary wit, was educated at Trinity College but soon moved to London. The poet, playwright and statesman William Butler Yeats (1865-1939) won the Nobel Prize for literature in 1938 – an honour shared by fellow Dubliners George Bernard Shaw in 1925 and Samuel Beckett in 1969. Bram Stoker (1847-1912), the creator of Dracula, was also a product of Dublin.

James Joyce is the city's most famous literary son. References to his great Dublin novel *Ulysses* can be found all over the city and the book is the inspiration for annual Bloomsday celebrations (see p. 11).

In more recent times Dublin schoolteacher Roddy Doyle *(The Commitments)* has had much success, including winning the Booker Prize in 1993 for *Paddy Clarke, Ha Ha Ha*. John Banville also bagged the Booker for *Book of Evidence* in 1989. Brendan Behan, Patrick McCabe, Flann O'Brien, Liam O'Flaherty and Sean O'Faolain are other Irish writers of note, while young scribblers to look out for include Pat Boran, Philip McCann, Emer Martin and Emma Donoghue.

Music

From traditional music through to rock and pop, tiny Ireland has been disproportionately represented on the world stage. Perhaps the best known traditional Gaelic music group is the Chieftains. Other notables include Scullion, the Wolfe Tones and the Fureys. Though more a folk band than a traditional outfit, the Dubliners have been around for more than 30 years.

The godfather of Irish singer-songwriters is Christy Moore, who is hugely popular for his folk-style music. Daniel O'Donnell is a favourite with the over-40s. Female singers like Mary and Frances Black, Mary Coughlan and Eleanor McEvoy are now being challenged by new stars including Juliet Turner, Naimee Coleman and Gemma Hayes.

Belfast-born Van Morrison put Ireland on the world rock map in the 1960s, followed by the likes of Thin Lizzy and the Boomtown Rats in the 1970s and '80s. The Cranberries, from Limerick, and the Corrs, from Dundalk, emerged more recently, as did the controversial Sinéad O'Connor. But none has achieved the phenomenal success of U2, the megastar Dublin band that has been churning out hits for more than 20 years.

In the 'treacle-pop' category, Boyzone had thousands of 12-year-olds in tears when they split in 2000, but Westlife quickly filled the void with their big smiles and dance routines.

Architecture

With Viking, Norman and medieval Dublin barely visible today, the neoclassical style of the Georgian era remains Dublin's most dominant architectural feature. During this period roads were widened, gardens and elegant squares laid out, the Liffey banked with concrete quays and a number of fine residences and public buildings constructed.

Many foreigners were drawn to the city during the Georgian period. The German Richard Cassels designed Powerscourt Townhouse (p. 62), Russborough House (p. 57), Newman House (p. 37) and Leinster House (p. 36). Swedish-born Sir William Chambers designed Trinity's Examination Hall and Chapel (2, B2), Charlemont House (now Hugh Lane Gallery, p. 20) and Casino at Marino (p. 51). Englishman James Gandon's two riverside masterpieces, Custom House (p. 36) and the Four Courts (p. 36), remain two of Dublin's most enduring landmarks.

Buildings of note from the 20th century include: Busáras (4, F9), the International Modernist bus station designed by Michael Scott in the 1940s; Paul Koralek's 1967 Berkeley Library (2, C3) at Trinity; and Sam Stephenson's controversial Dublin Corporation buildings (4, J3) on Wood Quay. The 1990s redevelopment of Temple Bar (p. 31) signalled the start of a major architectural renewal that continues to this day.

Bloomsday

On 16 June each year, Joyce-lovers take to the streets in a re-enactment of Leopold Bloom's journey around Dublin in *Ulysses*. Various readings and dramatisations from Joyce's works take place around the city as folk in period costume, circa 1904, chow down on Gorgonzola cheese and glasses of Burgundy.

Points of activity include the James Joyce Museum at Sandycove (p. 22) where *Ulysses* begins, Sweny's Chemist Shop (2, E6), the Oval (p. 90) and Davy Byrne's (6, C7) pubs and the National Library (4, L8).

Wall mural, James Joyce Cultural Centre

Theatre

Dublin's theatrical history is almost as long as its literary one. The city's first theatre was founded in Werburgh St in 1637, though it was closed by the Puritans four years later. Today the city's most famous playhouse, and Ireland's National Theatre, is the Abbey (p. 98), established in 1904 by WB Yeats and Lady Gregory.

After years in the doldrums following the successes of famous playwrights Wilde, Yeats, Shaw and Beckett, Irish theatre is undergoing something of a renaissance. A number of new companies are staging thought-provoking, contemporary plays as well as new spins on old classics. Look out for the likes of Rough Magic, Pig's Back and Cornmarket, as well as playwrights Conor McPherson, Martin McDonagh and Mark O'Rowe.

SOCIETY & CULTURE

More than 50% of Dubliners are under 28 and almost a quarter are under 15 – a fact which goes a long way to explaining the city's vibrant, liberal outlook. While social stratification exists, years of British rule fostered a healthy contempt for snobbery and it is generally money, rather than breeding, which impresses here.

The population of Dublin is 953,000 but about 1.2 million live within commuting distance of the centre. Although the city is predominantly Roman Catholic, the substantial Protestant minority has been boosted in recent years by immigrants from Africa and Eastern Europe. But the rapid growth in immigration has also exposed the raw nerves of racism in the city, with attacks and abuse all too common.

Divorce was narrowly accepted in a referendum in 1995, making Ireland the last country in Europe to legalise it. While abortion remains illegal, women now have the right to unbiased information and to travel abroad for terminations. A ban on sex shops, the sale of condoms and the contraceptive pill has also recently been lifted.

The Name Game

Visitors with Irish ancestry can try tracing their family tree at the National Library's **Genealogical Office** (Kildare St; 4, L8; ☎ 603 0200; Mon-Fri 10am-4.45pm, Sat 10am-12.30pm). While the office won't do the work for you, it points you in the right direction, providing free information and expert advice. Make the search easier by collecting as much information as possible from relatives and family records before you leave home.

Descendants of the Irish diaspora flock back 'home' to Dublin.

Dos & Don'ts

Dublin is relaxed and easy-going with few rigid rules and regulations. Probably the most important social tips for the visitor are those that apply to Irish pub culture.

The rounds system is integral to pub life, and you'll quickly lose favour if you disrupt the balance. Opting out of rounds or only buying drinks for those who've bought ones for you are both no-nos. Getting a drink for yourself and no-one else is even worse. The next round is always due when the first person of the group has finished their drink – so try to keep up.

In conversation, be aware that there is a marked difference between the views of the older and the younger generations. Young Dubliners are often extremely liberal – and sometimes radical – in their opinions, but older people might be reluctant to talk about issues such as sex, contraception, divorce or abortion. Religion and politics can also be volatile subjects, so tread carefully.

highlights

Dublin's main sights might not visually rival those of flashier European capitals but they offer rich historical and literary tales for those who care to listen. Politics, war and oppression are common themes, but gentler tales of struggling writers, civic-minded collectors and, of course, a mighty stout empire, can also be had. Most of the major sights are south of the Liffey and within easy walking distance of each other.

During summer, queues can be horrendous, especially at popular attractions like Trinity College and Kilmainham Gaol. Arrive as early as possible to avoid the crush; if not, be prepared to wait. Most fee-paying sights offer discounts to students, the elderly, children and families. You can also get discounts by block-buying tickets for Dublin Tourism-administered sights. The **Heritage Card** from Dúchas (☎ 647 2453; **e** www.heritageireland.ie; €19/7.60-12.70/45), is only worthwhile if you're travelling around the rest of the country.

The hop-on-hop-off **Museumlink bus** (€2.50/1.30) runs between the National Museum, the Natural History Museum and Collins Barracks. Tickets are valid all day.

Stopping Over?

One Day Start early at Trinity College, catch the buskers along Grafton St, then take a stroll in St Stephen's Green. See the National Museum and National Gallery then catch a bus, or walk, through the Liberties to the Guinness Storehouse. Eat dinner at L'Ecrivain then retire to the Stag's Head for drinks.

Two Days Start at the Chester Beatty Library in Dublin Castle then join one of the Castle tours. Next see Christ Church and/or St Patrick's Cathedrals and Marsh's Library, before a spot of afternoon shopping around Grafton St and Temple Bar. Have dinner at the Trocadero before seeing a play, some live music or comedy. Take your nightcap at the Palace Bar.

Three Days Explore the northside with a walk up O'Connell St and along the Liffey quays. If the weather's nice, picnic in Phoenix Park or take the DART to the Joyce Museum at Sandycove. If not, head west to the Irish Museum of Modern Art and Kilmainham Gaol. Unwind with afternoon tea at the Shelbourne, then dine at the Mermaid Cafe.

Dublin Lowlights
Some things we could do without:

- Poor public transport
- Rampant bicycle thieves
- Dog owners who don't clean up after their pets
- Crass, soulless 'theme' bars
- Early-closing pubs and clubs
- The rain, the rain, the rain

Richard Cummins

Dublin's rivers of traffic

CHESTER BEATTY LIBRARY (6, B2)

The astounding collection of New York mining magnate Sir Alfred Chester Beatty (1875-1968) is the basis for one of Dublin's best, if less-visited, museums. An avid traveller and collector from an early age, Beatty amassed more than 20,000 manuscripts, rare books, miniature paintings, clay tablets, costumes and other objets d'art. Just one per cent of the collection is on display at any one time and exhibits are rotated every six months. Beatty, who bequeathed the collection to the state on his death, became Ireland's first honorary citizen in 1957.

INFORMATION

- ✉ Dublin Castle, Ship St
- ☎ 407 0750
- 🚌 50, 51b, 54a, 56a, 77, 77a, 78a, 123
- ⏱ Mon-Fri 10am-5pm, Sat 11am-5pm, Sun 1-5pm; Oct-Apr closed Mon
- ⑤ free
- ⓘ free tours Wed 1pm, Sun 3 & 4pm; book ahead for monthly kids' workshops
- e www.cbl.ie
- ♿ good
- ✗ Silk Road Café

Emma Miller

Relaxing with a book in the Celtic garden of the Chester Beatty Library

Spread across two floors as an annexe to Dublin Castle's old clock tower, the museum is testament to Beatty's exquisite taste and his eye for beauty in its most intricate, delicate form. The first-floor gallery begins with memorabilia from Beatty's life, before embarking on an exploration of the art of Mughal India, Persia, the Ottoman Empire, Japan and China. Audiovisual displays explain the process of bookbinding, paper and print making along the way.

The second floor is devoted to major world religions – Judaism, Islam, Christianity, Hinduism and Buddhism. If you can tear yourself away from the cool cultural-pastiche video at the entrance, head for the collection of Korans from the 9th to the 19th centuries, considered to be among the best illuminated Islamic texts. You'll also find ancient Egyptian papyrus texts (including love poems from 1100BC), early Christian texts dating from the 3rd century, exquisite scrolls and artwork from Burma, Indonesia and Tibet. From the tranquil rooftop garden on the third floor, try to spot the slithering Celtic snakes cut into the grass of the garden below.

DON'T MISS
- Japanese samurai armour • Qing dynasty Dragon Robe
- illuminated Persian Korans • 17th-century snuff bottles
- landscaped roof garden

CHRIST CHURCH CATHEDRAL   ·   (4, K3)

Dublin's most imposing church, Christ Church lies within the city's original Norse settlement and the old heart of medieval Dublin. Built on the site of an existing wooden Viking church, the stone cathedral was commissioned in 1172 by the Anglo-Norman conqueror of Dublin, Richard de Clare ('Strongbow') and Archbishop Laurence O'Toole.

Although the north wall, transepts and western part of the choir remain from the original, the cathedral was restored several times over the centuries. Much of the building now dates from 1871-78, when the cathedral was rescued from ruin by a £230,000 donation (£2.3 million today) from whiskey distiller Henry Roe. The result is that Christ Church's architectural styles range from Romanesque to 19th-century English Gothic.

From its inception Christ Church was the State Church of Ireland. When Henry VIII dissolved the monasteries in 1537, the Augustinian priory who managed the church were replaced with a new Anglican clergy who remain to this day.

Highlights include the **Baroque tomb** of the 19th Earl of Kildare, the **Chapel of St Laud**, containing the embalmed heart of Archbishop O'Toole, and the **Lady Chapel**.

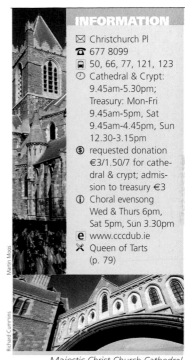

INFORMATION

- ✉ Christchurch Pl
- ☎ 677 8099
- 🚌 50, 66, 77, 121, 123
- 🕐 Cathedral & Crypt: 9.45am-5.30pm; Treasury: Mon-Fri 9.45am-5pm, Sat 9.45am-4.45pm, Sun 12.30-3.15pm
- 💲 requested donation €3/1.50/7 for cathedral & crypt; admission to treasury €3
- ⓘ Choral evensong Wed & Thurs 6pm, Sat 5pm, Sun 3.30pm
- 🖥 www.cccdub.ie
- 🍴 Queen of Tarts (p. 79)

Martin Moos

Richard Cummins

Majestic Christ Church Cathedral

Strongbow

Although Strongbow is buried in the cathedral, the **Strongbow tomb** in the southern aisle is a 14th-century replacement of the original, which was destroyed when part of the building collapsed in 1562. The half-figure beside the tomb is thought to be either part of his original effigy or a representation of Strongbow's son who was brutally cut in two by his father for displaying cowardice in battle.

The arched **crypt** dates from the original Viking church and is the oldest structure in Dublin. It houses curiosities such as a mummified cat and rat, and the stocks once used by church authorities to punish wrongdoers. The **Treasury exhibit** in the crypt includes rare coins, the Stuart coat of arms and gold given to the church by William of Orange after the Battle of the Boyne. It also shows how the Vikings built the original cathedral.

COLLINS BARRACKS   (3, E7)

Once the home of British forces in Dublin, Collins Barracks now houses the **Decorative Arts & History collection** of the National Museum of Ireland. The imposing greystone building on the Liffey's northern banks was built by Thomas Burgh in 1704 on the orders of Queen Anne.

INFORMATION

✉ Benurb St
☎ 677 7444
🚌 25, 25a, 66, 67, 90 or Museumlink shuttle bus
🕐 Tues-Sat 10am-5pm, Sun 2-5pm
$ free
ⓘ special events and educational work-shops for children held regularly
e www.museum.ie
♿ excellent
✗ Cooke's Cafe

Inside, the museum houses arte-facts ranging from silver, ceramics and glassware, to weaponry, furni-ture and folk-life displays. While the exhibition is a little haphazard, many individual pieces are very interesting. Some of the best are gathered in the **Curator's Choice Exhibition**, which brings together such disparate objects as a 2000-year-old Japanese ceremonial bell and the gauntlets worn by William of Orange at the Battle of the Boyne in 1690. The ornate 17th-century **Fleetwood Cabinet** was a gift from Oliver Cromwell to his daughter, Bridget, on her marriage to General Fleetwood in 1652.

The two-storey **Out of Storage gallery** displays items which were locked away in storerooms until Collins Barracks opened in 1997. Touch-screen computers provide information on the items here.

On the first floor is the museum's **Irish silver collection**, the second floor houses **Irish period furniture**, while the third floor has simple and sturdy **Irish country furniture**. A recent acquisition, **The Way We Wore exhibit** displays Irish clothing and jewellery from the past 250 years. The brooches, rings and necklaces – some made with human hair, horsehair, jet, shell or glass – highlight the symbolism jewellery had in bestowing mes-sages of mourning, love and learning.

Collins Barracks, a branch of the National Museum of Ireland

DON'T MISS
- Fonthill vase • Lord Chancellor's mace • the Domville Doll's House
- Eugene Rousseau's carp vase • the South Block's giant clock

DUBLIN CASTLE   (6, B2)

The stronghold of British power in Ireland for 700 years, Dublin Castle is principally an 18th-century creation built on Norman and Viking foundations. Of the 13th-century Anglo-Norman fortress built on the site, only the Record Tower remains. The most fascinating part of the castle is underground – recent flooding in the castle prompted excavations of the former Powder Tower, which revealed a chunk of the old city walls and moat.

Once the official residence of the British Viceroys in Ireland and now used by the Irish Government, access is by tour only. Tours include **drawing rooms** with their beautiful plasterwork, once used as bedrooms by visitors to the castle. The castle **gardens** end in a high wall said to have been built for Queen Victoria's visit to block the sight of the Stephen St slums.

The **Apollo Room**, or Music Room, has an ornate ceiling taken from a house on Merrion Row, while the **State Drawing Room** was restored with period furniture and paintings after a fire in 1941. The **Throne Room**'s large gold

INFORMATION

- ✉ Cork Hill, Dame St
- ☎ 677 7129
- 🚌 50, 54, 56a, 77, 77a
- 🕐 Mon-Fri 10am-5pm, Sat-Sun & holidays 2-5pm
- 💲 €4/1.50-3
- ⓘ tours run every 20-30 mins. State Apartments can be closed at short notice; call ahead to check
- ♿ partial access
- 🍴 on-site cafe

Richard Cummins

Doug McKinlay

Seat of power: the Throne Room

throne is said to have been presented to the castle by William of Orange on winning the Battle of the Boyne. The room's centrepiece, the decorative **Act of Union chandelier**, weighs more than a tonne.

The 25m-long **St Patrick's Hall** is where Irish presidents are inaugurated and is also used for state receptions. In the Lower Yard is the **Church of the Holy Trinity**, built in Gothic style by Francis Johnston from 1807-14. The interior is wildly exuberant, while the exterior is decorated with the carved heads of Irish notables and saints.

Justice for all?

The **Figure of Justice** that faces the castle's Upper Yard from the Cork Hill entrance has a controversial history. The statue was seen as a snub by many Dubliners, who felt Justice was symbolically turning her back on the city. If that wasn't enough, when it rained the scales would fill with water and tilt over, rather than remaining perfectly balanced. Eventually a hole was drilled in the bottom of each pan, letting the water drain out and restoring balance, of sorts.

GLASNEVIN (3, A9)

The northern suburb of Glasnevin is worth a visit for two historic sights, adjoining each other just south of the River Tolka.

INFORMATION

- ✉ Glasnevin; enter Botanic Gardens from Botanic Ave, Prospect Cemetery from Finglas Rd
- ☎ Gardens: 837 4388; Cemetery 830 1133
- 🚌 Gardens: 13, 19, 134; Cemetery: 40, 40a
- ⌚ Gardens: Apr-Oct Mon-Sat 9am-6pm, Sun 11am-6pm; Nov-Mar Mon-Sat 10am-4.30pm, Sun 11am-4.30pm. Cemetery: Mon-Sat 8am-4.30pm, Sun 9am-4.30pm
- 💲 both free
- ℹ free garden tours Sun 2.30pm from Visitor Centre (☎ 857 0909); free cemetery tours (☎ 830 1133) Wed & Fri 2.30pm
- 🖥 www.heritageireland .ie; www.glas nevin-cemetery.ie
- ♿ Gardens: excellent; Cemetery: good
- 🍴 Gardens on-site cafe

Emma Miller

The lush and lovely **National Botanic Gardens** have been an important centre of horticultural and botanical study for more than 200 years. The Gardens' pioneering work includes the first successful attempt to raise orchids from seed (1844) and the introduction of pampas grass and lilies to the lawns of Europe.

The highlight of the 19.5-hectare gardens is a series of spectacular curvilinear **glasshouses** built from 1843 to 1869 by Richard Turner. Within these Victorian masterpieces are ferns, cacti, succulents, orchids, palms and other exotic foreign plants, from which new varieties were bred. In summer, don't miss the **Giant Amazon Water Lily** in the Victoria House. Food lovers should seek out the prolific vegetable gardens.

South of the gardens is **Prospect Cemetery**, the largest cemetery in Ireland. It was established in 1832 for Roman Catholics, who faced opposition from Protestant cemeteries. Many of the monuments are overtly patriotic, adorned with high crosses, harps, shamrocks and other Irish national symbols.

The oldest section, near Prospect Square, is the most interesting. The watchtowers built into the walls were once used to watch for body snatchers working for the city's 19th-century surgeons. Part of *Ulysses* is set in the cemetery and there are several Joycean clues to follow among the tombstones.

Famous Graves

Prospect Cemetery is the final resting place of many of Ireland's most famous citizens: politicians Charles Stewart Parnell, Michael Collins, Eamon de Valera, Daniel O'Connell and Countess Markievicz, as well as the poet Gerard Manley Hopkins and writer Brendan Behan. The most imposing memorial is that of Cardinal McCabe (1837-1921), archbishop of Dublin and primate of Ireland.

GUINNESS STOREHOUSE (3, F7)

Like Disneyland for beer lovers, the Guinness Storehouse is an all-singing, all-dancing extravaganza combining sophisticated exhibits with more than a pintful of marketing hype.

Housed in an old grain store-house opposite the original, still-operating, but off-limits **St James's Gate Brewery**, the Storehouse is an impressive enterprise that milks the worldwide fame of Guinness for all it's worth. More multimedia installation than provincial beer museum, the Storehouse uses high-tech audiovisual displays to tell the story of Guinness.

Founded by Arthur Guinness in 1759, St James's Gate brews an astounding 4.5 million hectolitres of Guinness a year (one hectolitre = 100 litres). Almost 50% of all beer consumed in Ireland – four million

INFORMATION

- ⊠ St James's Gate
- ☎ 408 4800
- 🚌 51b & 78a from Aston Quay; 123 from O'Connell St
- ⏰ Apr-Sept 9.30am-7pm; Oct-Mar 9.30am-5pm
- 💲 €12.00/2.50-8/26; under-6s free
- ⓘ Infoline ☎ 453 8364
- e www.guinnessstore house.com
- ♿ excellent
- ✗ Brewery Bar

Oliver Strewe

pints a day – is produced here, and the company exports to 150 countries.

Exhibits in the £30 million centre are spread over five storeys. On the ground floor a copy of **Arthur Guinness' original lease** – £45 a year for 9000 years – lies embedded in the floor. From there you enter 'the Experience' and see how water, barley, hops and yeast combine to create the world-famous stout.

Cooperage is one of the simplest and most informative exhibits, showing how highly skilled coopers once cut, steamed and hammered each and every cask into shape. In **Advertising** you can replay your favourite Guinness ads, see classic posters and paraphernalia, then pop downstairs to the superstore and buy yourself a monogrammed tie.

Like the creamy head on a pint of Guinness, the circular, rooftop **Gravity Bar** is the best part. With a free glass of the black stuff in hand, a comfy chair to lounge in and the city spread out before you, it's what everyone really comes here for.

Working for Yer Man

In the 1930s when there were more than 5000 people working at St James's Gate, Guinness was the largest employer in the city. For nearly two centuries it was also one of the best places to work, paying 20% more than the minimum wage and offering subsidised housing, health benefits, pension plans, longer holidays and life insurance. Today, automation has reduced the workforce to around 600.

Enjoying a Guinness at the Gravity Bar.

HUGH LANE GALLERY   (4, D5)

The Hugh Lane Gallery's fine collection bridges the gap between the National Gallery's old masters and the cutting-edge works on show at the Irish Museum of Modern Art.

INFORMATION

- ✉ Charlemont House, Parnell Sq N
- ☎ 874 1903
- 🚌 3, 10, 11, 13, 16, 19
- 🚉 Connolly
- 🕐 Tues-Thurs 9.30am-6pm, Fri-Sat 9.30am-5pm, Sun 11am-5pm
- 💲 gallery free; Francis Bacon Studio €7.60/2.55-3.80, under-12s free
- ℹ holiday workshops for 6-10 year olds
- e www.hughlane.ie
- ♿ partial access
- ✗ on-site cafe

Martin Moos

Doug McKinlay

Housed in a spacious 18th-century townhouse designed by Sir William Chambers, the gallery displays mainly French Impressionist and early 20th-century Irish artists. Sculptures by Rodin and Degas, and paintings by Corot, Courbet, Manet and Monet sit alongside the works of Jack B Yeats, William Leech and Nathaniel Hone.

The gallery's newest exhibit, the **Francis Bacon Studio**, was painstakingly moved, in all its shambolic mess, from 7 Reece Mews, South Kensington, London, where the Dublin-born artist lived for 31 years. Bacon, who famously hated Ireland, would no doubt have found it amusing that a team of conservators spent years cataloguing scraps of newspaper, horse whips, old socks, dirty rags, dried-up paint and mouse droppings, to reverently reassemble it all in Dublin.

The gallery was founded in 1908 by wealthy art dealer Sir Hugh Lane. When Sir Hugh died on the *Lusitania* after it was torpedoed by a German U-boat in 1915, a bitter row erupted between the National Gallery in London and the Hugh Lane Gallery over

Hugh Lane: knocking between the classical and the modern

the jewels of his collection. Today, after years of wrangling, half the works are displayed in Dublin and half in London, on a rotating basis.

One of the best times to visit the gallery is on a Sunday when **classical concerts** are held in the sculpture hall at noon. In summer, concerts are usually on every week, while in winter there's about one a month. Call for details.

DON'T MISS
- Manet's *Eva Gonzales* • Pissarro's *Printemps* • Renoir's *Les Parapluies* • Morisot's *Jour d'Été* • Burne-Jones' *The Sleeping Princess*

IRISH MUSEUM OF MODERN ART

The country's foremost gallery for contemporary art, the Irish Modern Art (IMMA) is spectacularly housed in the form **Hospital Kilmainham**, once home to veteran soldiers.

Built between 1680 and 1684, the site languished for much of the century until it was extensively restored and reopened, first as an arts and ture centre, then as the present gallery. The museum juxtaposes the work major established artists with that of young up-and-comers, with a particular emphasis on the 1940s onwards.

Regular touring exhibitions accompany ever-changing shows from the gallery's 4000-strong collection which includes works by Picasso, Miró and Vasarely, and contemporary artists Gilbert and George, Gillian Wearing and Damien Hirst. Modern Irish art is always on display and Irish and international artists live and work on-site in the **converted coach houses** behind the south wing. The **New Galleries**, in the recently restored Deputy Master's House, should also not be missed.

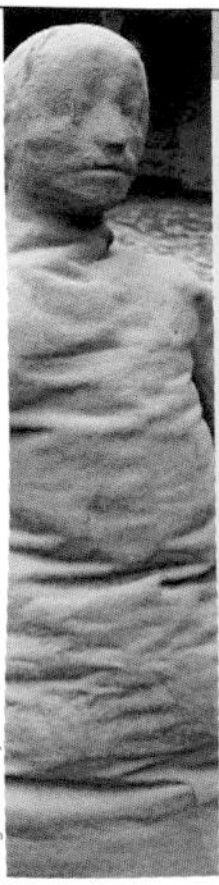

Doug McKinlay

INFORMATION

- ✉ Military Rd, Kilmainham
- ☎ 612 9900
- 🚌 68, 68a, 69, 78a, 79, 90, 123
- 🕘 Tues-Sat 10am-5.30pm, Sun and hols noon-5.30pm
- $ free
- ⓘ free exhibition tours Wed & Fri 2.30pm, Sun 12.15pm
- e www.modernart.ie
- ♿ good
- ✕ on-site cafe

While the art is often top-notch, it is the building that wows most visitors. With its striking classical facade and large central courtyard, the Royal Hospital was designed by Sir William Robinson whose other Dublin work includes Marsh's Library (p. 24). Inspired by Les Invalides in Paris, the Royal Hospital is felt to be the city's finest surviving 17th-century building.

The museum is surrounded by lush green grounds and is bordered on the north side by a perfectly laid out **Formal Garden** which has views across the Liffey to Phoenix Park. The tree-lined avenue west of the museum passes a **medieval burial ground** and some meadows before ending at the **Kilmainham Gate.** The gate was moved here in 1846 from Victoria Quay because it obstructed traffic flow to Heuston station.

IMMA's Hidden Treasures

Guided Heritage Tours of the museum (€3.15/1.90) are worth taking to see parts of the building normally closed to the public. Highlights include the **Banqueting Hall**, lined with portraits of 22 monarchs and viceroys, and the **Chapel** which has an elaborate Baroque ceiling and a set of Queen Anne gates. Tours run from June to September; call the museum for details.

Statues by Juan Muñoz

JOYCE MUSEUM (1, B5)

Martello tower overlooking Dublin Bay, the James Joyce combines memorabilia from the celebrated writer's life with a setting that has a story all its own.

INFORMATION

- Martello tower, Sandycove, Co. Dublin
- ☎ 280 9265
- 🚌 59 from Dun Laoghaire
- 🚉 Sandycove & Glasthule
- ⏰ April-Oct: Mon-Sat 10am-1pm & 2-5pm, Sun & hols 2-6pm; Nov-Mar by arrangement only
- 💲 €5.50/3-5/15
- ℹ️ open 8am-6pm Bloomsday (June 16), with special events and readings
- ♿ partial access
- ✕ Caviston's (p. 86)

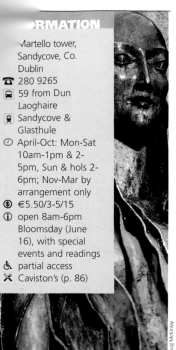

Anna Livia, Joyce's spirit of the Liffey

Doug McKinlay

The ground-floor museum has several first-edition Joyce books, as well as photographs, letters and one of two plaster death masks made of Joyce when he died in Zurich in 1941. Other items include an edition of *Ulysses* with illustrations by Henri Matisse, Joyce's guitar and hunting vest, and a page of original manuscript from *Finnegan's Wake*.

A set of tiny, winding stone steps take you up to the **Round Room** where the 22-year-old Joyce stayed for a few days in September 1904. Joyce was the guest of poet Oliver St John Gogarty – caricatured as the 'stately, plump Buck Mulligan' in *Ulysses* – who rented the tower for £8 a year.

Another set of steps leads to the tower's roof, the setting of the opening scene of *Ulysses*. A large cannon was once fixed here, as the tower was one of 26 built along the Dublin coast to defend against a threatened invasion by Napoleon.

Just below the Martello tower is the **Forty Foot Pool**, named after the army's 40th Foot Regiment, which was stationed nearby. At the close of the first chapter of *Ulysses*, Buck Mulligan heads to the pool for a morning swim, an activity which is still a local tradition. For years the spot was reserved for male-only nude bathing, but women are allowed now. Though a sign warns that 'Togs must be worn', die-hard men still keep it up – the tradition, that is – before 9am.

The Round Room Incident

By the time Joyce arrived to stay at the tower, Gogarty was less than happy to see him, having been branded a snob in Joyce's latest poem, *The Holy Office*. One night, Gogarty's other guest, Samuel Trench (Haines in *Ulysses*), had a nightmare about a panther and, half asleep, fired a shot at the fireplace. Gogarty took the gun from him, yelled 'Leave him to me' and shot down the saucepans on the shelf above Joyce's bed. Joyce took the hint and left the next morning.

KILMAINHAM GAOL (3, F4)

One of Dublin's most sobering sights, Kilmainham Gaol oozes centuries of pain, oppression and suffering from its decrepit limestone hulk. The scene of countless emotional episodes along Ireland's rocky road to independence, the jail was home to many of the country's political heroes, martyrs and villains.

Opened in 1796, Kilmainham Gaol saw thousands of prisoners pass through its corridors, including Robert Emmet and Charles Stewart Parnell. The uprisings of 1799, 1803, 1848, 1867 and 1916 all ended with the leaders' confinement in Kilmainham.

The **East Wing**, modelled on London's Pentonville Prison, was the setting for several scenes in the 1993 film *In the Name of the Father*, starring Daniel Day Lewis. Its design – with metal catwalks suspended around a light-filled, vaulted room – allowed guards full view of all the cells and brought the redeeming qualities of light and heaven, as the Victorians saw it, to the incarcerated. The prisoners' scratched and scrawled graffiti in the cells here is moving stuff.

Prisoners from the Civil War struggles were also held in Kilmainham, by their fellow Irishmen. One such inmate was Ireland's future prime minister and president, Eamon de Valera, who was the last person released when the jail closed for good in 1924. Kilmainham was left to ruin until the 1960s, when a team of volunteers set about the massive task of restoration.

Visits to Kilmainham include an excellent **museum**, the **prison chapel**, the exercise and execution yards and the dark, dank old wing. During the Great Famine, thousands of poor, petty thieves, as well as children, were crammed in here. It's advisable to rug up for your visit, as parts of the jail are several degrees colder than outside.

INFORMATION

- ✉ Inchicore Rd, Kilmainham
- ☎ 453 5984
- 🚌 51b, 78a & 79 from Aston Quay
- 🕐 Apr-Sept 9.30am-6pm, Oct-Mar Mon-Fri 9.30am-5pm, Sun 10am-6pm
- $ €4.45/1.90-3.20/10.15
- ⓘ last admission 1hr before closing; summer family tours Sun midday & 3pm
- e www.heritageireland.ie
- ♿ limited access; call ahead
- ✕ on-site tearoom

Do a stint in Kilmainham Gaol.

Richard Cummins

Doug McKinlay

The Uprising Executions

After the 1916 Easter Rising, 14 of the 15 rebel executions took place at Kilmainham. James Connolly, who was so badly injured during fighting he couldn't stand, was strapped to a chair to face the firing squad. The ruthlessness of the killings outraged the public, both in Ireland and England, and boosted the nationalist cause.

MARSH'S LIBRARY (4, M3)

Virtually unchanged for 300 years, Marsh's Library is a glorious example of an 18th-century scholar's den. The beautiful, dark oak **bookcases**, each topped with elaborately carved and gilded gables, are filled with some 25,000 books dating from the 15th to the early 18th centuries.

Founded in 1701 by Archbishop Narcissus Marsh (1638-1713), it is the oldest public library in Ireland. Designed by Sir William Robinson, its collection also includes maps, manuscripts and *incunabula*, or books printed before 1501. In its one nod to the 21st century, the library's current 'Keeper', Dr Muriel McCarthy, is the first-ever woman to hold the post.

Apart from theological books and Bibles in dozens of languages, there are tomes on medicine, law, travel, literature, science, navigation, music and mathematics. The oldest, and one of the most beautiful, books in the library is Cicero's *Letters to his Friends*, printed in Milan in 1472.

The most important of the four main collections held here is the 10,000-strong **library of Edward Stillingfleet**, bishop of Worcester. It was bought by Marsh in 1705 for UK£2500. Marsh's own extensive collection is also here, though he bequeathed his Oriental manuscripts to Oxford's Bodleian Library.

INFORMATION

- ✉ St Patrick's Close
- ☎ 454 3511
- 🚌 50, 50a, 56a from Aston Quay; 54, 54a from Burgh Quay
- 🕐 Mon & Wed-Fri 10am-12.45pm & 2-5pm, Sat 10.30am-12.45pm
- 💲 €2.50/1.25-2
- e www.marshlibrary.ie
- ✗ Gallic Kitchen (p. 80)

Doug McKinlay

Tony Wheeler

The oldest public library in Ireland

The library's books, some of which are in old Hebrew, Arabic, Turkish and Russian, were once chained to wooden rods attached to each shelf. As a further precaution, readers were locked into one of three wired **alcoves** at the back of the library while they perused rare volumes.

The **Delmas Conservation Bindery**, which repairs and restores rare books, manuscripts, prints, drawings and maps, operates from the library and it makes an appearance in *Ulysses*.

Swift Ambitions

Several items of the master satirist Jonathan Swift are kept in the library, including his copy of *History of the Great Rebellion*. His margin notes include a number of disparaging comments about Scots, of whom he seemed to have a low opinion. Swift, yet to become Dean of St Patrick's Cathedral, also held a low opinion of Archbishop Marsh, whom he blamed for his failure to achieve the lofty heights he felt he deserved. Both Swift and Marsh are buried in St Patrick's Cathedral.

NATIONAL GALLERY OF IREL...

The National Gallery opened in 1864 and has built ...
of Irish, British and European art. Its original collectr...
has grown, mainly through bequests, to around 12,500
ing oils, watercolours, drawings, prints and sculptures.

On the ground floor is the glittering **Shaw Room**, name...
wright George Bernard Shaw who was a major gallery benefa...
room, with its full-length portraits, busts and Waterford-crystal c...
liers, hosts weekend summer concerts by the Academy of Music
National Chamber Choir.

The **Yeats Museum** displays
paintings by Jack B Yeats (1871-
1957), his father, the noted por-
traitist John B Yeats (1839-1907),
and sisters Anne and Lily. The
ground-floor **Milltown Wing**
houses Irish art, while the **North
Wing** has Irish portraiture, big-
name Brits such as Hogarth,
Gainsborough and Turner, and the
Print Gallery which holds changing
exhibitions. The Spanish collection
is here too, featuring works by El
Greco, Goya, Velázquez and Picasso.

On the upper levels, periods
covered include Italian early
Renaissance to 18th century, French
17th to 19th centuries, as well as
Flemish, Dutch and German art. A
highlight is Caravaggio's *The Taking
of Christ*, which lay undiscovered for
more than 60 years in a Jesuit house
in Leeson St until spotted by the
chief curator of the gallery, Sergio
Benedetti, in 1990. Fra' Angelico,
Titian and Tintoretto are among the other Italian artists represented, while
Degas, Delacroix, Millet, Monet and Pissarro fly the flag for France.

The ultra-modern **Millennium Wing** on Clare St (to open early 2002)
has two floors of galleries for visiting exhibitions, a multimedia room and
a centre for the study of Irish art. The gallery also has excellent kids'
programs on Saturdays and almost daily activities in summer.

INFORMATION

- ✉ Merrion Sq W
- ☎ 661 5133
- 🚌 5, 6, 7, 7a, 8, 10, 13, 44, 48a, 62
- 🚉 Pearse
- ⏱ Mon-Wed, Fri & Sat 9.30am-5.30pm, Thurs 9.30am-8.30pm, Sun noon-5.30pm
- 💲 free
- ℹ free guided tours Sat 3pm, Sun 2, 3 & 4pm; Jul-Aug 3pm daily
- 🅴 www.nationagallery.ie
- ♿ fully accessible
- 🍴 Fitzer's Restaurant; winter garden restaurant

Doug McKinlay Doug McKinlay

Palladian pillars of the National Gallery

DON'T MISS
- Jack B Yeats' *The Liffey Swim* • Vermeer's *Lady Writing a Letter*
- Gainsborough's *The Cottage Girl* • Mantegna's *Judith and Holofernes* • Picasso's *Still Life with Mandolin*

...is home to a fabulous bounty of Bronze Age gold,
...work, Viking artefacts and some impressive ancient
...e Victorian Palladian-style building is a fine setting for

...
...444
...a, 8, 10, 11, 13
...earse
Tues-Sat 10am-5pm,
Sun 2-5pm

$ free

ⓘ regular guided tours
€1.25; family
programs Sun 3-4pm
(call ahead)

♿ ground floor only

✕ museum restaurant

Doug McKinlay

Doug McKinlay

National Museum of Ireland facade

the collection, with its 62-ft
domed rotunda, classical marble
columns and mosaic floors.

The exhibition begins in
Prehistoric Ireland, with Stone
Age burial mounds and Bronze
Age tools, spearheads and domestic
objects. An early Iron Age **bog
body**, its leathery skin gruesomely
preserved, is sure to impress kids.

An exceptional amount of
Bronze Age Irish gold, much of it
unearthed from bogs by farmers'
ploughs or peat-cutters' saws, is on
show in **Ór – Ireland's Gold**. The
stunning jewellery, dating from
2000-700BC, ranges from simple
lunulae – sun disks and crescents –
to elaborate bracelets, earrings and
neckpieces.

Two of the museum's best
pieces are in the **Treasury**. The
Ardagh Chalice, found by a
farmer in 1868, is made of 354
pieces of gold, silver, bronze, brass,
copper and lead. Engraved with
the names of the 12 Apostles, the
chalice is considered the finest
example of Celtic art ever found.
Also here is the **Tara Brooch**,
intricately decorated with filigree gold wire, enamelled studs, amber bands
and amethyst. The brooch is believed to have been made for a leading Celt
at the court of the Irish high kings at Tara.

When the Dublin Corporation began building its headquarters at
Wood Quay in the 1970s, excavations uncovered part of Dublin's original
Viking settlement. While the building controversially went ahead, some of
the recovered objects are now displayed in **Viking Ireland**. A model of a
Viking house accompanies jewellery, tools, swords, combs and the skeleton
of a warrior.

DON'T MISS
- Broighter Hoard • Cross of Cong • Loughnashade Trumpet
- Lurgan logboat • 'Ten Years Collecting' exhibit

NATURAL HISTORY MUSEUM   (4, L8)

Entering the Natural History Museum is like stepping into the year 1857. Scarcely changed since then, when Scottish explorer Dr David Livingstone delivered the inaugural lecture, this place is pure kitsch. Almost as interesting as the outrageously outdated displays is the realisation that the Victorians actually *liked* this kind of thing. But most visitors today will still find it fascinating, and most kids love it.

The creaking interior gives way to an overwhelming display of stuffed animals and mounted heads, crammed in like something from a Hitchcock movie. Of the two million species on display, around half are insects and many are long extinct.

INFORMATION

- ✉ Merrion St
- ☎ 677 7444
- 🚌 7, 7a, 8
- 🚆 Pearse
- ⏱ Tues-Sat 10am-5pm, Sun 2-5pm
- 🅢 free
- ♿ ground floor only
- ✗ Ely (p. 84); Bang (p. 83)

On the ground floor the **Irish Room** features a sizeable collection of mammals, birds and butterflies, including three skeletons of giant **Irish elk** which became extinct about 10,000 years ago. Suspended from the ceiling is a large basking shark, while some rather intriguing jars below contain parasites found in cats, dogs, pigs and sheep.

The World Animals Collection, spread across the upper three levels, has as its centrepiece a 20m-long skeleton of a **fin whale** caught in Bantry Bay, County Cork. Other notables include a **Tasmanian tiger** (mislabelled as a Tasmanian wolf), the probably extinct but still much-searched-for Australian marsupial, a **giant panda** from China and several African and Asian **rhinoceroses**.

Evolutionists will love the line-up of orang-utan, chimpanzee, gorilla and human skeletons in a glass cabinet on the first floor. The wonderful **Blaschka Collection** features finely detailed glass models of marine creatures, whose zoological accuracy is incomparable.

African explorer TH Parke, commemorated in the Natural History Museum's gardens

Doug McKinlay
Richard Cummins

DON'T MISS
- giant sunfish • elephant skeleton • spiky porcupine fish
- Great Irish wolfhound • dodo bird skeleton

PHOENIX PARK   (3, D2)

Dwarfing New York's Central Park and London's Hampstead Heath, Phoenix Park is one of the largest city parks in the world. Along with gardens, lakes and 300 deer, there's hurling, cricket and football grounds, a motor-racing track and some fine 18th-century residences. A pleasant place to stroll during the day, it is unsafe after dark.

Doug McKinlay

INFORMATION

- ✉ Phoenix Park
- ☎ Visitor Centre 677 0095
- 🚌 37 to Visitor Centre; 10, 25, 26, 66, 67 68, 69 to Park Gate
- ⏱ Visitor Centre June-Sept 10am-6pm, Oct 10am-5pm, Apr-May 9.30am-5.30pm, Nov-Mar 9.30am-4.30pm
- ⑤ park grounds free; Visitor Centre €2.50/ 1.25-1.90/6.35
- ① free 1-hr tours of president's residence Sat 10.30am-4pm depart from Visitor Centre
- 🄴 www.heritageire land.ie
- ♿ good
- ✗ Visitor Centre restaurant

From Anglo-Norman times the park was owned by St John's Priory in Kilmainham, but the land was seized by the crown after the Reformation, becoming a royal deer park. It wasn't until 1745 that the viceroy, Lord Chesterfield, opened it to the public.

Near the Parkgate St entrance is the 63m-high **Wellington Monument** (3, E5), a tribute to the Dublin-born Duke of Wellington. The **People's Garden** dating from 1864, the **Victorian bandstand** in the Hollow and **Dublin Zoo** (p. 48) are all nearby. On the park's southern edge is a derelict, 18th-century **Magazine Fort**.

Heading north-west along Chesterfield Ave, the **Áras an Uachtaráin** (3, C3), the Irish president's residence, is on the right. Built in 1751, it housed British viceroys from 1782-1922. On the left, the **Papal Cross** (3, C1) marks the site where Pope John Paul II preached to more than a million people in 1979.

In the centre of the park is the **Phoenix Monument** (3, C2), said to mark the site of a spring of *fionn uisce*, or clear water, from which the park's name may derive.

The **Visitor Centre** (3, B1), housed in former stables, has exhibits on the history and wildlife of the park. Tours include the adjacent **Ashtown Castle**, a 17th-century tower-house that was concealed inside another building until renovations revealed it in 1986.

Murder in the Park

In 1882 Lord Cavendish, the British chief secretary for Ireland, and his assistant were stabbed to death in Phoenix Park by members of a Fenian splinter nationalist group called The Invincibles. The assassins escaped but one of their comrades betrayed them and they were hanged at Kilmainham Gaol.

Lord Cavendish's home is now called Deerfield, and is used as the US ambassador's residence. Cavendish's murder occurred outside what is now the Irish president's residence.

ST PATRICK'S CATHEDRAL (4, M3)

St Patrick's Cathedral stands on one of Dublin's earliest Christian sites. St Patrick is said to have baptised converts at a well within the cathedral grounds. Although a church stood on the site from the 5th century, the present building dates from 1191, and several major alterations have been made since.

A series of natural disasters plagued the cathedral in the 14th century, including a storm that collapsed the spire and a fire that destroyed the original tower. In the 16th century, religious turmoil took its toll. When Henry VIII dissolved the monasteries in 1537, St Patrick's was ordered to hand over all of its estates, revenues and possessions and it was demoted to the rank of parish church.

In 1649 Oliver Cromwell ordered that the nave be used as a stable for his horses, and in 1666 the Lady Chapel was given to the newly arrived Huguenots in whose hands it remained until 1816. Although the church's most famous dean, writer Jonathan Swift, did his utmost to preserve the integrity of the building, by the end of the 18th century it was close to collapse. Salvation came in the form of the Guinness family who funded a major restoration in 1864.

Swift's grave, and that of his long-term companion, Esther Johnston, or Stella, are just inside the main entrance. The **Swift memorials** in the South Aisle include his epitaph, a selection of his writings, his death mask and the pulpit he preached from.

St Patrick's proudly soaring interior

INFORMATION

⊠ St Patrick's Close
☎ 453 9472
🚌 49, 50, 54a, 56a, 77, 77a
🕐 Mar-Oct 9am-6pm; Nov-Feb: Mon-Fri 9am-6pm, Sat 9am-5pm, Sun 9am-3pm; closed Dec 24-26 & Jan 1
⑤ €3.40/2.55/8.25
ⓘ entry for worshippers only during services
e www.stpatrickscathedral.ie
♿ by prior arrangement
✕ Gallic Kitchen (p. 80)

The **monument to Sir Benjamin Guinness' daughter** is a tribute to the family's role in the cathedral's restoration. Fittingly, it stands beneath a window that bears the words 'I was thirsty and ye gave me drink'.

DON'T MISS • Boyle monument • the organ • Celtic grave slabs • Chapter House door • Archbishop Marsh monument

ST STEPHEN'S GREEN   (4, M7)

Once a common where public whippings, burnings and hangings took place, the nine hectares of St Stephen's Green now provide a popular lunchtime escape for city workers. Geese, ducks and waterfowl splash about the ponds, there is a good children's playground and the bandstand hosts concerts in summer.

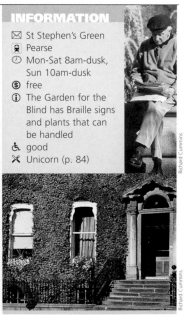

INFORMATION

- ✉ St Stephen's Green
- 🚋 Pearse
- ⏰ Mon-Sat 8am-dusk, Sun 10am-dusk
- ⑤ free
- ⓘ The Garden for the Blind has Braille signs and plants that can be handled
- ♿ good
- ✕ Unicorn (p. 84)

The green's backdrop of Georgian facades

The fine Georgian buildings around the square date mainly from Dublin's 18th-century boom, when the north side was known as the Beaux Walk because of the genteel types who strolled there. Today the grand **Shelbourne Hotel** (p. 104) remains a popular society meeting place. A few doors along is a small **Huguenot Cemetery** (6, F10), established in 1693 for French Protestant refugees.

The south side is home to beautifully restored **Newman House** (p. 37) and the Byzantine-inspired **Newman University Church** (p. 43). On the western flank is the 1863 **Unitarian Church** (☎ 478 0638; Mon-Fri 12.30-2.30pm) and the striking facade of the **Royal College of Surgeons** (closed to public).

The present look of the green harks back to 1880 when Lord Ardilaun, of the Guinness clan, financed its relandscaping. The lord was also responsible for revoking an annual entrance fee of one guinea, introduced in 1814.

Statues and memorials dot the green, including those of **Sir Arthur Guinness**, Irish patriot **Robert Emmet** and **James Joyce**. Around the central fountain are busts of **Countess Markievicz** and the poet **James Clarence Mangan**, and a 1967 Henry Moore sculpture of **WB Yeats**. In the north-east corner is 'Tone-henge', a slab-like **memorial to Wolfe Tone**, and the **Great Famine memorial**.

Surgeons' Seizure

During the 1916 Easter Rising, a band of Irish rebel forces occupied St Stephen's Green. They were led by Countess Constance Markievicz, the colourful Irish nationalist, and later the first woman elected to the Irish Parliament. Though Markievicz, who was married to a Polish count, failed to take the Shelbourne Hotel, the rebels seized the Royal College of Surgeons building. If you look closely at its columns you can still see the bullet marks.

TEMPLE BAR (5,

It's tacky. It's touristy. It's packed with falling-down-drunks at night and carpeted with vomit of a morning. But Temple Bar, the city's prime entertainment and eating spot, still has a certain something.

One of the oldest areas of the city, Temple Bar's fortunes have ebbed and flowed for centuries. The western boundary of Temple Bar is formed by **Fishamble St**, the oldest street in Dublin, which dates to Viking times. From 1282 to 1537 the area was owned by Augustinian friars, then by Sir William Temple, provost of Trinity College and Temple Bar's namesake.

Crime and prostitution rackets moved in during the 18th century, followed by small craft and trade businesses in the 19th century. But by the first half of the 20th century Temple Bar had sunk into decline, along with most of central Dublin.

A 1960s plan to build a major bus depot here was put on hold when the recession struck, and by

Lining up the kegs in Temple Bar.

INFORMATION

- ✉ Temple Bar
- ☎ Cultureline 671 5717
- 🚌 all city-centre buses
- 🚉 Tara St
- ① Temple Bar Information Centre (18 Eustace St; 5, C3; ☎ 677 2255) publishes the *Temple Bar Guide*
- e www.temple-bar.ie
- ✗ See pp.78-9

the 1980s the dilapidated area was home to a thriving community of artists, artisans and cultural groups who paid low or no rents on the scruffy buildings. The government soon recognised that local energy was rehabilitating the area and in 1991 it began a major revamp.

Today, in amongst tourist-fodder restaurants and meat-market pubs, you'll find some excellent art galleries, offbeat stores, a body-piercing clinic, buskers, an independent cinema, cutting-edge theatre and an organic gourmet food market on Saturdays. You can eat foie gras or fish and chips, buy a fluffy toy sheep or an Austrian crystal necklace – basically, Temple Bar is what you make it.

Diversions

From May to September a number of outdoor events are held in Temple Bar, courtesy of Temple Bar Properties' **Diversions** program.

Cultural performances and a market (p. 68) are held on Meeting House Square (5, D3), and on Saturday nights, classic films are screened on Temple Bar Square (5, C5). Sunday is family day with circus performances, mime and acrobatics.

Though events are free, major shows are ticketed and issued on a first come, first served basis from TBP's office at 18 Eustace St (5, C3). Tickets are available from 9am on the Monday before an event.

RINITY COLLEGE (2)

Ireland's premier university is both a tranquil retreat from the bustle of the city, and the home of Dublin's biggest attraction, the Book of Kells. Established by Elizabeth I in 1592 on land confiscated from an Augustinian priory, Trinity College was the queen's attempt to stop Irish youth from being 'infected with popery'.

The college remains one of Europe's best universities, with a legion of notable graduates and a long-established affiliation with Oxford's Oriel

Corinne Humphrey

INFORMATION

- ✉ College Green
- ☎ 677 2941
- 🚉 Pearse; Tara St
- 🕐 grounds: 7am-midnight; Old Library/ Book of Kells: Mon-Sat 9.30am-5pm, Sun 9.30am-4.30pm (June-Sept), noon-4.30pm (Oct-May)
- 💲 grounds free; Book of Kells €5.70/5.10/11.45, under-12s free
- ℹ 30-min walking tours (☎ 608 1724; €8.50, inc. entry to Book of Kells; May-Sept from 10.15am) depart every 40min from Front Sq
- ♿ good
- 🍽 Buttery Café & Bar; cafeteria in Arts & Social Science bldg

College and St John's in Cambridge. Until 1793 Trinity College remained completely Protestant. Even when the university relented and began to admit Catholics, the Catholic Church forbade it – a restriction not completely lifted until 1970. Today most of its 13,000 students are Catholic.

Heading through the Regent House entrance on College Green, past statues of the poet **Oliver Goldsmith** (1730-74; 2, B1) and the orator **Edmund Burke** (1729-97; 2, B1), you come to a large square which is technically three separate squares. On its north side is the **Chapel** (2, B2), designed by Sir William Chambers (1723-96) and open to all denominations since 1972. The Chapel has fine plasterwork, Ionic columns and painted glass windows.

The square is dominated by the 30m-high **Campanile** (2, B2). Designed by Edward Lanyon and erected in 1853, the tower is said to mark the centre of the monastery that preceded the college. Legend has it that students who cross underneath it when the bells toll will fail their exams.

On the east side of Library Square, the red-brick **Rubrics building** (2, B3) dates from around 1690, making it the oldest building in the college, though it has been extensively altered. On the square's lawn is a 1969 **Henry Moore sculpture** (2, B3).

Behind Rubrics is New Square, featuring the highly ornate 1853-57 **Museum Building** (2, C4; ☎ 608 1477; open by arrangement only), which houses exhibits and a Geological Museum. The **Berkeley Library** (2, C3) next door was designed in 1967 by Paul Koralek in the solid, square, brutalist style. Behind the library are **College Park** (2, D4) and the **Rugby Ground** (2, C4), while at its entrance is Arnaldo Pomodoro's 1983 sculpture **Sphere Within Sphere** (2, C3).

Trinity's main attraction is housed in the **Old Library** (2, C3; ☎ 608 2320), which is entered from Fellows' Square. The **Book of Kells**, an illuminated manuscript dating from around AD800, is one of the oldest books in the world. Probably produced by monks at St Columba's Monastery on the remote Scottish island of Iona, it moved with the monks to Kells in County Meath in AD806 after repeated Viking raids. The book was brought to Trinity College for safekeeping in 1654.

The manuscript contains the four New Testament gospels, written in Latin, as well as prefaces, summaries and other text. The superbly decorated lettering and the complex, intertwining illustrations are impressive, though the lighting in the gallery is poor. The book is displayed underneath the library, along with the AD807 **Book of Armagh** and the AD675 **Book of Durrow**.

Admission to the Book of Kells includes the 65m-long **Library Long Room**, which contains numerous ancient texts. Lined with dark wood shelves containing 200,000 of the library's oldest books and manuscripts, it also displays one of the oldest harps in the country, dating from around 1400. A rare copy of the **Proclamation of the Irish Republic**, read by Patrick Pearse at the beginning of the 1916 Easter Rising, is also here.

Hallowed halls: Trinity's Long Room

South across Fellows' Square is the **Arts & Social Science building** (2, D3), also designed by Paul Koralek and home to the **Douglas Hyde Gallery** (p. 40). **The Dublin Experience** (2, D3; ☎ 608 1688; €4.15/2.20-3.50/8.25; June-Sept, hourly 10am-5pm) provides a 45-minute audiovisual introduction to the city.

Trinity Scholars

Famous alumni of Trinity College include politicians Edmund Burke, Wolfe Tone, Douglas Hyde and Robert Emmet, and writers Jonathan Swift, Oliver Goldsmith, Samuel Beckett, Bram Stoker and Oscar Wilde. More recent graduates include former President Mary Robinson and her successor Mary McAleese, both of whom studied law.

Women were first admitted to the college in 1903, but only after a bitter battle with George Salmon, the college's provost from 1886 to 1904. Salmon, whose statue (2, B2) stands just west of the Campanile, famously carried out his threat to permit women 'over his dead body' by dropping dead when the worst happened.

sights & activities

Dublin's city centre is compact and best seen on foot, though at times the footpaths are so crowded it seems the entire population of the capital is on the move.

South of the Liffey the main promenade and the heart of town is pedestrianised **Grafton St**, where flower stalls, buskers, pavement artists and beggars compete to divert your gaze from the upmarket shops. The well-heeled streets **east of Grafton St** offer gastronomic pubs, cafes, bookshops, jewellery stores and art galleries for flush folk. The younger and funkier crowd lounge outside the cafes **west of Grafton St** where the tangle of streets offer offbeat clothing, gourmet delis, clubs and pubs. Directly north of here is **Temple Bar** (p. 31), one of Dublin's rowdiest, most alcohol-fuelled areas.

Out towards the Guinness Brewery (p. 19), **the Liberties** is one of the city's oldest areas and an interesting place to stroll – try Thomas St, Francis St and Meath St. Across the river, **O'Connell St** was laid waste in the 1916 Easter Rising and was extensively rebuilt last century. Today it's lined with cheap department stores and burger joints. Crossing O'Connell St, **Henry St** and **Talbot St** are lined with chain stores and discount outlets, while **Moore St** hosts an outdoor fruit and vegetable market (p. 68). West of here the ramshackle factories and shops of **Smithfield** are slowly being converted into modern apartments, trendy bars and galleries.

To get a sense of how sprawling and diverse Dublin is, catch the DART to the quiet, affluent **seaside suburbs** (pp. 46-7) north and south of the centre, such as Dalkey and Howth.

Off the Beaten Track

Dublin's city centre can get horribly congested with both people and cars, but it's not difficult to find some peace. For a real escape head to the seaside suburbs, or try these more central idylls:

- Iveagh Gardens (p. 44)
- Newman University Church (p. 37)
- Cafe at Hodges Figgis (p. 72)
- Chester Beatty Library & Garden (p. 14)
- College Park at Trinity (p. 33)
- RHA Gallagher Gallery (p. 41)
- Grand Canal towpaths (p. 44)

The 30m-high Campanile (1853) in Trinity College

LITERARY LANDMARKS

Dublin Writers' Museum (4, D5)

In a house once owned by the Jameson family (of whiskey fame), the museum celebrates Ireland's literary history. The displays could do with an update, both in presentation and content, but fans will enjoy the collection of letters, photographs, first editions and quirky memorabilia. The lavishly decorated Gallery of Writers upstairs has portraits and busts of famous scribblers.

⊠ 18 N Parnell Sq
☎ 872 2077
e www.visitdublin.com
🚌 11, 13, 16, 19, 36, 40
🚉 Connolly
🕐 June-Aug: Mon-Fri 10am-6pm, Sat 10am-5pm, Sun 11am-5pm; Sept-May: Mon-Sat 10am-5pm, Sun 11am-5pm
⑤ €5.50/3-5/15

James Joyce Cultural Centre (4, D6)

Dedicated to promoting the life and works of James Joyce, the centre has exhibition rooms, a reference library, Joyce family portraits and photos of some of the real Dubliners fictionalised in his books. The house itself has some fine plasterwork. It is where the dancing instructor Denis Maginni, who appears several times in *Ulysses*, taught students. The centre also runs Joyce tours (p. 59).

⊠ 35 Great George's St N
☎ 878 8547
e www.jamesjoyce.ie
🚌 3, 10, 11, 13, 16, 19, 22, 123 🚉 Connolly
🕐 Mon-Sat 9.30am-5pm, Sun 12.30-5pm
⑤ €3.80/2.50

Plaque reflects the city.

James Joyce Museum

See p. 22.

Oscar Wilde House

(4, L9) The first Georgian residence built on Merrion Square, No 1 was the home of surgeon Sir William Wilde, his wife (the poet Lady 'Speranza') and their son, Oscar, from 1855 to 1878. New owners, American College Dublin, now run tours of the restored first and second floors, but information about the family is scant.

⊠ 1 Merrion Sq N
☎ 662 0281
e www.amcd.edu
🚌 7, 8, 45, 84
🚉 Pearse
🕐 Mon, Wed & Thurs 10.15 & 11.15am
⑤ €2.50

Shaw Birthplace

(3, H9) The birthplace of playwright George Bernard Shaw is now an atmospheric museum that is as interesting for its almost creepy recreation of Victorian middle-class life as for its literary links. The excellent self-guided audio tour is available in several languages.

⊠ 33 Synge St
☎ 475 0854
e www.visitdublin.com
🚌 16, 19, 122
🕐 Easter-Oct: Mon-Sat 10am-1pm & 2-5pm, Sun 11am-1pm & 2-5pm
⑤ €5.50/3-5/15

Wilde by name, wild by nature

GEORGIAN DUBLIN

Casino at Marino
(3, A14) See p. 51.

City Hall (6, A2)
Recently restored to its Georgian glory, City Hall is adorned with neoclassical columns, a domed, gilded rotunda and patterned marble floors. Built by Thomas Cooley as the Royal Exchange from 1769 to 1779, City Hall was the setting for the funerals of both Michael Collins and Charles Stewart Parnell. The *Story of the Capital* exhibition in the arched vaults traces Dublin's history through artefacts, models and multimedia displays.
✉ **Cork Hill, Dame St**
☎ 672 2204 **e** www .dublincorp.ie/cityhall 🚌 50, 50a, 54, 56a, 77, 77a, 77b
🕐 Mon-Sat 10am-5.15pm, Sun 2-5pm
$ €3.80/1.25/8.90
♿ excellent

Custom House (4, G8)
A breathtaking Dublin landmark, Custom House was built to house the city's tax commissioners. James Gandon's first architectural triumph, the 18th-century building has a copper dome set with clock faces and neoclassical columns typical of the era. While the building now houses the Department of the Environment, the Visitor Centre explains Custom House's history.
✉ **Custom House Quay**
☎ 888 2538 🚉 Tara St; Connolly 🕐 mid-Mar-Oct: Mon-Fri 10am-12.30pm, Sat-Sun 2-5pm; Nov-mid-Mar: Wed-Fri 10am-12.30pm,

City Hall Building (1779)

Doug McKinlay

Sun 2-5pm
$ €1.30/free/3.80 adults & children/students/family ♿ access throughout; call ahead

Fitzwilliam Square
(4, O9) The smallest and the last of Dublin's great Georgian squares, Fitzwilliam is home to a quiet and elegant block of immaculate terraces, boasting some elaborate doors and fanlights. While by day the square houses doctors' surgeries and solicitors' offices, by night prostitutes wait for customers near the seedy Leeson St nightclubs. Only residents have access to the central garden.
✉ **Dublin 2**
🚌 10, 11, 13b, 46a, 58

Four Courts (4, H2)
With its 130m-long facade and neoclassical proportions, the Four Courts was built between 1786 and 1802 to the design of James Gandon. In 1922 the building was captured

by anti-Treaty republicans; pro-Treaty forces shelled the site to try to dislodge them. Displays on the building's history and reconstruction are on the first floor; court hearings can be observed from public galleries only.
✉ **Inns Quay**
☎ 888 6441 🚌 134
🕐 Mon-Fri 9am-4.30pm
$ free ♿ good

King's Inns (4, E3)
Home to Dublin's legal profession, King's Inns is yet another Georgian classic from the drawing board of James Gandon. Over its 15-year construction several other architects were recruited, including Francis Johnston who added the cupola. Only members and their guests can go inside.
✉ **Henrietta St**
☎ 874 4840
e www.kingsinns.ie
🚌 25, 25a, 66, 67, 90, 134

Leinster House (4, L8)
The Dáil and Seanad both meet at Leinster House, Ireland's parliament, when it sits for 90 days a year. Designed by Richard Cassels for the duke of Leinster, the Kildare St frontage is intended to look like a town house, while from Merrion St it appears to be a country estate.
✉ **Kildare St**
☎ 618 3000, 618 3271 for tour information
e www.irlgov.ie /oireachtas 🚌 7, 7a, 8, 10, 11, 13 🚉 Pearse
🕐 public gallery open when parliament in session, usually Nov-May
$ free ♿ good

Merrion Square

(4, M10) Merrion Square is lined with stately Georgian buildings whose doors, peacock fanlights, ornate door knockers and foot-scrapers epitomise the elegance of the era. Former residents include the Wilde family (p. 35), WB Yeats and Daniel O'Connell. Its lush central gardens are perfect for a picnic or peaceful pit stop.

⊠ **Merrion Sq**
🚌 5, 7, 7a, 8, 45
🚊 Pearse
♿ good

Mountjoy Square

(4, C7) Once the heart of Dublin's fashionable and affluent northside, today Mountjoy Square is a reminder of the area's urban decay. Former residents include Sean O'Casey, who set his play *The Shadow of a Gunman* here, though he referred to it as Hilljoy Square.

⊠ **Mountjoy Sq**
🚌 11, 16, 41
🚊 Connolly
♿ good

Newman House

(4, N6) Part of University College Dublin, Newman House consists of two exquisitely restored Georgian town houses with spectacular 18th-century stucco interiors. Of note are the Apollo Room and the Saloon by Paulo and Filipo LaFranchini, and later work by Robert West. Former students here include James Joyce and Eamon de Valera.

⊠ **85-86 St Stephen's Green** ☎ 706 7422
🚌 10, 11, 13, 14, 14a, 15a, 15b 🚊 Pearse
🕐 **by guided tour June-Sept: Tues-Fri noon, 2, 3 & 4pm, on** the hour Sat 2-5pm, Sun 11am-2pm
💲 €3.80/2.50

Number 29 (4, M10)

Built in 1794 for the widow of a wine merchant, Number 29 is a reconstruction of genteel Dublin home life circa 1790 to 1820. From the rat traps in the basement kitchen to the handmade wallpaper upstairs, the attention to detail is impressive. Ironically, the museum only exists because the Electricity Supply Board, having demolished most of the block for its new offices, restored it in recompense.

⊠ **29 Fitzwilliam St Lwr**
☎ 702 6165
🌐 www.esb.ie
🚌 6, 7, 8, 10, 45
🚊 Pearse

🕐 Tues-Sat 10am-5pm, Sun 2-5pm; closed 2 weeks over Christmas
💲 €3.20/1.25; under-16s free

Rotunda Hospital

(4, E5) The first maternity hospital in the British Isles, the Rotunda was built in 1757 to cope with Dublin's burgeoning urban population and high infant-mortality rates. The hospital's architect, Richard Cassels, re-used his design for Leinster House but added a three-storey tower. The stucco cherubs, flowers and draperies in the chapel are a sight to behold.

⊠ **Parnell St**
☎ 873 0700 🚌 36, 36a, 40, 40a, 40b
🕐 2-3pm & 7-8pm
💲 free ♿ excellent

By George

The Georgian period is roughly defined as the years between the accession of George I in 1714 and the death of George IV in 1830. Its inspiration was the work of the 16th-century Italian architect Andrea Palladio, who believed reason and the principles of classical antiquity should govern building.

In Dublin, the austere formality of the style was tempered by the use of coloured doors, delicate fanlights, intricate ironwork and exuberant interior plasterwork.

Martin Moos

Gracious Georgian doorways

MUSEUMS

Dublin Civic Museum

(6, C5) In the 18th-century City Assembly House, the Dublin Civic Museum has an eclectic collection of bric-a-brac that relates to the city's history. Most interesting is the carved head of Lord Nelson, all that remains of a statue toppled from its plinth in O'Connell St by an IRA bomb in 1966.

✉ **58 William St S**
☎ **679 4260**
🚌 **all city-centre buses**
🕐 **Tues-Sat 10am-6pm, Sun 11am-2pm** 💲 **free**

Fry Model Railway

(1, A5) The railway engineer and draughtsman Cyril Fry began this collection of handmade models in the 1920s and '30s – now the O-gauge replica of Ireland's transport system covers 240 sq metres. The model includes buses, trains, trams, barges, bridges and stations, and in the control room you can see how it all works.

✉ **Malahide Castle Demesne, Malahide, Co. Dublin**
☎ **846 3779**
🖥 **www.visitdublin .com** 🚌 **42 from Beresford Pl**
🚊 **from Connolly to**

Malahide

🕐 **Apr-Oct: Mon-Sat 10am-1pm & 2-5pm, Sun & hols 2-6pm; Nov-Mar: Sat, Sun & hols 2-5pm**
💲 **€5.50/3-5/15**
♿ **excellent**

GAA Museum (3, B11)

Sporting enthusiasts will enjoy this museum at Croke Park stadium, which explores the history of hurling, Gaelic football, camogie and handball from their ancient roots to the present day. Interactive screens let you test your own skills, listen to recordings from special matches and replay historic moments.

✉ **New Stand, Croke Park** ☎ **855 8176**
🚌 **3, 11, 11a, 16, 16a & 51a from O'Connell St**
🚊 **Connolly**
🕐 **May-Sept: 9.30am-5pm (New Stand ticket holders only on match days); Oct-Apr: Tues-Sat 10am-5pm, Sun noon-5pm**
💲 **€ 3.80/2.55/7.60**
♿ **excellent**

Heraldic Museum

(4, K8) Run by the National Library, the Heraldic Museum's collection includes seals, coins, stamps, livery buttons, armour and banners. The building, designed in 1865 in the Venetian style, features stone carvings of monkeys playing billiards – the only clue that this was once a gentleman's club.

✉ **2-3 Kildare St**
☎ **677 7444**
🖥 **www.nli.ie** 🚌 **10, 11, 13** 🕐 **Mon-Wed 10am-8.30pm, Thurs-Fri 10am-4.30pm, Sat 10am-12.30pm** 💲 **free**

Hot Press Irish Music Hall of Fame (4, G5)

One for the die-hard fans only, this museum is crammed with memorabilia from 1960s Van Morrison to 1990s Westlife. You can see U2 drummer Larry Mullen Jnr's first drum kit, Bono's 'Fly' sunglasses, the original Live Aid contract, and other stuff from Thin Lizzie, The Corrs, Riverdance, Boyzone and others.

✉ **57 Abbey St Middle**
☎ **878 3345**
🖥 **www.imhf.com**
🚌 **25, 26, 37, 39, 66, 67, 70, 134** 🕐 **10am-6pm** 💲 **€7.60/5.10/20.30**
♿ **excellent**

Irish-Jewish Museum

(3, H9) Dublin's dwindling Jewish population is remembered through photographs, paintings, certificates, books and other memorabilia in this terrace house in the former Jewish district of Portobello. The museum recreates a typical 19th-century Dublin kosher kitchen, while upstairs is an old synagogue, in a state of disuse since the 1970s.

✉ **3-4 Walworth Rd**
☎ **490 1857** 🚌 **14, 15, 16, 19, 65, 122, 155**
🕐 **May-Sept: Tues,**

Ha'penny Bridge

One of the city's most enduring symbols, Ha'penny Bridge (5, B5) – officially Wellington Bridge – has recently been restored to its former glory. Crossing the bridge is a time-honoured Dublin tradition, though doing so no longer attracts the halfpenny toll levied in the 19th century – the origins of its quaint moniker. The bridge, cast in Shropshire, England, was opened in 1816 and was the only pedestrian bridge across the Liffey until the Millennium Bridge opened in 2000.

Thurs & Sun 11am-3.30pm, Oct-Apr: Sun 10.30am-2.30pm ⑤ free ⓐ ground floor only

Museum of Banking
(5, C6) In the former Armoury and Guard House annexe to the Bank of Ireland, this small museum explores the history of banking, with particular emphasis on the bank's role in Ireland's economic and social development over the past 200 years.
✉ Bank of Ireland Arts Centre, Foster Pl
☎ 671 1488 ⓔ www .bankofire land.ie
🚌 all city-centre buses

Bank of Ireland: pillars of commerce

🕐 by tour only: Tues-Fri 10am-4pm ⑤ €1.90/1.30

National Print Museum (3, G13)
Housed in an old barracks, the print museum pays homage to the skills, tools and techniques of the printer's art from the age before computers. Ornate printing presses, type sets, linotype machines and historic newspaper pages are on display, and you can learn how books were once bound and stitched.
✉ Garrison Chapel, Beggars Bush ☎ 660 3770 🚌 5, 7, 7a, 8, 45 🚇 Grand Canal Dock or Landsdowne Rd
🕐 May-Sept: Mon-Fri 10am-12.30pm & 2.30-5pm, Sun noon-5pm; Oct-Apr: Tues, Thurs, Sat & Sun 2-5pm
⑤ €3.20/1.90/6.35 ⓐ ground floor only

Old Jameson Distillery (4, G1)
Housed in the original Jameson distillery where the famous Irish whiskey was produced from 1791 to 1966, the museum tells the story of the site and the drink. A heavy dose of marketing is thrown in, but

fans will enjoy the ⬤ ed old factory, the c⬤ explanations of the ⬤ ing process and, of co⬤ the free glass of Jamesc⬤ at the end of the tour.
✉ Bow St, Smithfield ☎ 807 2355 🚌 67, 67a, 68, 69, 79, 134
🕐 9.30am-6pm; by tour only ⑤ 6.30/1.90-3.80/12 ⓐ good

Waterways Visitor Centre (3, F13)
Known as 'the box in the docks' for its cubist design, Waterways provides an insight into the history and importance of Ireland's inland canal systems. Positioned on the docks with the lapping water visible from inside, it uses video, models, interactive computers and displays to tell the story of the waterways and the people who worked on them. The roof offers great views of the area which is undergoing major renewal.
✉ Grand Canal Quay ☎ 677 7510
🚌 3 from O'Connell St 🚇 Grand Canal Dock
🕐 June-Sept 9.30am-6.30pm; Oct-May Wed-Sun 12.30-5pm
⑤ €2.50/1.25-1.90/6.35 ⓐ ground floor only

GALLERIES

Arthouse (5, D4)
A multimedia centre as well as a gallery, Arthouse exhibits provocative new work that often incorporates the latest technology. The centre also runs training programs and events, and has an online database of 800 contemporary Irish artists.
✉ Curved St, Temple Bar
☎ 605 6800

ⓔ www.arthouse.ie
🚌 all city-centre buses
🚇 Tara St 🕐 Mon-Fri 9.30am-5.30pm, Sat 9.30am-2pm ⑤ free
ⓐ excellent

Cross Gallery (4, M2)
Among the top-end antique stores of the Liberties, Cross is a relaxed

modern gallery that promotes the work of both established and up-and-coming artists from Ireland and abroad. Expect abstract expressionism, muted landscapes and figurative work that tends towards the surreal.
✉ 59 Francis St
☎ 473 8978
ⓔ www.crossgallery.ie

8a, 123, 206
-Fri 10am-6pm,
am-4pm
e
ood

Douglas Hyde
gallery (2, D2)
It might be on-campus at Trinity, but this ain't no half-baked student gallery. One of the city's more cutting-edge contemporary spaces, this gallery tends towards conceptual art, including installations and performance-driven pieces.
✉ Trinity College
☎ 608 1116
e www.douglashyde gallery.com
🚌 all city-centre buses
🚉 Pearse; Tara St
🕐 Mon-Wed & Fri 11am-6pm, Thurs 11am-7pm, Sat 11am-4.45pm

Gallery of Photography (5, D3)
Ireland's premier photographic gallery, this place has ever-changing exhibits, often with Irish themes. Directly across the square is the National Photographic Archive (Mon-Fri 10am-5pm, Sat 10am-2pm) which displays mainly historical photographs from the National

Library's collection.
✉ Meeting House Sq
☎ 671 4654 e www .irish-photography.com
🚌 all city-centre buses
🕐 Tues-Sat 11am-6pm, Sun 1-6pm ⑤ free
♿ good

Green on Red (2, B7)
This fashionable warehouse space houses cutting-edge, mainly Irish shows that range from prints, photography and sculpture to more 'out-there' installations.
✉ 26-28 Lombard St E
☎ 671 3414 🚌 1, 2, 3, 48a 🚉 Pearse
🕐 Mon-Fri 10am-6pm, Sat 11am-5pm
⑤ free

IB Jorgensen Fine Art (6, D9) Run by former Danish fashion designer IB Jorgensen, this gallery specialises in well-mannered European fine art from the 19th and 20th centuries. Prices are high and names are suitably big.
✉ 29 Molesworth St
☎ 661 9758 e www .jorgensenfineart.com
🚌 10, 11, 14, 15
🚉 Pearse
🕐 Mon-Fri 9am-5.30pm, Sat 9.30am-2pm
⑤ free ♿ poor

Kerlin Gallery (6, D7)
Hidden behind a nondescript door in a dingy little lane, the Kerlin Gallery is the ultimate statement in cool. Inside, the minimalist space, designed by English architect John Pawson, displays mainly conceptual and abstract art from some of Ireland's leading lights, including Dorothy Cross and Kathy Prendergast.
✉ Anne's La, Anne St S
☎ 670 9093
e www.kerlin.ie
🚌 10, 14, 14a, 15
🕐 Mon-Fri 10am-5.45pm, Sat 11am-4.30pm ⑤ free

Kevin Kavanagh Gallery (4, H5)
On a backstreet behind the Morrison Hotel, Kevin Kavanagh's intimate gallery carries on the tradition of unearthing emerging Dublin artists which was established by Kavanagh's previous venture, Jo Rain Gallery in Temple Bar. Kavanagh's eye has uncovered artists who now show at IMMA and abroad – catch them here first.
✉ 66 Great Strand St
☎ 874 0064
🚌 37, 70, 134, 172
🕐 Tues-Sat 11am-5pm
⑤ free ♿ good

Lemonstreet Gallery
(6, C7) Lemonstreet specialises in contemporary printmaking, including limited edition etchings, woodcuts, lithographs, screenprints and lino prints. Works by Francis Bacon, Michael Craig-Martin, Tony O'Malley and a host of local artists are available and you can order prints over the Internet.
✉ Lemon St
☎ 671 0244 e www .lemonstreet.com

In the frame at the Gallery of Photography

Doug McKinlay

🚌 all city-centre buses
🕐 Mon-Wed & Fri-Sat
10am-6pm,
Thurs 10am-8pm, Sun
noon-5pm
⑤ free ♿ poor

Doug McKinlay
A slice of the Solomon salon

Origin Gallery (4, N6)
A relaxed space on the first floor of a Georgian terrace, Origin functions primarily as a showcase for artists who've stayed at the gallery's County Kerry retreat, Cill Rialaig. That means lots of landscape painting, but shows with various themes are also held.
✉ 83 Harcourt St
☎ 478 5159 🚌 14, 15, 16, 19 🕐 Mon-Fri 11am-5.30pm, Sat noon-4pm ⑤ free

Original Print Gallery
(5, C4) The gallery's back catalogue of work from 150 Irish and international printmakers is available for viewing and buying, along with new, limited-edition work. You can also order prints online and have them shipped anywhere in the world.
✉ 4 Temple Bar
☎ 677 3657
e www.original print.ie 🚌 all city-centre buses 🚆 Tara St 🕐 Tues, Wed & Fri 10.30am-5.30pm, Thurs 10.30am-8pm, Sat 11am-5pm, Sun 2-6pm ⑤ free ♿ partial

RHA Gallagher Gallery (4, N8)
Established in 1823, the Royal Hibernian Academy has four galleries – three dedicated to curated exhibits of Irish and international art, and a fourth, the Ashford Gallery, which promotes the work of Academy members and

artists who haven't yet secured commercial representation. Works on show range from traditional to innovative.
✉ 25 Ely Pl ☎ 661 2558 e www.royal hibernianacademy.com 🚌 10, 11, 13b, 51x 🕐 Tues, Wed, Fri & Sat 11am-5pm, Thurs 11am-8pm, Sun 2-5pm ⑤ free ♿ excellent

Rubicon Gallery (6, E7)
Overlooking St Stephen's Green, the Rubicon is one of the city's more prestigious galleries, with mainly paintings from gallery artists and local up-and-comers.
✉ 1st fl, 10 St Stephen's Green ☎ 670 8055 e www .rubicongallery.ie 🚌 all city-centre buses 🕐 Mon-Fri 11am-5.30pm, Sat 11am-4.30pm ⑤ free

Solomon Gallery
(6, C5) Set in a restored Georgian salon on the top floor of the Powerscourt Centre, Solomon Gallery has established a reputation for showing fine figurative art that includes painting, ceramics, glass and mixed media. Along with contemporary pieces are traditional Irish period paintings. A new exhibition is launched every three weeks or so.
✉ Powerscourt Townhouse Centre, William St S ☎ 679 4237

e www .solomon gallery.com 🚌 all city-centre buses 🕐 Mon-Sat 10am-5.30pm ⑤ free

Taylor Galleries (6, F9)
Founded in 1978, Taylor Galleries is the successor to both the Dawson and Waddington galleries. Housed in a fine Georgian building near the Shelbourne Hotel, contemporary artists shown include Louis le Brocquy, Tony O'Malley and John Doherty, while old-school works by Jack B Yeats and William Leech sometimes make an appearance.
✉ 16 Kildare St ☎ 676 6055 🚌 10, 11, 13 🚆 Pearse 🕐 Mon-Fri 10am-5.30pm, Sat 11am-1pm ⑤ free ♿ good

Temple Bar Gallery & Studios (5, C4)
Contemporary, thoughtful shows in a variety of media from a broad range of local and international artists. Set up in 1983 as an artist-run space, the gallery dedicates its upper floors to on-site studios and interesting solo or group shows from emerging painters, sculptors and mixed media artists.
✉ 5-9 Temple Bar ☎ 671 0073 🚌 all city-centre buses 🚆 Tara St 🕐 Tues-Wed, Fri-Sat 11am-6pm, Thurs 11am-7pm, Sun 2-6pm ⑤ free ♿ good

NOTABLE BUILDINGS

Bank of Ireland (5, D7)
Built for the Irish Houses of Parliament, the Bank of Ireland moved in after the Act of Union in 1801. Though the elaborate House of Commons was remodelled, the House of Lords survived intact. Its Irish oak woodwork, mahogany standing clock, 18th-century crystal chandelier and tapestries are well worth a look. Free tours are held on Tuesday at 10.30 and 11.30am and 1.45pm.
✉ **College Green**
☎ **671 1488, 677 6801**
🚌 **all city-centre buses**
🚉 **Tara St** ⏰ **Mon-Wed & Fri 10am-4pm, Thurs 10am-5pm**
💲 **free** ♿ **poor**

General Post Office (4, G6) The GPO is an important landmark that has played a starring role in Ireland's independence struggles. The 1916 Easter Rising leaders read their proclamation of a republic from its steps – the facade is still pockmarked from the subsequent clash and also from fighting during the Civil War in 1922. Today the GPO still attracts protesting pressure groups and individuals on a personal crusade.
✉ **O'Connell St** ☎ **705 7000** 📧 **www.anpost.ie**
🚌 **O'Connell St**
🚉 **Tara St** ⏰ **Mon-Sat 8am-8pm, Sun & hols 10am-6.30pm** 💲 **free**
♿ **poor**

Government Buildings (4, M8)
The domed Government Buildings, built in an Edwardian interpretation of the Georgian style, were opened in 1911. Tours lasting around 40 minutes include the new wing, renovated in the 1990s at a cost of £17.4 million, with the Taoiseach's office and the ceremonial staircase. The much more atmospheric old wing houses the cabinet room where Irish Free State ministers met for the first time.
✉ **Merrion St Upper**
☎ **662 4888** 📧 **www .irlgov.ie/taoiseach**
🚌 **7, 7a, 8, 45**
🚉 **Pearse** ⏰ **Sat 10.30am-3.30pm; tickets from National Gallery on day of visit**
💲 **free**
♿ **by arrangement**

National Library (4, L8)
The library's extensive collection includes valuable early manuscripts, first editions, maps and other items of interest. Temporary exhibitions are often held on the ground floor, and the library's gorgeous domed reading room is mentioned in Joyce's *Ulysses* – to see it get a visitor's ticket from the front desk. On the second floor is the Genealogical Office (p. 12).
✉ **Kildare St** ☎ **603 0200** 📧 **www.nli.ie**
🚌 **10, 11, 13**
⏰ **Mon-Wed 10am-9pm, Thurs-Fri 10am-5pm, Sat 10am-1pm**
💲 **free** ♿ **poor**

Sunlight Chambers (5, C1) Sunlight Chambers, on the southern banks of the Liffey, stands out among the Georgian and modern architecture for its beautiful Art Nouveau friezework. Sunlight was a brand of soap made by Lever Brothers, who built the late 19th-century building. The frieze shows the Lever Brothers' view of the world: men make clothes dirty, women wash them.
✉ **Essex Quay**
🚌 **all city-centre buses**

Windmill Lane Studios (3, E12)
Fans of U2 still flock to the recording studio where the group produced their early albums. Much to the chagrin of other businesses in Windmill Lane, the entire street has become a graffiti homage to the band – despite signs pleading punters to 'spray it on the real wall'.
✉ **4 Windmill La, Sir John Rogerson's Quay**
🚌 **1, 3** 🚉 **Pearse; Tara St** 💲 **free**

Bank of Ireland punters at the home of the punt

Doug McKinlay

PLACES OF WORSHIP

Newman University Church (4, N6)

The Catholic Newman University Church was built between 1854 and 1856 in an elaborate Byzantine style that features multicoloured marble and copious gold leaf, making it very fashionable for society weddings. Cardinal Newman, who founded the city's first Catholic University next door at Newman House (p. 37), is honoured with a bust.

✉ 83 St Stephen's Green
☎ 478 0616 🚌 10, 11, 13, 14, 14a, 15a, 15b
🕐 Mon-Sat 8am-6pm
💲 free

St Audoen's Church

(4, K2) The only surviving medieval parish church in the city, St Audoen's was built between 1181 and 1212, though the site is thought to be much older. Enlarged in its 15th-century heyday, it shrunk to its present size in the 18th and 19th centuries, when the eastern wing and St Anne's Chapel were left to ruin. Today the chapel houses an excellent visitor centre, and guides run tours of the much-renovated church and tower.

✉ High St
☎ 677 0088
🚌 51b, 78a, 123, 206
🕐 June-Sept 9.30am-5.30pm; last admission 4.45pm 💲 €1.90/0.75-1.25/5.10 ♿ good

St Mary's Pro-Cathedral (4, F7)

Dublin's Catholic cathedral is tucked away on tiny Marlborough St – a deliberately inconspicuous site. Built between 1816 and 1825, the cathedral's facade is modelled on the Temple of Theseus in Athens. Its carved altar is very impressive. Oddly, Marlborough St was once the biggest red-light district in Europe with an estimated 1600 prostitutes.

✉ Marlborough St
☎ 874 5441 📧 www.procathedral.ie 🚌 27, 31b, 42a, 42b, 130
🚊 Connolly
🕐 8am-7pm; closed Sun 2-4pm 💲 free

St Michan's Church

(4, H2) St Michan's was founded by Danes in 1095, though major rebu... 1686 and 1828 has... little of the original. ...church has a fine oak organ that may have bee... played by Handel, but the star attraction is the underground vault, where buried bodies have been gruesomely mummified by the magnesium limestone walls.

✉ Church St Lwr
☎ 872 4154 🚌 134
🕐 Mar-Oct: Mon-Fri 10am-1pm & 2-5pm, Sat 10am-1pm; Nov-Feb: Mon-Fri 12.30-3.30pm, Sat 10am-1pm
💲 €2.50/1.30-1.90 ♿ church only, vaults inaccessible

St Stephen's Church

(3, G12) Built in 1825 in Greek Revival style – complete with cupola – St Stephen's is commonly known as the 'Peppercanister church' because of its shape. It hosts classical concerts from time to time.

✉ Mount St Crescent
☎ 288 0663
🚌 5, 7, 7a, 8, 45, 46
🚊 Grand Canal Dock
🕐 services only: Sun 11am & Wed 11.30am; Jul-Aug extra service Fri 11am 💲 free

Whitefriar Street Carmelite Church

(6, E3) Built on the site of a previous Carmelite monastery, the church houses a 16th-century Flemish oak statue of the Mother and Child which is thought to be the only one of its kind to survive the Reformation. The altar contains the remains of St Valentine, donated by Pope

Dublin's Guilds

St Audoen's was one of several churches which served Dublin's crafts guilds from medieval times. Tradesfolk such as butchers, felt makers, cooks, skinners and bakers formed guilds to increase their political influence and to establish standards of practice in their craft, which apprentices then had to meet. Guilds often paid for the construction of chapels where Mass could be conducted at their request. The only remaining guildhall in Dublin is the Tailors' Guild Hall (4, K2) on Back Lane. It now houses the offices of the National Trust.

... 1835.
...gier St
...321 🚌 16,
..., 19, 19a, 65, 83
...n & Wed-Fri
...5.30pm, Tues
...-9.30pm, Sat 8am-
...m, Sun 8am-7.30pm
🅳 free ♿ good

St Werburgh's Church (6, B1)

On the west side of Dublin Castle, St Werburgh's Church stands on ancient foundations (probably 12th century). It was rebuilt in 1662, 1715 and again in 1759 and Lord Edward Fitzgerald, a leader of the 1798 Rising, is interred in the vault.

✉ Werburgh St
☎ 478 3710
🚌 50, 56a, 150
🕐 Mon-Fri 10am-4pm; ring bell for caretaker
🅳 free

PARKS & GARDENS

Garden of Remembrance (4, D5)

Established for the 50th anniversary of the 1916 Easter Rising, the garden commemorates those who sacrificed their lives in the long struggle for Irish independence. The centrepiece is a 1971 sculpture by Oisin Kelly depicting the myth of the Children of Lir, who were turned into swans by their wicked stepmother.

✉ Parnell Sq
☎ 874 3074 🚌 36, 40

🚉 Connolly
🕐 May-Sept 9.30am-dusk, Oct-Apr 11am-dusk
🅳 free ♿ poor

Herbert Park (3, J13)

This is a pleasant swathe of lush green lawns, ponds and flower beds near the Royal Dublin Society Showgrounds. Sandwiched between prosperous Ballsbridge and Donnybrook, the park runs alongside the River Dodder.

✉ Ballsbridge
🚌 5, 7, 7a, 8, 45, 46

🚉 Sandymount; Lansdowne Rd
🕐 dawn to dusk
🅳 free ♿ good

Iveagh Gardens (4, O6)

Just behind Newman House are the landscaped Iveagh Gardens, accessible from Earlsfort Terrace or Harcourt St. Designed by Ninian Niven in 1863, they include a rustic grotto, cascade, fountain, maze and rosarium. They used to be one of Dublin's best kept secrets but the word's out – so you'll have plenty of company on a sunny day.

✉ Clonmel St
☎ 475 7816
🚌 14, 14a, 15a, 15b
🕐 Mon-Sat 8am-dusk, Sun 10am-dusk
🅳 free ♿ good

War Memorial Gardens (3, F3)

Just north of Kilmainham Gaol, the gardens are dedicated to the memory of the 49,400 Irish soldiers who died in WWI. Designed by architect Sir Edwin Lutyens, highlights are the sunken rose gardens and herbaceous borders.

✉ South Circular Rd, Islandbridge
☎ 677 0236
🚌 25, 26, 51, 66, 68, 69
🕐 Mon-Fri 8am-dusk, Sat-Sun 10am-dusk
🅳 free ♿ poor

Dublin's Canals

True Dubliners, it is said, are born within the confines of the two canals which encircle the inner city. The older Grand Canal, which began operation in 1779, stretches from Ringsend, through south Dublin, to the River Shannon in the centre of Ireland. Barges, towed by horses, carried cargo and passengers along the canal until 1960 when its commercial life came to an end. It is still used today by leisure craft.

North Dublin's Royal Canal, built in 1790, never made money and was later sold to a railway company.

Both canals have pleasant stretches that are great for strolling or cycling. Join the Royal Canal towpath at North Strand Rd (3, C12), and follow it to the suburb of Clonsilla over 10km away. Or take the Grand Canal towpath west from Mount St Lower (3, G12) to the Robert Emmet Bridge (3, H8), stopping at one of the canalside pubs along the way.

Taking a lunch break in a park along the Grand Canal

Monumental Failures

Dublin's civic history is littered with public monuments that have been blown up, defaced, ridiculed and bungled.

William III's statue on College Green was mutilated so often it was sold for scrap in 1929, as was one of George II soon after. In 1957 Lord Gough was blown off his horse in Phoenix Park, and in 1966 Lord Nelson's head exploded onto the footpath on O'Connell St (it's now in the Dublin Civic Museum, p. 38).

Even patriots were not immune. In 1971 St Stephen's Green's **Wolfe Tone monument** (4, M8) became intimate with a stick of gelignite but was restored by the artist. It's no wonder that the authorities soon turned their attentions to less controversial figures. The **statue of Molly Malone** (2, C1; see below) at the north end of Grafton St represents the legendary cockles and mussels vendor who is the subject of Dublin's most famous song. But her plunging neckline soon earned her the tag 'the tart with the cart'. **James Joyce's statue** (4, F6) on O'Connell St depicts him strolling with a walking stick. So Dublin's greatest writer became 'the prick with the stick'.

The **Anna Livia monument** (4, F6; p. 22) on O'Connell St is meant to symbolise the spirit of the Liffey. But Dubliners found the woman lying in water so ugly they labelled it 'the floozy in the Jacuzzi', and 'the hoo-er in the sewer'.

Oscar Wilde, reclining on a rock in Merrion Square (4, L9; p.35), became 'the fag on the crag', while a statue of **two women with shopping bags** (5, A4) on the north side of Ha'penny Bridge is known as 'the hags with the bags'.

In the lead up to 2000, Dublin Corporation placed a luminous clock in the Liffey. It was meant to count down the hours to the millennium. Unfortunately the Liffey's grime kept clogging the clock up and 'the time in the slime' was removed.

Dublin's latest civic project, a 120m-high spike with no obvious purpose or symbolism, is due to replace Nelson's Column on O'Connell St. But Dubliners are not impressed by plans for 'the skewer by the sewer', or 'the stiletto in the ghetto'.

Some things do remain sacred though, including the O'Connell St **statues of Daniel O'Connell** (4, G7) and **Charles Stewart Parnell** (4, E6), and the **Famine Statues** (4, G9; p. 7) outside Custom House, which commemorate the millions who died during the 1845-51 Potato Famine.

Tapping a hearty tune to the 'tart with the cart'

SEASIDE SUBURBS

Bray   (1, C5)

The Brighton of Dublin, Bray has a long seafront parade of fast food places, tacky amusement arcades, fairy floss vendors and happily screeching kids. Developed in the 1850s when the railway arrived, Bray is 19km south of Dublin. Home to a Martello tower owned by Bono from U2, Bray also has fine views of the Wicklow Mountains and an 8km cliff walk around Bray Head to Greystones further south. The Porterhouse pub (☎ 286 0668) on the foreshore is a branch of the Temple Bar microbrewery (p. 93) which makes its own excellent beers and serves hearty meals from 5pm. Catch the DART to Bray.

Clontarf   (1, A5)

Just 5km north-east of the centre, Clontarf is a pretty bayside suburb whose main attractions are birds and golf. The **North Bull Wall**, which extends about 1km into Dublin Bay, was built in 1820 to stop Dublin Harbour from silting up. Marshes and dunes developed behind the wall, creating **North Bull Island** which is now a Unesco biosphere reserve. The bird population can reach 40,000 – watch for shelducks, curlews and oystercatchers on the mud flats – and a range of plants and other animals can be seen. An interpretive centre (☎ 833 8341; free; times vary – call ahead) on the island is reached by walking across the 1.5km-long northern causeway. Driving is the best option for getting there as transport to the island is poor. Catch the DART to Raheny, from where it's a 40-minute walk to the northern causeway, or bus 130 from Lower Abbey St to the Bull Wall stop, within a 25-minute walk.

Dalkey   (1, B5)

In medieval times Dalkey was Dublin's most important port town and boasted seven castles, of which only two remain. Today it's home to Dublin's rich and famous, including several members of U2, racing driver Damon Hill and film director Neil Jordan. As well as good restaurants and pubs on Castle St, the villagey main drag, the coastline and beaches nearby are superb.

The roofless **Archibold's Castle** on Castle St is closed except at Christmas, when a nativity crib is open to visitors. Across the road is the 15th-century **Goat Castle** which houses an interesting visitor centre (☎ 285 8366; €4/3.50/2.50; Apr-Oct: Mon-Fri 9.30am-5pm, Sat, Sun & hols 11am-5pm; Nov-Apr weekends only). Exhibits explain the castle's defence systems, the history of the area's transport and various myths and legends. The remains of the 11th-century **St Begnet's Church and Graveyard** are also here.

The waters around **Dalkey Island** are popular with scuba divers; catch one of the small boats touting for business at Coliemore Harbour. To get to Dalkey from Dublin, catch the DART.

Howth (1, A5)

Howth (rhymes with 'both'), at the northern end of Dublin Bay, offers visitors a quaint fishing village, walks on the windswept peninsula and a nearby island to explore. **Howth town**, 15km north-east of central Dublin and accessible by DART, has a pleasant port with three piers, some good pubs and excellent fish and chip joints.

Looming above it is the **Hill of Howth**, wonderful for a leisurely half or full-day's walk with views of Dublin city and the bay. In spring the peninsula is ablaze with unusual wildflowers, and seabirds caterwaul around the shore. Grab the Howth Heritage Trust's *The Howth Peninsula* map and guide from Eason's (p. 72) in O'Connell St before you go.

About 1.5km offshore is **Ireland's Eye**, a rocky, seabird sanctuary with the ruins of a 6th-century monastery. There's a Martello tower at the island's north-western end, while at the eastern end a spectacular rock face plummets into the sea. Seals can also be spotted. Doyle & Sons (☎ 831 4200) run boats out to the island from the East Pier of Howth Harbour during summer from around 10.30am on weekends. Return trips cost €6.50/3.50.

Malahide (1, A5)

A pretty town with a marina and several good restaurants, Malahide's main attraction is **Malahide Castle** (☎ 846 2184; €5.50/3-5/15), set in 101 hectares of parklands. The castle served as the Talbot family home from 1185 to 1976 and incorporates a hotchpotch of architectural styles from the 12th to the 18th centuries. On the grounds is the **Fry Model Railway** (p. 38) and **Tara's Palace** (☎ 846 3779; €3.80/1.25-2.50/8.90), an elaborate, over-sized doll's house whose rooms are furnished with fittings from around the world. The **Talbot Botanic Gardens** (☎ 872 7777; €2.50), also within the grounds, has a varied collection of plants, many from the southern hemisphere. Catch bus 42 from Busáras or the DART from Connolly.

Doug McKinlay

Howth's harmonious harbour

UBLIN FOR CHILDREN

Dublin is a reasonably child-friendly city but it does have its drawbacks. The main problem is infrastructure – poor transport means lots of walking, there are few public spots to stop and rest (particularly on the northside), and trendification means many pubs are not as family-friendly as they used to be. There's also a dearth of public toilets in the city centre, although the major shopping centres have toilets and baby change facilities. On the upside, the increased wealth of Dubliners has spurred a variety of children's activities. And a good number of restaurants accept child diners, though it's best to arrive early in the evening.

The Ark (5, D3)

A four-storey cultural centre with a theatre, gallery and workshop, the Ark is aimed at kids aged four to 14. Its programs promote an interest in science, the environment and the arts, and its 15 core staff are supplemented by artists from a variety of disciplines. A good chance for kids to mix with their Dublin counterparts – but book well ahead to ensure a place.
✉ 11a Eustace St
☎ 670 7788
e www.ark.ie 🚌 all cross-city buses
🕐 Mon-Fri 9.30am-5.30pm ⑤ €2.50-6.50
& excellent

Dublin's Viking Adventure (5, D1)

Fittingly located just off Wood Quay, the old heart of Norse Dublin, DVA is an interactive recreation of 'Dyflin', led by guides in costume. The smells, sounds and streets of the city come to life and you can chat with 'locals' along the way. An extensive collection of artefacts recovered during excavations at Wood Quay is also on display.
✉ Essex St W ☎ 679 6040 e www.visitdublin.com 🚌 51, 51b, 78a, 79 🕐 Mar-Oct: Tues-Sat 10am-4.30pm; Nov-Feb:

Tues-Sat 10am-1pm & 2-4.30pm ⑤ €7.50/4-7/20 & good

Dublin Zoo (3, D5)

The second-oldest public zoo in Europe, Dublin Zoo is home to more than 700 animals, including rhinos, gorillas, leopards, penguins and polar bears. Apart from the animal antics, kids will enjoy the regular feedings, the mini-train ride through the grounds, the informative discovery centre and, if all else fails, the play equipment.
✉ Phoenix Park
☎ 677 1425
e www.dublinzoo.ie
🚌 10 from O'Connell St, 25 or 26 from Abbey St Middle
🕐 Mar-Oct: Mon-Sat 9.30am-6pm, Sun 10.30am-6pm; Nov-Feb: Mon-Sat 9.30am-5pm, Sun 10.30am-5pm

Other Kids' Stuff

Some other choice children's activities can be found at:

- weekend or holiday programs at the National Gallery of Ireland (p. 25)
- National Museum (p. 26)
- Irish Museum of Modern Art (p. 21)
- Temple Bar (p. 31)

⑤ €9.50/6-7.25/27; under-3s free & good

Dvblinia (4, K3)

Inside what was once Christ Church's Synod Hall, Dvblinia recreates medieval Dublin, using models, music, streetscapes and interactive displays. Adults might find it a bit kitsch,

When you can't bear any more whingeing, try the zoo.

but kids enjoy the recreated medieval fair — with simple but fun activities at each stall — and the models of the medieval quayside and a cobbler's shop. You can climb St Michael's Tower for panoramic views of the city.

✉ **Christ Church**
☎ **679 4611** 🚌 **51b, 78a, 123, 206** 🕐 **Apr-Sept 10am-5pm; Oct-Mar: Mon-Sat 11am-4pm, Sun 10am-4.30pm** 💲 **€5/3.80/12.70; under-5s free** ⚹ **good**

Hey, Doodle Doodle

(5, C5) Budding young artists get their chance to create at this paint-your-own ceramics studio. Kids pick a piece of pottery, paint it and you pick it up two or three days later, after it's been fired and glazed. Design time is free but painting time is charged by the hour; all materials are supplied and staff are happy to help.

✉ **14 Crown Alley**
☎ **672 7382** ℮ **www .heydoodle doodle.com** 🚌 **all cross-city buses** 🚉 **Tara St** 🕐 **Tues-Sun 11am-6pm** 💲 **€6.35/hr, plus ceramics (from €7.50); studio rates also available**

Lambert Puppet Theatre (1, B4)

The puppets are all handmade, the theatre has been running since 1972, and the performers span three generations of the same family. It's not hard to see why Lambert is a Dublin institution. Shows include old favourites like Hansel and Gretel, and newer works written by the company. During the

International Puppet Festival in September, international acts take the stage with their weird and wonderful creations.

✉ **Clifton La, Monkstown, Co. Dublin**
☎ **280 0974** 🚉 **Monkstown** 🕐 **box office: 10am-5pm; puppet show: Sat & Sun 3.30pm** 💲 **€7.60** ⚹ **excellent**

National Sealife Centre (1, C5)

The old and pitiful National Aquarium was taken over by a British company a couple of years ago and is now a much more pleasant place to visit. Aquariums are stocked with 70 different sea and freshwater species, from seahorses to sharks.

✉ **Strand Rd, Bray**
☎ **286 6939** ℮ **www .sealife.com** 🚉 **Bray** 🕐 **10am-6pm** 💲 **€7/5** ⚹ **good**

National Wax Museum (4, D4)

Dublin's version of the ubiquitous wax museum combines the usual parade of stars with Irish historical figures. Jack and the Beanstalk, Aladdin, the Flintstones and ET will suit the youngest, while older kids who aren't squeamish might prefer the Chamber

of Horrors. Joyce, Yeats, Robert Emmet and several Irish presidents are on show, but kids will probably prefer Michael Jackson, Madonna and U2.

✉ **Granby Row, Parnell Sq** ☎ **872 6340** 🚌 **all cross-city buses** 🚉 **Connolly** 🕐 **Mon-Sat 10am-5.30pm, Sun noon-5.30pm** 💲 **€4.50/ 3.20/2.50** ⚹ **poor**

Newbridge House & Farm (1, A5)

Newbridge House combines a historic Georgian manor with a large traditional farm. The house has an elaborate interior, with fine plasterwork, period furniture, a museum and an ornate coach in the stables. The self-sufficient, 18th-century farm has cows, pigs and birds, as well as rare breeds like the Connemara pony, Jacob sheep and some exotic chickens with punk hairdos.

✉ **Donabate, Co. Dublin** ☎ **843 6534** 🚌 **33b from Eden Quay** 🚉 **Northern Suburban to Donabate** 🕐 **Apr-Sept: Tues-Sat 10am-5pm (house closed 1-2pm), Sun 2-6pm; Oct-Mar: Sat-Sun & hols 2-5pm** 💲 **house & farm: €5/2.50-3.80/14; farm only: €1.25/1/2.50** ⚹ **poor**

KEEPING FIT

Dubliners love watching and talking about sport, but aren't nearly as fanatical when it comes to exercising their own bodies. It's not difficult to see why – poor weather and a dearth of accessible, affordable, quality sporting venues means that the few good public facilities in town are perennially crowded. To cope with the strain, many places charge peak and off-peak rates.

Ashtown Riding Stables (3, A1)
From here you can trail ride in Phoenix Park, on horses suited to a range of expertise. Hour-long rides take in the park's main sights, and the more experienced can gallop through the wilder areas where fallow deer roam. Lessons are provided in the sandy arena and protective helmets are supplied.
✉ **Ashtown Rd, Ashtown, Castleknock**
☎ **838 3807** 🚌 **37, 38, 39** 🚊 **Western Suburban to Ashtown**
🕐 **park rides: Sat & Sun 1, 2 & 3pm; classes: Sat & Sun 2 & 3pm, adults only Wed 6.30 & 7.30pm** 💲 **€19/15hr**

Deer Park Golf Course (1, A5)
Ten kilometres north-east of the city centre on the Howth Peninsula, this public course is set within the grounds of Howth Castle, affording some fabulous views.
✉ **Howth, Co. Dublin**
☎ **832 2624**
🚌 **31, 31b from Abbey St Lwr** 🚊 **Howth**
🕐 **8am-dusk**
💲 **Mon-Fri €13, Sat-Sun €24 for 18 holes**

Herbert Park Tennis Club (3, J13)
The 12 tarmac courts are operated by the Parks Association on a pay-as-you-play basis. You can't book (there's no phone); simply turn up and grab a court. There are no floodlights, so it's all over at dusk.
✉ **Herbert Park, Ballsbridge** 🚌 **5, 7, 7a, 8, 18, 45**
🚊 **Lansdowne Rd or Sandymount**
🕐 **10am-dusk**
💲 **€1.90\hr**

Irish National Sailing School (1, B5)
This place has sailing courses for adults and children, from beginners to advanced. Kids' five-day courses run at Easter, weekdays during summer, and in the October mid-term break.
✉ **West Pier, Dun Laoghaire** ☎ **284 4195**
📧 **www.inss.ie**
🚊 **Dun Laoghaire**
🕐 **call for course dates; no courses Dec-Mar** 💲 **adults €182/wk May-Sept, €165 Oct-Nov & Apr; children €160/wk**

Jackie Skelly Fitness Centre (6, C5)
This light and airy gym has treadmills, bikes, steppers, rowers and free weights. Morning and evening fitness classes include step, aerobics, spinning, yoga and pilates. Day passes only give you off-peak access (weekends and 6.30am-4pm Mon-Fri), and you'll need to book classes during peak times (Mon-Fri 4-9pm).
✉ **41-42 Clarendon St**
☎ **677 0040**
📧 **www.jackieskelly fitness.com**
🚌 **all cross-city buses**
🕐 **Mon-Fri 6.30am-9.30pm, Sat 9am-6pm, Sun 10.30am-5pm**
💲 **day pass €12.70**

Markievicz Leisure Centre (4, H8)
The best public leisure centre in the city, Markievicz

A Sporting Chance
The *Golden Pages* is a useful place to find listings of sports facilities near you. Dublin Tourism publishes the free *Golfing Around Dublin* guide, available at their office in Suffolk St. Check out 📧 www.golfdublin.com for information about the city's public courses.The following associations can also point you in the right direction:

The Irish Sailing Association (☎ 280 0239)
Pitch & Putt Union of Ireland (☎ 450 9299)
Irish Waterski Federation (☎ 285 5205)
Tennis Ireland (☎ 668 1841)
Irish Squash (☎ 450 1564)
Irish Basketball Association (☎ 459 0211)

has a fully-equipped gym, daily aerobic classes and an 25m indoor heated swimming pool (bathing caps compulsory). Casual gym sessions include a quick dip (at a rather regimented quarter to the hour), while those with a swim-only ticket can paddle pretty much as long as they like. Peak and off-peak rates apply.
✉ Townsend St ☎ 672 9121 🚊 Tara St
🕐 Mon-Fri 7am-10pm, Sat 9am-6pm, Sun 10am-4pm ⑤ pool: €3.80/2.50, gym: €4.45; peak times €0.65 more

Surfdock (3, F13)
Windsurfing enthusiasts and novices alike can hit the water at Surfdock, a water sports retailer and training centre which operates from a barge at Grand Canal Dock. Courses run all year; beginners can try three-hour 'taster' sessions, while 12-hour intensive training caters to the more experienced. You can also rent windsurfing gear and go out on your own.
✉ South Docks Rd, Grand Canal Dock, Ringsend
☎ 668 3945
e www.surfdock.ie
🚌 1, 3 🚊 Grand Canal Dock 🕐 shop: Mon-Fri 10am-6pm, Sat 10am-5pm; call for course times ⑤ windsurfing: €45 for 3hrs, €140-150 for 12hrs; sailboards €15.50/hr

QUIRKY DUBLIN

Casino at Marino
(3, A14) Roman temple from the outside and kooky Georgian house inside, the Casino at Marino is one of Ireland's finest – and weirdest – Palladian buildings. The house was built by Sir William Chambers for the eccentric James Caulfield (1728-99), later earl of Charlemont. While externally the building appears to contain just one room, the interior is a convoluted maze of rooms.
✉ off Malahide Rd, Marino ☎ 833 1618
e www.heritageire land.ie 🚌 20a, 20b, 27, 27b, 42, 42c, 123 🚊 Clontarf Rd
🕐 June-Sept 10am-6pm; May & Oct 10am-5pm; Feb, Mar & Nov: Thurs & Sun noon-4pm; April: Thurs & Sun noon-5pm
⑤ €2.50/1.25-1.90/6.35

The Decent Cigar Emporium (6, E6)
When the buzz of Grafton St gets too much, slip up this discreet staircase, recline in a plush leather armchair and light up a hand-rolled, long-filler cigars. A glass of red wine and a cup of Illy coffee later, you'll barely remember the clamour below. Humidors, pipes, designer lighters and ashtrays are on sale too.
✉ 46 Grafton St
☎ 671 6451 e www .decent-cigar.com
🚌 all city-centre buses 🕐 Mon-Wed, Fri & Sat 10am-6pm, Thurs 10am-8pm, Sun 1.30-5.30pm ⑤ free

The Doll Store & Hospital (6, C4)
Broken arms, severed heads, missing eyes and gaping wounds are all lovingly treated at the Dolls' Hospital, where experts repair a whopping 23,000 dolls and teddies each year. This is also the place to kit out your doll's house with an enormous range of furniture, fittings and other essentials, like miniature tins of Heinz baked beans. For glamour pusses gone PC, they can also turn your old fur coat into a teddy bear.
✉ 62 Great George's St S ☎ 478 3403
e ww.dollstore.ie
🚌 16, 16a, 19, 19a, 65, 83 🕐 Mon-Sat 10am-5pm ⑤ free ⑤ good

Golf D2 (4, J4)
No time to make it to the course? Then virtual golf could be the answer. You hit real balls with real clubs (yours or theirs, no extra charge) into a computer-generated course on a huge screen. Play matches on over 30 famous courses, including St Andrew's and Pebble Beach, or practice your swing on the virtual driving range. Lessons provided by a real, human PGA professional. Booking essential.
✉ Cow's La ☎ 672 6181 🚌 50, 54a, 56a, 150 🕐 Mon-Fri noon-10pm, Sat 10am-8pm
⑤ €26/hr for one person, €19/hr each for two, €15.50/hr for three, €10/hr for four, €8/hr for five

Temple Bar's funky street art

Richard Cummins

out & about

WALKING TOURS
Perambulate with Pints

Begin at Dublin's oldest pub, the Brazen Head **1** on Bridge St, turn right onto the quays and walk to Parliament St where you turn right to the Porterhouse **2** microbrewery. Turn left into Essex St, noting the stained glass *Ulysses* window of the Norseman **3**, and continue east to the traditional Palace Bar **4**. Turn left at Westmoreland St, then right at the quays for the enormous Messrs Maguire **5** microbrewery. Take Hawkins St right, then left into Poolbeg St where Mulligans **6** is said to serve Dublin's best pint of Guinness. Head back to Hawkins St and turn left. Cross over Pearse St to College St and follow the south side of College Green until you see an arched laneway – go through it to the magnificent Stag's Head **7**. Take Dame Court south then turn left at Exchequer St and pause at the International Bar **8**. At Grafton St turn right,

then left into Duke St for Davy Byrne's **9**. Back on Grafton, turn right at Harry St for Art Nouveau–style Bruxelles **10** and Brendan Behan's old boozer, McDaid's **11**. Continue south down Grafton again and turn left into Anne St S past Kehoe's **12**. Turn right at Dawson St, then left at St Stephen's Green, continuing down Merrion Row to take in some tunes at O'Donoghue's **13** or, if you are up to it, one more pint at Toner's **14** or Doheny & Nesbitt **15**.

distance 4km **duration** 2hrs
▶ **start** 🚌 25, 26, 69, 79, 90
● **end** 🚌 10, 11, 13b, 51x

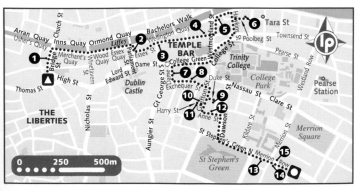

Take a Walk on the Northside

From Mountjoy Square ❶, head south-west down Gardiner Place and turn left into Great George's St N, one of the best-preserved Georgian streets in the north. Visit the Cobalt Gallery & Cafe ❷ and James Joyce Cultural Centre ❸. Turn right onto Parnell St, pass the Charles Stewart Parnell statue ❹ and do a clockwise loop of Parnell Square. You'll pass the Rotunda Hospital ❺ on the south side, and the Hugh Lane Gallery ❻ and Dublin Writers' Museum ❼ on the north side. Near the towering Abbey Presbyterian Church ❽ is the Garden of Remembrance ❾. Continue around the square past

SIGHTS & HIGHLIGHTS

Mountjoy Square (p. 37)
Cobalt Gallery & Cafe (p. 77)
James Joyce Cultural Centre (p. 35)
Charles Stuart Parnell Statue (p. 45)
Rotunda Hospital (p. 37)
Hugh Lane Gallery (p. 20)
Dublin Writers' Museum (p. 35)
Garden of Remembrance (p. 44)
Gate Theatre (p. 99)
Anna Livia & James Joyce statues (p. 45)
General Post Office (p. 42)
Daniel O'Connell Monument (p. 45)
Hags with the Bags statue (p. 45)
Ha'penny Bridge (p. 38)
Winding Stair Bookshop & Cafe (p. 77)
Four Courts (p. 36)
St Michan's (p. 43)

A sitting post at the GPO

distance	3km	duration	2hrs
▶ start	🚌 11, 16, 41 🚉 Connolly		
● end	🚌 134		

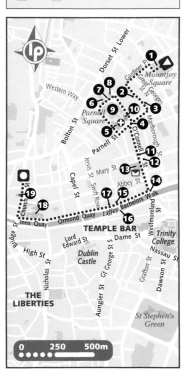

the Gate Theatre ❿ to O'Connell St where you'll find the Anna Livia ⓫ and James Joyce ⓬ statues and the GPO ⓭. Continue down O'Connell St to the Daniel O'Connell monument ⓮ then turn right onto the quays, stopping to admire the 'hags with the bags' ⓯ and Ha'penny Bridge ⓰. Browse and refuel at the Winding Stair Bookshop & Cafe ⓱, then continue along the quays, admiring the view, to James Gandon's dramatic Four Courts ⓲. At Church St turn right to see the grisly vaults at St Michan's ⓳.

he Liberties to Kilmainham

art outside Dublin Corporation ❶ on Wood Quay, and take Fishamble
t to Christ Church Cathedral ❷. Backtrack to Werburgh St and St
Werburgh's Church ❸. Continue south, turn right at Kevin St Upper, then
right again at St Patrick's Close for Marsh's Library ❹ and St Patrick's
Cathedral ❺. Cross Patrick St and head to the antique shops of Francis St.

Doug McKinlay

distance 4.4km **duration** 2hrs
▶ **start** 🚌 50, 66, 77, 121, 123
● **end** 🚌 68, 69, 78a, 79, 90, 123

Pause for a snack at the Gallic Kitchen ❻. Turn right at Thomas Davis St to Back Lane, with Mother Redcaps Market ❼ and the Tailor's Guildhall ❽. Turn left at Cornmarket, passing St Audoen's Catholic ❾ and St Audoen's Protestant ❿ Churches on your right. Continue west along Cornmarket, past John's Lane Augustinian Church ⓫ and St Catherine's ⓬ outside which the patriot Robert Emmet was beheaded. Turn left at Crane St and follow the signs to the Guinness Storehouse ⓭. Turn right at Grand Canal Place, then right at Echlin St to rejoin Thomas St opposite the Guinness Brewery ⓮. Cross the road, veer right onto Bow Lane W and turn right again into Steeven's Lane. St Patrick's ⓯ and Dr Steeven's ⓰ Hospitals are both on your left. At Heuston station turn left into Military Rd for the Irish Museum of Modern Art ⓱.

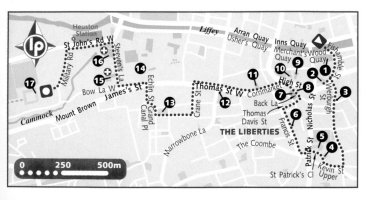

Waterside Wander

Start at the Bleeding Horse pub ❶ on Camden St Lower, built in 1710 as a farrier inn, and walk south to the Portobello ❷, a pub built to house and feed canal workers. Turning left at the Grand Canal, begin your stroll along

the towpath, passing several old locks which still operate. About 300m past Leeson St, there's a statue of poet Patrick Kavanagh ❸ relaxing on a bench. At Macartney Bridge, turn right onto Baggot St and refuel at Searsons ❹. Return to the canal and continue east, diverting left at Mount Street Crescent for St Stephen's Church ❺. Back on the towpath, turn right at Northumberland Rd, then left at Haddington Rd for the National Print Museum ❻. Turn left at Grand Canal St Upper and divert right to Barrow St, where you can climb the steps of the DART station to see an ornate Victorian gas ring. Retrace your steps, then turn right at Grand Canal Quay for the Waterways Vistor Centre ❼. Turn left at Pearse St, right at Cardiff's Lane and left at Sir John Rogerson's Quay. To see U2's former studios ❽ turn left at Windmill Lane, then rest on a bench at City Quay with views of Custom House.

Early leather boat, Waterways Visitor Centre

distance 5.54km **duration** 3hrs
▶ **start** 🚌 16, 16a, 19, 19a, 65, 83
● **end** 🚉 Tara St

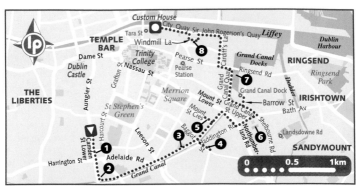

EXCURSIONS
Glendalough   (1, D4)

Spectacularly set in a deep valley beside two ancient lakes, Glendalough (pronounced 'glendalock') is an ancient monastic settlement that somehow retains its magic, despite the coachloads of tourists who visit. The **Visitor Centre** sets the scene with some interesting displays, a video on ancient Irish monasteries and a model of Glendalough in its prime.

INFORMATION

54km south of Dublin

🚌 St Kevin's Bus Service (☎ 281 8119), 11.30am daily from Royal College of Surgeons (6, F5)

✉ Glendalough

☎ 0404-45325, 45352

ⓘ *Exploring the Glendalough Valley* is a useful guide available from Dúchas (p. 13)

🕐 Visitor Centre: June-Aug 9am-6.30pm, Sept-mid-Oct & mid-Mar-May 9.30am-6pm, mid-Oct-mid-Mar 9.30am-5pm

⑤ Visitor Centre: €2.50/1.25-1.90/6.35

✗ Wicklow Heather Restaurant (☎ 0404-45157), Laragh

The beautifully preserved round tower

Richard Mills

One of the country's most important sites, Glendalough was founded by St Kevin in the 6th century AD. From this time on it was renowned for the monastic settlement, where hermit monks retired to contemplate in the quiet solitude of the valley. The settlement survived Viking raids and an English incursion in 1398, before it was dissolved during the Reformation.

The site is entered through Ireland's only surviving monastic gateway, to the east of **Lower Lake**. The ruins here include a 10th-century round tower, the Cathedral of St Peter and St Paul, a fine high cross and St Kevin's Church, a stone masterpiece.

Green Rd takes you to the ruins and breathtaking scenery of **Upper Lake** to the west. The remains of an early Christian stone fort, the 11th-century Reefert Church and **St Kevin's Bed**, a 2m-deep cave where the saint is said to have slept, are scattered around the lake's south-eastern edge.

Those with monastic tendencies might like the new Heritage Retreat Centre (☎ 0404-45140; €32 per night) which rents out individual hermitages to those seeking solitude and quiet contemplation. The one-person, self-catering accommodation includes a bed, bathroom, small kitchen and open fire but no electricity.

National Stud & Japanese Gardens

In the heartland of Ireland's hugely successful horse-breeding and racing industry, the National Stud was founded in 1900 by Colonel William Hall-Walker (of the Johnnie Walker distilling family). Home to some of Ireland's top breeding stallions, as well as a museum, you don't need to be a

INFORMATION
25km west of Du...
- 🚌 Bus Éireann (☎ 836...
  Kildare, several departe...
- 🚊 Arrow line from Heuston...
  Kildare
- ✉ Tully, Co. Kildare
- ☎ 045-521251
- e www.irish-national-stud.ie
- ⏱ mid-Feb-mid-Nov 9.30am-6pm
- $ €7.60/3.80-5.70, includes gardens
- ✗ Silken Thomas (☎ 045-522252),
  Market Sq, Tully

Co. Kildare's little patch of zen

racing aficionado to appreciate a visit – the setting is beautiful. Next door, the **Japanese Gardens** (☎ 045-521617) were laid out in 1906 by master gardener Tasso Eida and his son Minoru. The gardens chart the journey of life – from birth to death – through a series of symbolic landmarks, and are considered to be among the finest Japanese gardens in Europe.

Russborough House   (1, C3)

One of Ireland's finest stately homes, Russborough House was designed by Richard Cassels and built between 1740 and 1751. The magnificent Palladian villa's granite central building is flanked by two wings that are connected by curving, pillared collonnades.
Inside, the style is exuberantly Baroque, with ornate plasterwork by the LaFranchini brothers and period fittings and furnishings. In 1952 the house was bought by Sir Alfred Beit of De Beers, who brought his remarkable art collection with him. Works by Goya, Gainsborough, Rubens and Vermeer still hang in the grand rooms, though security is tight after high-profile robberies in 1974 and 1986. Many of the more valuable works now hang in the National Gallery (p. 25).

INFORMATION
40km south-west of Dublin
- 🚌 65 from Eden Quay (10 daily;
  6am-11.15pm)
- ✉ 5km south-west of Blessington,
  Co. Wicklow
- ☎ 045-865239
- ⏱ June-Aug 10.30am-5.30pm; May
  & Sept: Mon-Sat 10.30am-
  2.30pm, Sun 10.30am-5.30pm;
  Apr & Oct Sun & hols 10.30am-
  5.30pm
- $ €5/2.50-4
- ✗ on-site tearoom

..., the picturesque village of Enniskerry is Powerscourt ... by Richard Cassels on the site of a 13th-century castle. ... house accidentally burnt down in 1974 and has not been ... its former glory. It contains a small **historical exhibition**,

MATION

2km south of central Dublin
- 44 from Hawkins St to Enniskerry
- DART to Bray, then bus 85 to Enniskerry (€1.50 one way)
- ✉ Enniskerry, Co. Wicklow
- ☎ 204 6000
- e www.powerscourt.ie
- ⏰ house & gardens: 9.30am-5.30pm; waterfall: 9.30am-7pm (10.30am-dusk Nov-Feb)
- $ house: €2.50/1.50-2; garden: €6/3-5; house & garden: €8/4-6.50
- ✗ Avoca Restaurant on-site; Poppies Country Cooking (☎ 282 8869), The Square, Enniskerry

Powerscourt House: damaged by fire yet still impressive

several craft shops and an excellent restaurant, but the real attraction is the estate's fabulous 20-hectare **garden**. The owners still live in one wing of the house.

The terraced gardens descending the hill in front of the house are backed by the peak of the 506m-high Sugarloaf Mountain. The **Italianate front gardens** were begun in the 19th century when an enormous number of trees were planted. The grounds were adorned with elaborate statues and ironwork collected by the Wingfield family who held court here for more than 350 years.

The **Japanese garden** includes maples, azaleas and palms, as well as a pagoda, wooden bridges and stone lanterns. One of the oldest parts of the estate is the **Walled Gardens**, with Venetian gates and multicoloured rose bushes. One of the strangest features is the **Pet Cemetery**, complete with headstones mourning the passing of Tiny the dachshund and Eugenie the Jersey cow.

A 5km walk or shuttle bus ride away is the 130m **Powerscourt Waterfall** (€3.50/1.50-3), the highest in Britain and Ireland. It's most impressive after heavy rain. Several companies include Powerscourt on their tours, including Bus Éireann (☎ 836 6111; €26/23/13, including entry fees), which departs from Busáras at 10am Tuesday from June to mid-September.

ORGANISED TOURS

Dublin has loads of tours to choose from, with themes from literary landmarks to ghostly tales. Daytrips outside Dublin are easy with a variety of coach and rail tours that travel as far away as the Aran Islands in Galway.

BUS TOURS

Dublin Bus (4, F6)
A hop-on, hop-off tour around the major sights of Dublin. The whole tour lasts around 1¼ hours and you can get on and off as often as you like at any of the 16 designated stops.
✉ 59 O'Connell St Upper ☎ 872 0000, 873 4222 e www.dub linbus.ie ☺ 9.30am-6.30pm ⑤ €10.20/5.10

Bus Éireann (4, F6)
Daytrips go to major attractions near the capital, including Glendalough, Powerscourt, Newgrange, Waterford, the Boyne Valley and Avoca – setting for the TV hit *Ballykissangel*. You can book at Busáras (4, F9), Dublin Tourism on Suffolk St (6, A6), or online (e www.buseireann.ie).
✉ 59 O'Connell St Upper ☎ 836 6111 ☺ varies, call for details ⑤ most tours €25/12.70-23

Mary Gibbons Tours
Full-day tours of Powerscourt and Glendalough, as well as a celebrated tour of the Boyne Valley, including Newgrange and the Hill of Tara, the ancient seat of the Irish high kings. All tours depart from outside Dublin Tourism, Suffolk St (6, A6).
✉ Suffolk St ☎ 283 9973 ☺ Powerscourt & Glendalough: Thurs & Sat-Sun 10.45am; Boyne Valley: Mon-Wed & Fri 10.45am ⑤ €28

Wild Coach Tours
Small Mercedes coaches take you to Wicklow/ Glendalough, Malahide Castle or Powerscourt, with lots of diversions along interesting scenic routes that the bigger buses usually miss. Excellent, energetic guides create a fun and friendly atmosphere. Tours have a variety of pick-up points.
☎ 280 1899 e www .wildcoachtours.com ☺ Wicklow: 9am-5.30pm; Powerscourt: 2-6pm; Malahide: 10am-1.30pm ⑤ Wicklow: €28/ 25.50; Powerscourt or Malahide: €19/16.50

TRAIN TOURS

Railtours Ireland
Virtually every must-see sight in Ireland is accessible on Railtours' half and full-day trips which include the Aran Islands, Cliffs of Moher, Ring of Kerry, Connemara and Giant's Causeway. Trips start around 7am from Heuston or Connolly stations and return as late as 10.30pm. Booking essential.
✉ Railtours Desk, Dublin Tourism, 2 Suffolk St (6, A6) ☎ 856 0045 e www .railtoursireland.com ☺ varies ⑤ €25-125

CYCLING TOURS

Molly Malone Bike
Relaxed bike tours of the city centre, including the Grand Canal, the Liffey, St Stephen's Green and medieval Dublin.

Non-strenuous riding, covering around 6.5km in four hours, with sightseeing stops every 400m and a 45-minute rest. Bikes and rain gear are provided; no need to book.
✉ depart Molly Malone statue (2, C1) ☎ 086-604 2608, 087-621 2424 e www.mollybikes .com ☺ May-Aug 11.30am & 4pm; Sept-Oct 12.30pm ⑤ €21

LITERARY, MUSIC & HISTORY

Dublin Footsteps Walking Tours
A gentle two-hour walk through Dublin's Georgian and literary past, bringing you to Merrion Square and St Stephen's Green. Anecdotes about Joyce, Wilde, Shaw and Yeats highlight various points of interest. The tour ends back at Bewley's, with a free cuppa.
✉ departs James Joyce Room, Bewley's, Grafton St (6, C6) ☎ 496 0641, 269 7021 ☺ Mon, Wed & Fri-Sat 10.30am ⑤ €6.50

James Joyce Cultural Centre (4, D6)
One-hour walking tours of North Dublin, exploring Joyce's writings, his inspirations and various *Ulysses* landmarks. Tours depart from, and include, the James Joyce Cultural Centre (p. 35).
✉ 35 Great George's St N ☎ 878 8547 ☺ Mon, Wed & Fri 2.15pm ⑤ €8.25/6.35/ 15.25, inc entry to centre

Dublin Literary Pub Crawl

A night tour of four literary drinking holes, starting at the Duke pub (6, C7), just off Grafton St. The 2¼-hour tour is led by two actors who perform extracts by famous Dublin writers along the way. It's a popular tour so get to the pub by 7pm to secure a ticket, or book at Dublin Tourism (☎ 605 7700).
✉ **The Duke (upstairs), 9 Duke St ☎ 670 5602 e www.dublinpub crawl.com** ⏰ **Apr-Oct: 7.30pm nightly, Sun noon; Nov-Mar: Thurs-Sat 7.30pm, Sun noon & 7.30pm ⑤ €9/7.50**

Dublin Musical Pub Crawl

Two musicians play tunes and explain the evolution of Irish music in Temple Bar pubs, including the Palace Bar and the Norseman. Musicians, drawn from a pool of 25 pros, are all excellent, as is the music.
✉ **departs Oliver St John Gogarty's (upstairs), cnr Fleet & Anglesea St, Temple Bar (5, C6) ☎ 478 0193 e www.musical pubcrawl.com** ⏰ **May-Oct: 7.30pm; Nov & Feb-Apr Fri & Sat 7.30pm ⑤ €9/7.50**

Historical Walking Tours

Trinity College history graduates lead this 'seminar on the street' which explores the Potato Famine, Easter Rising, Civil War and Partition. Sights include Trinity, City Hall, Dublin Castle and Four Courts. In summer, themed tours on architecture, women in Irish history and the birth of the Irish state are also held.
✉ **departs Trinity College, College Green entrance (2, B1) ☎ 878 0227 e www.historical insights.ie** ⏰ **May-Sept: Mon-Fri 11am & 3pm, Sat-Sun 11am, noon & 3pm; Oct-Apr Fri-Sun noon ⑤ €7.60/6.40**

SPOOKY TOURS

The Walk Macabre

The Trapeze Theatre Company runs this excellent tour which combines theatre performance with a walk through the spooky corners of Georgian Dublin. Sinister writings by Bram Stoker, Oscar Wilde and James Joyce are brilliantly dramatised, as are some of the city's more brutal murders.
✉ **departs Fusiliers' Arch, St Stephen's Green (6, E6) ☎ 087-677 1512** ⏰ **7.30pm; by booking only ⑤ €7.60**

Zozimus Ghostly Experience

A 1½-hour tour of Dublin's superstitious and seedy medieval past. The guide – the blind and ageing character Zozimus – recounts stories of murders, great escapes and mythical events. Booking essential.
✉ **departs Dublin Castle gate, Dame St, opposite Olympia Theatre (6, A3) ☎ 661 8646 e www.zozimus.com** ⏰ **summer 9pm, winter 7pm, by arrangement ⑤ €8**

KOOKY TOURS

Viking Splash Tours

(4, L3) Possibly Dublin's kookiest tour, Viking Splash take you out on a reconditioned WWII amphibious vehicle that goes to Viking sites around the city before splashing into the Grand Canal Basin for a water tour. All the while your 'craaazy' guide in Viking costume spins tales of the city.
✉ **Bull Alley St ☎ 855 3000 e www.viking splashtours.com** ⏰ **Mar-Nov 10 tours daily ⑤ €12.70/7**

Horse & Carriage Rides

Along the west side of St Stephen's Green you can pick up a horse and carriage with a driver/commentator for an old-fashioned journey around town. Most tours last half an hour but you can negotiate with the driver for longer trips. Carriages hold four or five people.
✉ **St Stephen's Green, near Fusiliers' Arch (6, F6)** ⏰ **varies ⑤ around €36 per ½hr**

On the Rock Trail

Unknown to most visitors, much of Dublin's musical history is found in seemingly innocent – and very uncool – places. Dublin Tourism's *Rock 'n' Stroll* booklet (2 Suffolk St; 6, A6; €3.20) takes you on a walk past 21 everyday sites made extraordinary because of their musical connections. Stops include the restaurant where Sinead O'Connor waitressed, the shoe shop where Ronan Keating worked and the hearing aid shop whose name Bono nicked.

shopping

Dubliners might be relatively new to the shopping-as-pastime craze, but they've taken to it with a gusto normally reserved for last-drinks call at the pub. On weekends especially, the main shopping districts are chock-a-block with gaggles of teenagers, pram-pushing families, serious consumer couples, tourists and the odd elderly lady bravely making her way through the chaos.

Unless you enjoy the hustle and bustle, save your shopping for weekdays – the earlier the better – when window shopping is a realistic option and sales staff are relaxed enough to help you. Most shops open Monday to Saturday from 9 or 10am until 6pm, Sundays and bank holidays they are either closed, or open for limited hours, usually noon-5pm. Late shopping is on Thursday, until 8 or 9pm.

British and US chains dominate the high street and major shopping centres but there are also numerous small, independent shops selling high-quality, locally made goods. Irish designer clothing and street wear, hand-made jewellery, unusual home-wares and crafts, and cheeses to die for are readily available if you know where to look.

While souvenir hunters can still buy toy sheep, Guinness magnets and shamrock tea towels, a new breed of craft shop offers one-off or limited-edition pottery, glassware, leather goods, furnishings and art. Traditional Irish products, such as crystal and knitwear, remain popular choices, and you can increasingly find innovative modern takes on the classics.

Almost all shops accept credit cards and you are rarely more than 100m from an ATM in the main shopping districts.

Hot Shop Spots

Dublin's main shopping areas are:

Grafton St – boutiques, department stores, clothing and music chains
West of Grafton St – small, funky independent shops, street wear, designer and second-hand clothing, jewellery stores, cosmetics
East of Grafton St – antiques and silverware, art galleries
Temple Bar – record shops, vintage clothes, kooky knick-knacks
Henry St – high-street chains, department stores, sportswear
Talbot St – bargain-basement clothes, homewares, furnishings and hardware
Capel St – outdoor gear, car accessories, cheap furniture

Oliver Strewe

Bounteous blooms at Moore Street market

DEPARTMENT STORES & SHOPPING CENTRES

Arnott's (4, G5)
Occupying a huge block with entrances on Henry, Liffey and Abbey Sts, a recent overhaul has made this one of Dublin's best department stores. From garden furniture to high fashion, it's all here – and the basement bargains can be worth trowelling through.
✉ **12 Henry St** ☎ **805 0400** 🚌 **O'Connell St** ⏲ **Mon, Wed, Fri-Sat 9am-6.30pm, Tue 9.30am-6.30pm, Thurs 9am-9pm, Sun noon-6pm**

Brown Thomas (6, B7)
Dublin's most exclusive and expensive store has the best cosmetics counters in the city, stylish homewares, bed linen, luggage, electronics and a large selection of Irish crystal. Irish fashion designers represented here include John Rocha, Lainey Keogh, Philip Treacy and Orla Kiely. The 2nd-floor cafe is small and surprisingly relaxed, as

Sales

Dublin has two universally observed sales periods each year: July and January. But you'll find many shops offering discounts between times on stock they can't move. Dedicated bargain hunters should find Dublin's sales quite satisfying. Reductions can be sizeable (25-50% off) and prices are often reduced further (up to 75%) as the weeks wear on.

is Brown's Bar in the basement.
✉ **92 Grafton St** ☎ **605 6666** 🚌 **all cross-city** ⏲ **Mon, Wed & Fri-Sat 9am-6pm, Tue 10am-6pm, Thurs 9am-8pm, Sun noon-6pm**

Clery & Co (4, G6)
With its distinctive clock and prominent O'Connell St location, Clery & Co is traditional Dublin at its best. The old store has been made over in parts, but it still sighs wearily under the weight of its clothes, shoes, furniture, pots, pans and bedding. The first-floor restaurant does a nice afternoon tea.
✉ **O'Connell St** ☎ **878 6000** 🚌 **O'Connell St** ⏲ **Mon, Wed & Sat 9am-6.30pm, Tues 9.30am-6.30pm, Thurs 9am-9pm, Fri 9am-8pm**

Dunnes Stores (6, E6)
A favourite choice with Irish mothers wanting to outfit the whole family, Dunnes offers reasonably priced men's, women's and children's clothing that ranges from simple basics to less successful forays into current trends. For numerous branches around the city see the *Golden Pages*.
✉ **62 Grafton St** ☎ **671 4629** 🚌 **all cross-city** ⏲ **Mon-Wed & Fri-Sat 9am-6.30pm, Thurs 9am-9.30pm, Sun noon-6pm**

Ilac Centre (4, F5)
A dark, low-roofed monstrosity, Ilac houses a number of mainstream chains, including a Dunnes Store, as well as gangs of senior citizens competing for a seat

on one of the few benches available in the inner city.
✉ **Henry St** ☎ **704 1460** 🚌 **O'Connell St** ⏲ **Mon-Wed, Fri-Sat 9am-6pm, Thurs 9am-9pm, Sun noon-6pm**

Jervis Centre (4, G4)
An ultra-modern, domed mall that's a veritable shrine to the British chain store. Boots, Top Shop, Debenhams, Argos, Dixons, M&S, Dorothy Perkins and even Tesco all get a look-in. Flying the flag for Ireland is Bewley's, with a pleasant courtyard restaurant.
✉ **Jervis St** ☎ **878 1323** 🚌 **O'Connell St** ⏲ **Mon-Wed, Fri-Sat 9am-6pm, Thurs 9am-9pm, Sun noon-6pm**

Marks & Spencer (6, C7) Mid-priced, dependable men's and women's own-label clothing, shoes, and no-nonsense socks and underwear from this most British of stores. The basement food hall has takeaway snacks, a bottle shop and supermarket items. There's another branch at 24-29 Mary St (☎ 872 8833).
✉ **15-20 Grafton St** ☎ **679 7855** 🚌 **all cross-city** ⏲ **Mon-Wed & Fri-Sat 9am-7pm, Thurs 9am-9pm, Sun noon-6pm**

Powerscourt Townhouse (6, C6)
This upmarket shopping mall in an 18th-century town house is where discerning shoppers quietly visit boutiques, beauty salons and the first-floor art, craft and antique shops. Karen Millen and

fcuk are also here, as is Solomon Gallery, a vegetarian restaurant and a wig store. Mimo (☎ 679 7789), the courtyard restaurant, is a pleasant spot to gather yourself.
✉ 59 William St S ☎ 679 4144 🚊 all cross-city ⏰ Mon-Wed & Fri 10am-6pm, Thurs 10am-8pm, Sat 9am-6pm, Sun noon-6pm

St Stephen's Green Shopping Centre
(6, E5) A 1980s version of a 19th-century shopping arcade, the dramatic, balconied interior and central courtyard are a bit too grand for the nondescript chain stores within. There's a Boots, Benetton, TJ Maxx

The view from the stairs, Powerscourt Townhouse

and a Levi's shop, as well as a Dunnes Store with supermarket.
✉ main entrance cnr King St & St Stephen's Green W ☎ 478 0888 🚊 all cross-city ⏰ Mon-Wed, Fri Sat 9am-7pm, Thurs 9am-8pm, Sun noon-6pm

Westbury Mall (6, C6)
Wedged between the five-star Westbury Hotel and the expensive jewellers of Johnson's Court, this small mall has a handful of pricey, specialist shops, some thriving on reputation, others struggling with the slow passing trade.
✉ Clarendon St 🚊 all cross-city ⏰ Mon-Sat 10am-6pm, Sun 12-5pm

HIGH-END FASHION

Alias Tom (6, D7)
Dublin's best designer menswear store, where knowledgeable and friendly staff guide you through the impeccable mix of casuals by Prada, Armani, Burberry, Donna Karan and YSL Rive Gauche. Downstairs it's classic tailored suits and Patrick Cox shoes.
✉ Duke La ☎ 671 5443 🚊 all cross-city ⏰ Mon-Sat 9.30am-6pm, Thurs 9.30am-8pm

Allicano (6, D5)
Silky, diaphanous, dressy outfits for lithe-figured style queens from a crop of young, innovative Belgian, French, Danish and Irish designers, including Dubliner Una O'Reilly.
✉ 4 Johnsons Pl ☎ 677 3430 🚊 all cross-city ⏰ Mon-Sat 10am-6pm, Thurs 10am-7pm

Claire Garvey (6, A1)
A fantastical den of purples, golds and swirling paint is the perfect setting for the theatrical collection of Claire Garvey. The elf-like designer, who studied costume making in Moscow, creates one-off pieces on-site with hand-ruched silks, velvets, feathers, quilting, sequins and rosettes. The ultimate statement for the cashed-up extrovert.
✉ 6 The Music Hall, Cow's La, Temple Bar ☎ 671 7287 🚊 all cross-city ⏰ Tues, Wed & Fri-Sat 10am-5.30pm, Thurs 10am-7pm

Costume (6, C5)
From casuals to sparkly full-length dresses, Costume specialises in offbeat women's wear from mainly young Irish designers. Their own Costume label sits alongside pieces by Pauric

Sweeny and Antonia Campbell-Hughes, while Anna Sui and small Italian and French labels make up the foreign contingent.
✉ 10 Castle Market ☎ 679 4188 🚊 all cross-city ⏰ Mon-Sat 10am-6pm, Thurs 10am-7pm

Cuan Hanly (5, D1)
Owned by Irish menswear designer Cuan Hanly, this concrete-floored, minimalist store combines pieces by young up-and-comers with more established designers. Along with menswear from John Rocha, Paul Smith and Hanly, are innovative pieces by recent Irish fashion graduates, as part of Hanly's 'Design Link' project. Traditional bespoke tailoring is also available.
✉ 1 Pudding Row ☎ 671 1406

Feet first at Cuan Hanly's boutique

himself works at the original Capel St store; the others are at 29-30 Pembroke St Lower (4, N9) and 18-19 Wicklow St (6, B6).
✉ **39-41 Capel St**
☎ **872 1600** 🚌 **37, 70, 134, 172** ⏰ **Mon-Sat 9am-5.30pm (7.30pm Thurs)**

Platform (6, C5)
This cool, white store has an unusual mix of stylish women's wear, with an off-beat bent. Irish designers, including Philip Treacy, are joined by Dutch and Italian labels and a good selection of accessories.
✉ **50 William St S**
☎ **677 7380** 🚌 **all cross-city** ⏰ **Mon-Sat 10am-6pm, Thurs 10am-8pm**

Thomas Pink (6, E7)
Plain men's shirts in a wide selection of vibrant hues, including, ahem, pink, and all excellent quality. Jazz up a dark suit or team them with casuals – you can't really go wrong.
✉ **29 Dawson St**
☎ **670 3647** 🚌 **10, 14, 14a, 15** ⏰ **Mon-Sat 9.30am-6pm, Thurs 9.30am-7pm**

🚌 **all cross-city**
⏰ **Mon-Sat 10am-6.30pm**

The Design Centre
(6, C6) Dedicated to Irish-only designer women's wear, this is the place for well-made, conservative outfits, including suits, evening wear and knitwear. Labels include Ramsay, Roisin Gartland, Aideen Bodkin and Rita Daly.
✉ **Powerscourt Townhouse** ☎ **679 5718** 🚌 **all cross-city** ⏰ **Mon-Wed & Fri 10am-6pm, Thurs 10am-8pm, Sat 9.30am-6pm**

FX Kelly (6, E6)
Smart casuals and Italian designer suits for men who like to look fashionable, but not too fashionable. Along with a gorgeous range of silk ties, casual and dressy shoes, belts and socks, are the more sober offerings from the ready-to-wear collections of

Hugo Boss, Armani, Helmut Lang and Replay.
✉ **48 Grafton St**
☎ **677 8211** 🚌 **all cross-city** ⏰ **Mon-Wed & Fri-Sat 9.30am-6pm, Thurs 9.30am-8pm, Sun 1.30-5.30pm**

Louis Copeland
(4, G4) A Dublin tradition for off-the-peg suits and casual menswear, with Lacoste, Burberry, Dior, Louis Ferraud and Canali featuring. Louis

Passion for Fashion
After years in the wilderness, Irish designers are making a name for themselves on the international fashion stage. John Rocha, whose own-label clothes have been high fashion for the past decade, has recently branched out into hotel design (The Morrison, p. 104) and homewares (Waterford Crystal). Orla Kiely's colourful bags are a hit in London and New York, while Philip Treacy makes extravagant hats for international clients and the cat-walk. Lainey Keogh's weathered, shorn and torn knitwear has graced the lithe bodies of supermodels and even Madonna.

STREET WEAR

Aspecto (6, D7)
Boys who like their style with some attitude head to this UK store, stocked with Duffer, Evisu, Carhartt and Paul Smith casuals, and shoes by Camper, Vans and Timberland.
✉ **6 Anne St S** ☎ **671 9302** 🚌 **all cross-city** 🕐 **Mon-Sat 10am-6pm, Thurs 10am-8pm, Sun 1-6pm**

BT2 (6, C6)
Brown Thomas' young and funky offshoot, with expensive casuals for men and women and a modern cafe upstairs overlooking Grafton St. Brands include DKNY, Diesel, Ted Baker and Tommy Hilfiger.
✉ **88 Grafton St** ☎ **679 5666** 🚌 **all cross-city** 🕐 **Mon-Wed 10am-6.30pm, Thurs 10am-8pm, Fri-Sat 10am-7pm, Sun noon-6pm**

Cuba (6, A5)
High-end street wear that's sleek and sexy rather than big and baggy. Jeans, tees, jackets and dresses from Boxfresh, You Must Create, Pash, Evisu and Irish label Optix. Also a good selection of colourful clothes, bags and wallets from monkey-man Paul Frank.
✉ **13 Trinity St** ☎ **672 7489** 🚌 **all cross-city** 🕐 **Mon-Wed & Fri-Sat 9.30-7pm, Thurs 9.30am-8pm, Sun noon-6pm**

Flip (5, D4)
This hip Irish label takes the best (male) fashion moods of the 1950s and serves them back to us, minus the mothball smell.

US college shirts, logo T-shirts, oriental and Hawaiian shirts, Fonz-style leather jackets and well-cut jeans mix it with the genuine second-hand gear upstairs.
✉ **4 Fownes St** ☎ **671 4299** 🚌 **all cross-city** 🕐 **Mon-Wed & Fri-Sat 9.30am-6pm, Thurs 9.30am-7pm, Sun 1-5.30pm**

Hairy Legs (4, F7)
Bargains galore at this sale outlet for Irish street labels Susst and Nope. Denim jeans and jackets, windcheaters and T-shirts which have recently fallen from grace with the front-running style-gurus can be had for a song.
✉ **102 Talbot St** ☎ **872 7106** 🚌 **all cross-city** 🕐 **Mon-Sat 9.30am-6pm**

Hobo (6, A5)
Irish-owned label, with fun and funky clobber for clubbers, young bucks on the make and girls who prefer understated cool to glam. Well-made hooded tops, T-shirts, flared jeans and accessories, adorned with the Hobo name or their cute logo.
✉ **6-9 Trinity St** ☎ **670 4869** 🚌 **all cross-city** 🕐 **Mon-Wed & Fri-Sat noon-7pm, Thurs noon-9pm, Sun noon-6pm**

Urban Outfitters
(5, C4) Expensive street wear and funky designer labels mix with offbeat gadgets and homewares at this branch of the Philadelphia chain. As the DJ spins tunes from the 3rd-floor record outlet, boys can browse G-Star denims, Pringle knits and Fiorucci trousers, while girls choose between Claudie Pierlot, W&LT and Mandarina Duck.
✉ **7 Fownes St** ☎ **670 6202** 🚌 **all cross-city** 🕐 **Mon-Wed & Sat 10am-7pm, Thurs, Fri 10am-8pm, Sun noon-6pm**

Grab a bargain at George's St Arcade.

Doug McKinlay

LLERY

(6, C6)

ed into the tiniest of s, Angles has cabinets ving with handmade, ntemporary Irish jewellery, most of it by up-and-coming Dublin craftspeople. Commissions are taken and pieces on display can be custom fitted and sent on to you abroad.

✉ 10 Westbury Mall, Johnson's Court ☎ 679 1964 🚌 all cross-city ⏱ Mon-Wed & Fri 10am-6pm, Thurs 10am-7pm, Sun noon-6pm

Consumer R&R

There's no need to shop till you drop while pounding the mean streets of Dublin. Several stores have quiet and comfortable cafes where you can refuel, take stock and plan your next move. These include:

Avoca Handweavers (p. 69)
Brown Thomas (p. 62)
BT2 (p. 62)
Clery & Co (p. 62)
Hodges Figgis (p. 72)
Kilkenny (p. 69)
Powerscourt Townhouse (p. 62)
Winding Stair Bookshop (p. 72)

Appleby Jewellers
(6, C6) Renowned for the high quality of its gold and silver jewellery, which tends towards more conventional designs, this is the place to shop for serious stuff – diamond rings, sapphire-

encrusted cufflinks and Raymond Weil watches.

✉ 5-6 Johnson's Court ☎ 679 9572 🚌 all cross-city ⏱ Mon-Wed & Fri 9.30am-5.30pm, Thurs 9.30am-7pm, Sat 9.30am-6pm

Barry Doyle Design Jewellers (6, B4)
Upstairs on the southern side of George's St Arcade, Barry Doyle works away in his light-filled, wooden studio producing beautiful, bold, handmade necklaces, bracelets and rings in Celtic and modern designs. Individual pieces can be commissioned – prices are steep but the work is of excellent quality.

✉ George's St Arcade ☎ 671 2838 🚌 all cross-city ⏱ Mon-Sat 9am-6pm, Thurs 9am-8pm

Designyard (5, C3)
Exclusive and exceptional handmade jewellery by Irish and international artists who use all sorts of media. Anything from beautifully crafted rings to brooches that look like nipples will be on offer, and there are themed jewellery exhibitions held regularly. Original pieces, big price tags.

✉ 12 Essex St E ☎ 677 8453 🚌 all cross-city ⏱ Mon & Wed-Sat 10am-5.30pm, Tues 11am-5.30pm

Rhinestones (6, A6)
Exceptionally fine antique and quirky costume jewellery from the 1920s to 1970s, with pieces priced from €12 to €1200. Victorian jet, 1950s enamel, Art Deco turquoise,

1930s mother-of-pearl, cut-glass and rhinestone necklaces, bracelets, brooches and rings are displayed by colour in old-fashioned cabinets.

✉ 18 St Andrew St ☎ 679 0759 🚌 all cross-city ⏱ Mon-Wed & Fri-Sat 9.30am-6pm, Thurs 9.30am-8pm, Sun noon-5pm

Vivien Walsh (4, L5)
One of Ireland's best-known jewellery designers, Vivien Walsh uses Swarovski crystal, glass, feathers, pearls and beads to create delicate, fantastical pieces that hark back to the 1920s and beyond. The elaborate necklaces, in vivid turquoise, pink, purple and green, are quite an investment, but simple bracelets can be had for under €30. French and Italian leather bags and shoes complement the displays.

✉ 24 Stephen St Lwr ☎ 475 5031 🚌 all cross-city ⏱ Mon-Sat 10am-6pm, Thurs 10am-7pm

Weir & Sons (6, B7)
The largest jeweller in Ireland, this huge store on Grafton St first opened in 1869 and still has its original wooden cabinets and a workshop on the premises. There's new and antique Irish jewellery (including Celtic designs) and a huge selection of watches, Irish crystal, porcelain, leather and travel goods.

✉ 96-99 Grafton St ☎ 677 9678 🚌 all cross-city ⏱ Mon-Sat 9am-5.30pm, Thurs 9am-8pm

RETRO STORES

A Store is Born (6, D5)
Hidden for six days a week
behind a garage roller-door,
this store opens up on
Saturdays to reveal a bounty of paisley dresses, peas-
ant tops, belts, beads, cash-
mere cardies, sequined sin-
glets, wide-collared men's
shirts and suit pants.
✉ **34 Clarendon St**
☎ **679 5866** 🚌 **all
cross-city** ⏲ **Sat 10am-
6pm**

Eager Beaver (5, D5)
In a creaky wooden build-
ing that looks even older
than the fashions, the
Beaver provides rack upon
rack of no-nonsense,
second-hand gear. There
are cords galore, Levis,
combats, leathers, golf
slacks, army jackets,
wedding suits and a huge
range of Hawaiian shirts.
✉ **17 Crown Alley**
☎ **677 3342** 🚌 **all
cross-city** ⏲ **Mon-Wed
& Fri-Sat 9.30am-6pm,
Thurs 9.30am-7.30pm,
Sun 1-6pm**

Euphoria (4, P5)
Homewares and kooky
collectibles from the 1940s
to 1960s, including arc
lamps, a huge range of multicoloured glassware, clocks,
figurines, lamps and mirrors.
✉ **41a Camden St**
☎ **475 24461** 🚌 **all
cross-city** ⏲ **Mon-Sat
11am-6pm, Thurs
11am-9pm, Sun 2-6pm**

Harlequin (6, C5)
Some exquisite vintage gems
as well as the standard stock
of second-hand jeans, T-shirts,
shoes, bags and suits.
✉ **13 Castle Market**
☎ **671 0202**

Emma Miller

Classic comebacks at Jenny Vander

🚌 **all cross-city**
⏲ **Mon-Sat 10.30am-
6pm, Thurs 10.30am-7pm**

Jenny Vander (6, B4)
More Breakfast-at-Tiffany's
chic than the castoffs from
Hair, this second-hand store
oozes elegance and sophis-
tication. Exquisite beaded
handbags, fur-trimmed
coats, richly patterned
dresses and costume
jewellery priced as if it were
the real thing are snapped
up by discerning fashion-
istas looking for something
quirky to wear with their
Chloe pantsuits. A reverent
air ensures you handle the
precious goods with care.
✉ **George's St Arcade**
☎ **677 0406** 🚌 **all
cross-city** ⏲ **Mon-Sat
10am-6pm, Thurs
10am-7pm**

Wild Child (4, L5)
If you're in the market for
Crimplene flares and a
tangerine body shirt, then
this is the place. Good
quality men's and women's
clothing, from the '60s,
'70s and '80s is supple-
mented by new retro
jewellery and glitter nail
polish. A second branch is
at 61 Great George's St S.
✉ **77 Aungier St**
☎ **475 7177** 🚌 **16,
16a, 16c, 19, 19a, 65,
83** ⏲ **Mon-Sat 10am-
6pm, Thurs 10am-7pm**

**20th Century
Designs** (4, L2)
Among the antique stores
of Francis St is this place,
which takes over where the
other dealers stop. You'll
find classic decorative art
from the 1920s to the
1970s – some impressive
and unusual, others sharp
reminders never to discard
anything ugly your mother
once owned.
✉ **31 Francis St**
☎ **454 6161**
🚌 **49, 50, 51b, 77,
78, 123**
⏲ **Mon-Sat 11am-6pm**

MARKETS

George's Street Arcade (6, B4)

Dublin's best non-food market (there's sadly not much competition) is sheltered within an elegant Victorian Gothic arcade. Apart from shops and stalls selling new and old clothes, second-hand books, hats, posters, jewellery and records, there's a fortune teller, some gourmet nibbles and a fish and chipper who does a roaring trade.

✉ **between Great George's St S & Drury St** 🚌 **all cross-city** 🕐 **Mon-Sat 10am-6pm**

Meeting House Square Market (5, D3)

One of the best places to spend your Saturday morning, this market buzzes with visitors and locals stocking up on organic, gourmet and imported foodstuffs while buskers provide the soundtrack. Munch on sushi, paella, waffles, crepes and sizzling sausages, while perusing the stalls of farmhouse cheeses, hand-pressed juices, organic meats and tubs of garlic pesto.

✉ **Meeting House Sq** 🚌 **all cross-city** 🕐 **Sat 9am-5pm**

More value at the Moore Street market

Moore St Market

(4, F5) A raucous, open-air market that remains steadfastly 'Old Dublin', Moore St has flowers, fruit, vegetables and fish, and people hawking cheap cigarettes, tobacco and chocolate. Don't try to buy just one banana though – if it says 10 for €1, that's what it is.

✉ **Moore St** 🚌 **all cross-city** 🕐 **Mon-Sat 9am-4pm**

Mother Redcaps

(4, K2) Tucked away off Francis St in the heart of the Liberties, Mother Redcaps has a colourful collection of stalls selling everything from antiques to records.

✉ **Back La** ☎ **454 0652** 🚌 **50, 54a, 56a, 150** 🕐 **Fri-Sun 10am-5.30pm**

Smithfield Market

(4, H3) Housed in a pretty, covered arcade, this fruit and vegetable market runs along both sides of St Michan's St, near the Four Courts. It caters mostly to the wholesale trade, but it's a nice place for a wander. Paddy's Place, inside the market, sells traditional Irish grub.

✉ **St Michan's St** ☎ **872 1248** 🚌 **134** 🕐 **Mon-Thurs 6.30am-4.30pm, Fri 6.30am-5pm, Sat 6.30am-1pm**

Taxes & Refunds

A value-added tax (VAT) of 20% applies to most goods and services in Ireland. Residents of the EU cannot claim back VAT, but non-EU visitors can get a refund on large purchases at airports or ports when they are leaving the EU. The 'Cashback' voucher you receive when you make your purchase can be refunded at Dublin or Shannon airport, or in some circumstances will be posted to you or credited to your credit card.

ARTS & CRAFTS

As well as mass-produced tourist fodder, a great number of Dublin shops now specialise in high-end crafts made by local artisans. If fine art is what you're after, try the commercial galleries (pp. 39-41).

The Art Store (6, C5)
Taking art to the people at reasonable prices is the aim of the Art Store which has unframed artwork by emerging Irish and international artists from as little as €60. More shop than gallery, you can flick through the hundreds of paintings, photographs and drawings at leisure while perusing the latest exhibition.
✉ 56 William St S
☎ 672 7284 🚌 all city-centre ⏱ Mon-Wed & Fri 10am-6am, Thurs 10am-7pm, Sat 11am-6pm

Avoca Handweavers
(6, A7) Combining clothing, homewares, a basement food hall and an excellent top-floor cafe (p. 80), Avoca promotes a stylish but homey brand of modern Irish life. Many of the garments are woven, knitted and naturally dyed at their Wicklow factory. The children's section, with unusual knits, fairy outfits, theatrical capes, bee-covered gumboots and toys, is fantastic.
✉ 11-13 Suffolk St
☎ 677 4215 🚌 all cross-city ⏱ Mon-Wed & Fri-Sat 10am-6pm, Thurs 10am-8pm, Sat 10am-6.30pm, Sun 11am-6pm

The Bridge (4, J3)
Housed in a Georgian terrace on the quays, this place is part art gallery, part high-end crafts store. Regular exhibitions are held out the back, while the shop sells paintings, ceramics, woodcarvings and jewellery.
✉ 6 Ormond Quay Upper ☎ 872 6969 🚌 all cross-city ⏱ Mon-Sat 10am-6pm, Sun 2-5pm

Dublin Woollen Mills
(5, A4) At the northern end of the Ha'penny Bridge, this is one of Dublin's major wool outlets. It has a large selection of sweaters, cardigans, scarves, rugs, shawls and other woollen goods and runs a tax-free shopping scheme.
✉ 41 Ormond Quay Lwr ☎ 677 5014 🚌 all cross-city ⏱ Mon-Sat 9.30am-6pm, Sun 1-6pm

Crafts Council Gallery (5, C3)
Apart from its regular exhibitions, this gallery-shop, above Designyard (p. 66), showcases work by a number of artists and includes sculpture, pottery, glassware and textiles. The council also has a database of its members' work, which can be viewed on request.
✉ 1st fl, 12 Essex St E
☎ 677 8453
🚌 all cross-city
⏱ Mon & Wed-Sat 10am-5.30pm, Tues 11am-5.30pm

House of Ireland
(6, B8) Traditional, tourist-oriented Irish crafts, including chunky Aran knits, checked rugs and throws, tea cosies, crystal, Royal Tara porcelain and unusual figurines carved out of turf.
✉ 38 Nassau St
☎ 671 4543
🚌 all cross-city
⏱ Mon-Wed & Fri 9am-6.30pm, Thurs 9am-8pm, Sat 9am-6pm, Sun 10.30am-6pm

Kilkenny (6, C9)
Contemporary, innovative takes on classic Irish crafts, including multicoloured, modern Irish knits, designer clothing, Orla Kiely bags and some lovely silver jewellery with bold Celtic motifs. The glassware and pottery is beautiful and sourced from workshops around the country. The upstairs cafe serves hot

Irish Crystal
Once prized items in the dining room cabinets of grandmothers across the Western world, Irish crystal has undergone something of an overhaul in recent years. While the traditional designs are still available, Irish designer John Rocha has created some sleek, contemporary styles for Waterford Crystal that would never look right resting on a doily. Minimalist, angular and – dare we say it – funky, this is glass with pure class.

food and snacks.
✉ **5-6 Nassau St**
☎ **677 7066** 🚌 **all cross-city** 🕐 **Mon-Wed & Fri 8.30am-6pm, Thurs 8.30am-8pm, Sat 9am-6pm, Sun 11am-6pm**

Powerscourt Townhouse
See p. 62.

Tower Craft Design Centre (3, F12)
Buy crafts direct from the artist at these studios in an old sugar refinery opposite the Waterways Visitor Centre. Around 20 artisans work on-site producing jewellery, ceramics, textiles, rugs and leather goods.
✉ **Pearse St (enter via Grand Canal Quay)**
☎ **677 5655** 🚌 **1, 2, 3** 🚉 **Grand Canal Dock; Pearse St** 🕐 **Mon-Fri 9am-5pm**

Whichcraft (6, A1)
A high-end, craft-as-art shop where everything you see is one-off and hand-made in Ireland. There's gorgeous silverware, pottery, leather goods, glassware and weird and wonderful decorative items. Another branch (☎ 670 9371), with less exclusive gear, is around the corner at 5 Castle Gate, Lord Edward St.
✉ **Cow's La**
☎ **474 1011**
🚌 **all cross-city**
🕐 **Mon-Sat 9am-6pm, Sun 10am-6pm**

ANTIQUES

Dublin's antique dealers tend to stick together, making browsing all the more easy. Most reside in Francis St (4, L2) in the Liberties. Other areas include Anne St S (6, D7) or Johnson's Court (6, C6) for silverware and jewellery, or the antiques gallery on the first floor of the Powerscourt Townhouse (p. 62). Every second Sunday, Newman House (p. 37) hosts an antiques and collectibles fair from 11am-6pm (€2).

Daly & Eacrett (4, M2)
Paintings, prints, objets d'art and trinkets as well as furniture from the Regency and Victorian periods.
✉ **58 Francis St**
☎ **454 9467**
🚌 **49, 50, 51b, 77, 78, 123**
🕐 **Mon-Sat 9am-5.30pm**

Fleury Antiques
(4, M2) Oil paintings, vases, candelabras, silverware, porcelain and decorative pieces from the 18th century to the 1930s.
✉ **57 Francis St**
☎ **473 0878**
🚌 **49, 50, 51b, 77, 78, 123**
🕐 **Mon-Sat 9am-6pm**

H Danker (6, D7)
Chock-full of exquisite treasures, this shop specialises in Irish and English antique silver, jewellery and objets d'art.
✉ **10 Anne St S** ☎ **677 4009** 🚌 **all cross-city**
🕐 **Mon-Sat 9am-6pm**

Michael Connell Antiques (4, L2)
A huge range of antique light fittings, as well as Edwardian furniture, silver, brassware and china.
✉ **53 Francis St**
☎ **473 3898** 🚌 **49, 50, 51b, 77, 78, 123**
🕐 **Mon-Sat 9.30am-5.30pm**

Renaissance (4, P5)
Art, antiques and quality reproductions from diverse corners of the globe. Statues of Ganesh rub shoulders with Chinese painted urns, Delftware, pot-bellied stoves, Pakistani rugs, gilded mirrors and some incredibly elaborate chandeliers.
✉ **41 Camden St**
☎ **475 24461** 🚌 **all cross-city** 🕐 **Mon-Sat 11am-6pm, Thurs 11am-9pm, Sun 2-6pm**

Timepiece (4, M3)
Antique Irish clocks from the 18th and 19th centuries, including a superb collection of Georgian and Victorian grandfather clocks.
✉ **57-58 Patrick St**
☎ **454 0774** 🚌 **49, 50, 51b, 77, 78, 123**
🕐 **Mon-Sat 10am-5pm**

The Real Deal

The Irish Antique Dealers' Association (☎ 679 4147) has 80 members around Ireland and holds an annual fair in September/October. You can pick up a booklet which lists its members from any registered shop or by calling the association.

MUSIC

Celtic Note (6, B9)
The largest Irish music store in the country, with everything from classic Irish pub songs to traditional ballads and harp music. Staff are knowledgeable and many are musicians. CDs, cassettes, DVDs and videos are available.
✉ **14-15 Nassau St**
☎ **670 4157** 🚌 **all cross-city** ⏱ **Mon-Wed & Fri-Sat 9am-6.30pm, Thurs 9am-8.30pm, Sun 11am-6.30pm**

Claddagh Records
(5, D4) An intimate, well-loved shop with knowledgeable staff, Claddagh specialises in folk, traditional and ethnic music from Ireland, the US and South America.
✉ **2 Cecilia St** ☎ **677 0262** 🚌 **all cross-city** ⏱ **Mon-Fri 10.30am-5.30pm, Sat noon-5.30pm**

Comet Records (5, D5)
You can't miss this store, with its huge, colourful, graffiti-inspired mural. Specialist in independent label releases – including metal, indie, ska and techno – they also stock house, hip-hop and some early U2 releases.
✉ **5 Cope St** ☎ **671 8592** 🚌 **all cross-city** ⏱ **Mon-Sat 10am-6pm, summer Sun noon-5pm**

HMV (6, D6)
This megastore gives you all the top mainstream rock hits plus almost every other music genre known to man. Spread over three floors, the shop has reasonably on-the-ball staff but it can often get too

busy for them to help you.
✉ **65 Grafton St**
☎ **679 5334** 🚌 **all cross-city** ⏱ **Mon-Wed & Fri-Sat 9am-7pm, Thurs 9am-9pm, Sun 11am-7pm**

Road Records (6, C4)
Independent music shop with a discerning mix of alternative, indie, mostly non-chart CDs, along with a huge amount of reggae on vinyl.
✉ **16b Fade St** ☎ **671 7340** 🚌 **16, 16a, 19, 19a, 65, 83** ⏱ **Mon-Sat 10am-6pm (7pm Thurs)**

Rhythm Records
(5, A7) Grungy little store on the quays with a large U2 section, including major releases, singles, special tour editions, remix albums and some suspicious-looking cassette tapes with photocopied covers. Also posters, videos, postcards and a big 7-inch collection from big names in contemporary rock and pop.
✉ **1 Aston Quay**
☎ **671 9594** 🚌 **all cross-city** ⏱ **Mon-Sat 11am-6pm**

Tower Records (6, B6)
A broad selection of CDs, records and DVDs, from the latest mainstream releases to good alternative rock, jazz, soul and classical sounds.
✉ **16 Wicklow St**
☎ **671 3250** 🚌 **all cross-city** ⏱ **Mon & Wed 9am-10pm, Tues 10am-10pm, Thurs-Sat 9am-10.30pm, Sun 11.30am-7.30pm**

Virgin Megastore
(5, A7) Dublin's biggest

record store, covering new releases, an extensive back catalogue of rock, pop, alternative and dance albums, classical and jazz. If you can put it in a CD player, they've probably got it.
✉ **14 Aston Quay**
☎ **677 7361** 🚌 **all cross-city** ⏱ **Mon-Wed 9am-6pm, Thurs 9am-8pm, Fri-Sat 9am-6pm, Sun noon-6pm**

Walton's (6, B4)
These traditional Irish music specialists sell CDs, instruments (banjos, bodhráns, guitars), sheet music for Irish harp, flute and fiddle, and song books featuring tunes by the Wolfe Tones, the Fureys and the Dubliners. You can also take two-hour crash courses in the bodhrán or tin whistle at their music school.
✉ **69-70 Great George's St S** ☎ **475 0661** 🚌 **16, 16a, 19, 19a, 65, 83** ⏱ **Mon-Sat 9am-5.30pm**

Martin Moos

Get into the rhythm.

BOOKS

Cathach Books (6, C7)
Rare editions of Irish literature and history, including works by Wilde, Joyce, Yeats and Beckett, and a large selection of signed first editions in one of Dublin's best antiquarian bookshops.
✉ **10 Duke St** ☎ **671 8676** 🚌 all cross-city ⏰ Mon-Sat 9.30am-5.45pm

Dublin Bookshop
(6, C7) Its location on Grafton St can make for a bit of an unbookish crush, but the stock is good and there's a particularly good selection of books of Irish interest.
✉ **24 Grafton St** ☎ **677 5568** 🚌 all cross-city ⏰ Mon-Fri 9am-7pm (10pm in summer), Sat 9am-6pm, Sun 11am-6pm

Eason's (4, G6)
A massive and busy shop filled with mainstream popular fiction, new titles and books of Irish interest. Whole walls of magazines, some international newspapers, a selection of Irish roadmaps and stationery make up the mix.
✉ **40 O'Connell St** ☎ **873 3811** 🚌 all cross-city ⏰ Mon-Wed 8.30am-6.45pm, Thurs 8.30am-8.45pm, Fri 8.30am-7.45pm, Sat 8.30am-6.45pm, Sun 12.45-5.45pm

Forbidden Planet
(5, B5) Science fiction and fantasy specialist, with books, comics, magazines, figurines, posters and videos. Just the place for those Dr Spock ears or a Star Wars light sabre.
✉ **5-6 Crampton Quay** ☎ **671 0688** 🚌 all cross-city ⏰ Mon-Wed 10am-6pm, Thurs 10am-7pm, Fri-Sat 10am-6pm

Hodges Figgis (6, B8)
A huge range of titles over four floors, including a specialist Irish section covering art, architecture, literature and sport. The first-floor cafe has hot food and sandwiches and also serves as a casual reading room.
✉ **57 Dawson St** ☎ **677 4754** 🚌 all cross-city 🚊 Pearse ⏰ Mon, Wed & Fri 9am-7pm, Tues 9.30am-7pm, Thurs 9am-8pm, Sat 9am-6pm, Sun noon-6pm

Murder Ink (6, C8)
All manner of murder mystery and crime novels are in this small specialist bookstore that has categorisation down to a fine art – choose from historical mystery, romantic crime, sci-fi mystery, true crime and more.
✉ **15 Dawson St** ☎ **677 7570** 🚌 all cross-city 🚊 Pearse ⏰ Mon-Sat 10am-6pm, Thurs 10am-7pm, Sun noon-5pm

Waterstone's (6, B8)
Large and multistoried, Waterstone's manages to maintain that snugly, hide-in-a-corner ambience that book lovers adore. The broad selection is supplemented by five bookcases of Irish fiction, as well as poetry, drama, politics and history. Book signings every Thursday evening; check board outside for details.
✉ **7 Dawson St** ☎ **679 1415** 🚌 all cross-city 🚊 Pearse ⏰ Mon-Tues & Fri 9am-7pm, Wed 9.30am-7pm, Thurs 9am-8pm, Sat 9am-6.30pm, Sun noon-6pm

Winding Stair (5, A4)
This is a creaky old place oozing with character. It can be some effort to manoeuvre yourself past the bookish types to the heaving bookcases crammed with new and second-hand books. When you've had enough head up the winding stairs to the excellent cafe (p. 77).
✉ **40 Ormond Quay Lwr** ☎ **873 3292** 🚌 all cross-city ⏰ Mon-Wed & Sat 9.30am-6pm, Thurs-Fri 9.30am-8pm, Sun 1-6pm

Dublin Reads

Add the following Dublin-based books to those by Joyce (*Ulysses, Dubliners, Finnegan's Wake*) and Roddy Doyle (*The Commitments, The Snapper, The Van, Paddy Clarke, Ha Ha Ha*):

- *Circle of Friends* – Maeve Binchy
- *The Journey Home* – Dermot Bolger
- *Down all the Days* – Christy Brown
- *The Ginger Man* – JP Donleavy
- *The Quare Fellow* – Brendan Behan
- *Butcher Boy* – Patrick McCabe

FOOD & DRINK

The Big Cheese
(6, A5) Apart from a huge selection of cheeses – Irish, French, Italian and more – this large deli has gourmet breads, jars of delectable sauces, pestos, jams and spreads, kosher products and a number of US imports in hyper-coloured boxes.
✉ St Andrew's La
☎ 671 1399 🚌 all cross-city ⏰ Mon-Fri 10am-6.30pm, Sat 10am-6pm

Bretzel Bakery
(3, H9)
The bagels might be a bit on the chewy side, but they've got their charms – as do the scrumptious selections of breads, savoury snacks, cakes and biscuits that have locals queuing out the door on weekends. No longer kosher, the bakery has been on this Portobello site since 1870.
✉ 1a Lennox St
☎ 475 2724 🚌 14, 15, 65, 83 ⏰ Mon-Fri 8.30am-6pm, Sat 9am-5.30pm, Sun 9am-1pm

Epicurean Food Hall
See p. 77.

La Maison des Gourmets
(6, C5)
If you can resist lunch at the upstairs Salon de Thé (Mon-Sat noon-3pm), make your own Gallic feast from the downstairs deli's selection of cheeses, brioches, cakes, bread (flown in from Paris) and handmade chocolates. A second branch, Le Petit des Gourmets (☎ 878 1133) is in the Epicurean Food Hall (p. 77).
✉ 15 Castle Market
☎ 672 7258

🚌 all cross-city
⏰ Mon-Sat 9am-6pm, Thurs 9am-7pm

Magills
(6, C6)
With its characterful old facade and tiny dark interior, Magills' old-world charm reminds you how Clarendon St must have once looked. Family run, you get the distinct feeling that every Irish and French cheese, olive oil, packet of Italian pasta and salami was hand picked.
✉ 14 Clarendon St
☎ 671 3830 🚌 all cross-city ⏰ Mon-Sat 9am-5.45pm

Meeting House Square Market
See p. 68.

Mitchell & Son Wine Merchants
(6, E9)
Established in 1805, the store is still run by a sixth and seventh generation Mitchell father-and-son team. Wines, champagnes, Irish whiskey and Cuban cigars fill the cavernous space. You can also buy stylish wine racks, glasses, hip flasks and ice buckets.
✉ 21 Kildare St
☎ 676 0766 🚌 11, 11a, 14, 14a, 15a ⏰ Mon-Fri 9.30am-5.30pm, Sat 10.30am-5.30pm

Sheridans Cheesemongers
(6, D7) If heaven were a cheese shop, Sheridans would be it. The wooden shelves are laden with rounds of artisan farmhouse cheeses, individually sourced from around the country by Kevin and Seamus Sheridan who have almost single-handedly revived cheese making in Ireland. You can taste any one of the 60 cheeses on display and pick up some wild Irish salmon, Italian pastas and olives while you're at it.
✉ 11 Anne St S
☎ 679 3143 🚌 all cross-city ⏰ Mon-Sat 9am-6pm

Genuine Irish culture: County Cork's Coolea Cheese, from the Big Cheese Company

SHOPPING FOR CHILDREN

Baby Bambino (6, C6)
If you can afford the fabulously flamboyant designer gear in this shop, then let the kids go wild. Choose from funky leather jackets, cowboy boots, fake furs, ponchos, fake leopard skin shoes and more from DKNY, D&G, Joseph, Katherine Hamnett and Gianfranco Ferre. Girls from 0-16 years, boys 0-10 years.
✉ **41 Clarendon St**
☎ **671 1590** 🚌 **all cross-city** ☺ **Mon-Sat 10am-6pm, Thurs 10am-8pm**

Early Learning Centre (4, G5)
Fun with an educational bent for the tiniest tots, including ELC-brand plastic and wooden toys, spelling and numerical games, simple devices that honk and squeak and a good range of Thomas the Tank Engine stuff.
✉ **3 Henry St**
☎ **873 1945** 🚌 **all cross-city** ☺ **Mon-Wed & Fri-Sat 9am-5.30pm, Thurs 9am-8pm, Sun 1-5pm**

Gymboree (6, C6)
Good quality, own-brand clothes for boys and girls aged one to seven from this US chain store. The big TV screening children's programs at the back of the shop is the perfect place to deposit little tantrum-throwers while you look around.
✉ **75 Grafton St**
☎ **670 3331**
🚌 **all cross-city**
☺ **Mon-Wed & Fri-Sat 10am-6pm, Thurs 10am-8pm, Sun noon-6pm**

Careful shopping can score you some real treats.

Jacadi (6, E5)
Beautiful, smart outfits for babies and toddlers from this super-stylish French chain. Prices are high but they'll look like angels – for a few minutes at least.
✉ **32 King St S** ☎ **671 1418** 🚌 **all cross-city** ☺ **Mon-Sat 9.30am-6pm**

Mothercare (6, E6)
The ground floor of this British chain stocks good quality, own-label baby clothes, shoes, toys, books and sleepwear, while upstairs are cots and bedding, highchairs and maternity wear. There's another branch in the Jervis Centre (p. 62; ☎ 878 1184).
✉ **St Stephen's Green Shopping Centre**
☎ **478 4755** 🚌 **all cross-city** ☺ **Mon-Sat 9am-7pm, Thurs 9am-8pm, Sun noon-6pm**

Rainbow Crafts
(6, C6) Small but well-stocked toy shop, with puppets, educational aids, wooden and tin toys, traditional Irish dolls, doll's houses and furniture, kites, puzzles and a big range of rubber stamps.
✉ **Westbury Mall**
☎ **677 7632** 🚌 **all cross-city** ☺ **Mon-Wed & Fri-Sat 9am-6pm, Thurs 9am-7pm, Sun noon-5.30pm**

Smyths Toys (4, F4)
Toy superstore, with towering aisles full of Barbies, Lego, various action men, soft toys, puzzles, board games and a whole room devoted to Playstations, Gameboys and videos.
✉ **Jervis St** ☎ **878 2878** 🚌 **all cross-city** ☺ **Mon-Wed, Fri-Sat 9am-6pm, Thurs 9am-9pm, Sun 1-6pm**

T. Bear & Co (6, E6)
As its name suggests, T. Bear stocks teddy bears as well as other soft and cuddlies from the WWF toy collection. Hand puppets and paraphernalia from the Simpsons, Noddy and Winnie the Pooh are also on offer.
✉ **St Stephen's Green Shopping Centre**
☎ **478 1139** 🚌 **all cross-city** ☺ **Mon-Sat 9am-7pm, Thurs 9am-8pm, Sun noon-6pm**

SPECIALIST SHOPS

The Great Outdoors
(6, D6) Dublin's best outdoors store, with gear for hiking, camping, surfing, mountaineering, swimming and more. Fleeces, tents, inflatable dinghies, boots and gas cookers – they're all here.
✉ **20 Chatham St**
☎ **679 4293** 🚌 **all cross-city** ⏱ **Mon-Sat 9.30am-5.30pm, Thurs 9.30am-8pm**

Haus (5, D4)
Cutting-edge designer furniture and homewares from the drawing boards of the big names, such as Phillipe Starck and Le Corbusier.
✉ **3-4 Crow St** ☎ **679 5155** 🚌 **all cross-city** ⏱ **Mon-Sat 10am-6pm**

Irish Historical Picture Company
(5, B1) With a print collection that's second only to the holdings at the National Library, this place is jammed full with more than 12,000 pictures taken around Ireland at the turn of the 20th century. The prints cover all 32 counties and range from town streetscapes to images of bog cutters. Mounted prints can be framed within minutes.
✉ **5 Ormond Quay Lwr**
☎ **872 0144** 🚌 **all cross-city** ⏱ **Mon-Fri 9am-6pm, Sat 9am-5pm, Sun 10am-5pm**

Knobs and Knockers
(6, B9) Despite the saucy name, this shop offers a rather sober selection of reproduction Georgian door knockers, knobs, handles and locks. Here's

where you get that Dublinesque lion's head knocker you've always dreamed of. They also sell model sailing ships and petanque sets.
✉ **19 Nassau St**
☎ **671 0288** 🚌 **all cross-city** ⏱ **Mon-Wed & Fri 9.30am-6pm, Thurs 9.30am-8pm, Sun 11am-6.30pm**

The Mad Hatter
(4, L5) Hats in all shapes and sizes from Italy and England, plus Irish designs by Catherine Cooke. The Hatter also hires out hats for the day – perfect for that surprise wedding or race meet.
✉ **20 Stephen St Lwr**
☎ **405 4936** 🚌 **all cross-city** ⏱ **Mon-Sat 10am-5.30pm, Thurs 10am-7.30pm**

Blue Eriu (6, B5)
In a fantastic, otherworldly, white space, Blue Eriu sell top-end skincare, cosmetics and haircare from the likes of Prada, Shu Uemura and Kleins, as well as scented candles, oils and artisan perfumes. Their facials and massages are highly

regarded but pricey.
✉ **7 William St S**
☎ **672 5776** 🚌 **all cross-city** ⏱ **Mon-Wed, Fri-Sat 10am-6pm, Thurs 10am-8pm, Sun 2-6pm**

McNeill's (4, G4)
Very little has changed in this traditional music shop since it opened in 1834. The warped floors, rustic workshop and old wooden cabinets lend the perfect atmosphere for browsing for a new or vintage bodhrán, accordion, banjo, violin or whistle.
✉ **140 Capel St**
☎ **872 2159** 🚌 **37, 70, 134, 172** ⏱ **Mon-Sat 10am-6pm**

Natural Shoe Store
(6, C5) Give your feet a treat at this tiny, spartan shop that specialises in natural, comfortable shoes. Apart from therapeutic but cool Birkenstocks and Komodos, there are 'vegetarian' shoes and handmade shoes in two designs by a shoemaker in Cork.
✉ **25 Drury St** ☎ **671 4978** 🚌 **all cross-city** ⏱ **Mon-Sat 9am-5.30pm**

Spoil yourself silly at Blue Eriu.

Emma Miller

places to eat

Dublin's food and restaurant scene is finally moving with the times, spurred on by residents' new-found passion for dining out and the demands of foreign visitors. You can now eat anything from French haute cuisine to Nepalese, and spend as little as €5, or several hundred, on a meal. But while there's been much talk of the culinary revolution sweeping the city, most of the flag-waving is being done by the pricey gastronomic restaurants. Finding a decent mid-range meal, at a price you can stomach, can still be a difficult task.

Meal Costs

The pricing symbols used in this chapter indicate the average cost of a main course at dinner, or other peak times.

$	under €8
$$	€8-15
$$$	€16-25
$$$$	over €25

Martin Moos

The most concentrated restaurant area is **Temple Bar**, but apart from a handful of good places, the bulk of eateries offer bland, unimaginative fodder and cheap set menus for tourists. Better food and service can usually be found **east and west of Grafton St**, while the top-end restaurants are clustered around **Merrion and Fitzwilliam Squares**. Fast food chains dominate the **northside**, though some fine cafes and eateries are thankfully appearing there too.

Ireland has excellent beef, pork, seafood, dairy foods and winter vegetables, and many good restaurants now source their ingredients locally, from organic and artisan producers. The rediscovery and reworking of traditional Irish cuisine is slowly filtering down from the innovative chefs who man the stoves in the city's upmarket establishments. Stews, bangers and mash, poached and smoked salmon and hearty steaks are increasingly appearing on menus everywhere. Stick to the produce and dishes that Ireland does best and you will have more hits than misses.

Non-smokers

Very few Dublin restaurants make allowances for non-smokers, and even if there is a non-smoking section, it's usually in the same room as the smokers. If smoking really spoils your appetite, your best bet is the city's vegetarian restaurants, which all have non-smoking sections or ban it altogether.

Wine culture is undeveloped compared to continental Europe and most bars still dole out airline-size bottles of extremely rank wine. Mid-range restaurants usually have a reasonable selection of wines, while cheaper joints might offer a house red and white, or nothing at all. Bucking the trend yet again, most top restaurants have superb wine lists, and a sommelier on hand to advise you.

For many restaurants, particularly those in Temple Bar, it's worth booking for Friday or Saturday nights to ensure a table.

Anne St South's fresh air restaurants

Martin Moos

NORTH OF THE LIFFEY

101 Talbot (4, F7) **$$**
Modern European
Close to Busáras and Connolly station, 101 Talbot bravely brings good food north of the river. The Mediterranean and Middle Eastern-style cuisine includes beef, duck, pork and fish, as well as several interesting vegetarian offerings. The two-tiered space has a sunken no-smoking area.
✉ 101 Talbot St
☎ 874 5011 🚌 all cross-city ⏲ Tues-Sat 5-11pm ♿ V

Cobalt Cafe & Gallery (4, D6) **$**
Cafe
Though the gallery is little more than a few paintings on the wall, this has to be the nicest cafe on the northside. Sit in the front room of this beautifully restored Georgian town house, or head out back to the garden. The food is simple and good – well-stuffed sandwiches, cheap breakfasts, coffee, tea and juice.
✉ 16 Great George's St N ☎ 873 0313
🚌 all cross-city
⏲ Mon-Sat 10am-5pm ♿

Epicurean Food Hall (4, H5) **$**
Food Hall
Some of Dublin's best eateries have outlets in this food hall, where you can grab a snack or buy specialist products. Caviston's has fresh and cooked fish, La Corte has Italian deli items, Le Petit des Gourmets offers French patisserie and Nectar does juices and smoothies. There are also bagels, sushi and Mexican and Lebanese food.
✉ Liffey St Lwr
🚌 all cross-city
⏲ Mon-Wed & Fri 9am-6pm, Thurs 9am-7pm, Sat 10am-6pm ♿ V

Halo (4, H4) **$$$$**
French-Oriental
Housed in the slick Morrison Hotel, Halo is visually stunning – soaring ceilings, a wall of mirrors and striking artwork. The high-end fusion cooking reflects the East-meets-West interior, combining Oriental spices with French technique.
✉ The Morrison Hotel, Ormond Quay ☎ 878 2999 🚌 all cross-city
⏲ 12.30-2pm & 7-10.30pm

Kelly & Ping (4, G1) **$$**
Asian
Opposite the Old Jameson Distillery, this bright modern restaurant, decorated with the odd Buddha and bonsai, does sophisticated Asian fusion cooking that draws from Thai, Chinese, Malay and Japanese cuisine, with Irish microbrewery and Asian beers.
✉ Smithfield Village, Smithfield ☎ 817 3840
🚌 134 ⏲ Mon-Sat noon-10.30pm, Sun noon-6pm ♿

Panem (5, B3) **$**
Cafe
A tiny cafe that does pasta, focaccia and salads,

Books and cooks

Panem's speciality is wickedly good sweet and savoury pastries, all handmade on-site. The croissants and brioche – filled with Belgian chocolate, almond cream or hazelnut amaretti – are the perfect snack for a stroll along the quays.
✉ 21 Ormond Quay Lwr ☎ 872 8510
🚌 all cross-city
⏲ Mon-Fri 9am-5pm, Sat 10am-5pm ♿ V

Winding Stair (5, B4) **$**
Cafe
Upstairs from the bookshop of the same name (p. 72), this great cafe is spread over two floors with views of the Liffey. Murals, wooden benches and picnic tablecloths lend an artfully dishevelled air, while the kitchen dishes up soups, salads and sandwiches laden with brie, apple sauce, whiskey salami and Gorgonzola.
✉ 40 Ormond Quay Lwr ☎ 873 3292,
🚌 all cross-city
⏲ Mon-Wed & Sat 9.30am-6pm, Thurs-Fri 9.30am-8pm, Sun 1-6pm ♿ V

Tipping
A tip of 10-15% is customary, but not obligatory, for service in restaurants, though not for eateries that include a service charge (usually 10%) on the bill.

TEMPLE BAR

Ar Vicoletto
(5, D4)   **$$**
Italian
Cosy little osteria with good-value, authentic Italian standards that can be excellent, but not always. Apart from pastas, crostini and salads, there are the usual offerings of veal, beef and seafood.
✉ 5 Crow St
☎ 670 8662 🚌 all cross-city ⏰ Mon-Sat noon-4pm & 6-11.30pm, Sun 2-11.30pm ♿

Bad Ass Cafe
(5,C5)   **$$**
American
Yes, yes, Sinéad O'Connor once worked here as a waitress. But that's not the only reason to visit – bright, cheerful and family-friendly, the cafe has big, basic pizzas, pastas and burgers. Pulleys on the ceiling whisk orders to the kitchen. Wine and beer available.
✉ 9-11 Crown Alley
☎ 671 2596
🚌 all cross-city
⏰ 11.30am-midnight
♿ kids' menu **V**

Bar Italia (4, J4)   **$**
Italian Cafe
This tiny, glass-fronted cafe is incredibly appealing, despite the traffic roaring along the quays. Maybe it's the fantastic Alombini coffee, or the rich chocolate tart, daily pastas or deli counter. Probably though it's the buzz of the Italian staff, whizzing between tables in their frantic, friendly way.
✉ Unit 4, The Bookend, Essex Quay
☎ 679 5128 🚌 all cross-city ⏰ Mon-Sat 8am-6pm ♿ **V**

Bruno's (5, C3)   **$$$**
Modern European
The owner is French, all the chefs are Irish, and the menu is contemporary (some say overly so). The light, modern room is favoured as much for its raucous, friendly atmosphere as for the food.
✉ 30 Essex St E
☎ 670 6767 🚌 all cross-city ⏰ Mon-Fri 12.30-2.30pm & 6-10.30pm, Sat 6-10.30pm

Cafe Gertrude
(5, B6)   **$$**
Cafe
Just off the main Temple Bar drag, this relaxed cafe offers good sandwiches, salads and pizzas at reasonable prices although, oddly, their coffee is expensive.
✉ 3-4 Bedford Row
☎ 677 9043
🚌 all cross-city
⏰ Mon-Sat 9am-10pm, Sun 9am-9pm ♿ **V**

Cafe Irie (5, C4)   **$**
Cafe
A vague Rasta theme holds sway here – but only as far as the laid-back vibe and music. The food is basic cafe fare with cornflakes and the full cooked deal available at breakfast, while lunch is wraps, paninis and sandwiches.
✉ 11 Fownes St Upper
☎ 672 5090
🚌 all cross-city
⏰ 9am-8.30pm ♿ **V**

The Chameleon
(5, C4)   **$$**
Indonesian
Friendly, characterful and draped in exotic fabrics, Chameleon serves up Indonesian classics like satay, gado gado, nasi goreng and mie goreng. If you can't decide, try the *rijsttaffel* – a selection of several dishes and rice.
✉ 1 Fownes St Lwr, Temple Bar ☎ 671 0362
🚌 all cross-city
⏰ Tues-Sat 6-11pm, Sun 6-10pm ♿ **V**

Dish (5, D4)   **$$$**
Modern European
One of the new breed of über-trendy joints in Temple Bar, it has simple

Vegetarian Options
Dublin has a surprising number of good vegetarian restaurants as well as a considerable number of regular restaurants offering a reasonable selection of things to graze on. The following vegetarian restaurants also have vegan dishes:

Juice or **Cornucopia** (both on p. 80)
Govinda (4 Aungier St; 4, L5; ☎ 475 0309; Mon-Sat noon-9pm; $) – run by Hare Krishnas, with daily hot meals and salads
Cafe Fresh (Powerscourt Townhouse; 6, C6; ☎ 671 9669; Mon-Sat 9am-5pm; $) – hot meals, smoothies, juices, soups and great toasted focaccias
Blazing Salads (42 Drury St; 6, C5; ☎ 671 9552; Mon-Sat 9am-5.30pm; $) – excellent salad bar and sandwiches, but no seating

Lights of Eden

but contemporary meals, with a strong emphasis on organic produce. The menu is constantly changing and the set lunch is excellent value. Book for weekends.
✉ **2 Crow St** ☎ **671 1248** 🚌 **all cross-city** 🕐 **12.30-11.30pm** ♿ **V**

Eden (5, D3) $$$
Modern European
A big, stark space facing Meeting House Square, Eden is the epitome of Temple Bar chic. Its solid, well-cooked contemporary meals offer the usual fusion foods. Try to get a terrace seat in summer, especially when performances are held in the square. Book ahead.
✉ **Meeting House Sq** ☎ **670 5372** 🚌 **all cross-city** 🕐 **noon-3pm & 6-10.30pm** ♿

Elephant & Castle (5, C6) $$
American
Spicy chicken wings, burgers and omelettes are a speciality at this bustling eatery. Interesting ingredients lift the menu above the basic. There are also New York –style sandwiches, salads, soups and pastas. Sunday brunch is very popular.
✉ **18 Temple Bar** ☎ **679 3121** 🚌 **all cross-city** 🕐 **Mon-Fri 8am-11.30pm, Sat 10.30am-11.30pm, Sun noon-11.30pm** ♿ **V**

Gruel (5, E3) $
Diner
Gruel's soup kitchen decor suits perfectly the gourmet greasy spoon fare they dish up. The daily 'roast-in-a-roll' is a mighty mountain of meat doused in cranberry or apple sauce, while the daily 'deli roll' is a vegie version.
✉ **68a Dame St** ☎ **670 7119,** 🚌 **all cross-city** 🕐 **Mon-Fri 7.30am-9.30pm, Sat-Sun 10.30am-5.30pm** ♿ **V**

Il Baccaro (5, D3) $$
Italian
Tucked away in an atmospheric wine cellar on Meeting House Square, this trattoria's rustic cuisine is richly flavoured and authentic. The Irish owner imports wines by the barrel from northern Italy – so grab a carafe, order some bruschetta and settle in for some serious eating.
✉ **Diceman's Corner, Meeting House Sq** ☎ **671 4597** 🚌 **all cross-city** 🕐 **Sun-Fri 6-11pm, Sat noon-11pm**

Mermaid Cafe (5, E3) $$$
Modern European
One of the best restaurants in the city, Mermaid dishes up unusual and inspired top-end food in informal, friendly surrounds. Everything is homemade, artfully combined and well presented – from the crab cakes with piquant mayonnaise to the monkfish wrapped in prosciutto and rosemary. Book ahead.
✉ **70 Dame St** ☎ **670 8236** 🚌 **all cross-city** 🕐 **Mon-Sat 12.30-2.30pm & 6-11pm, Sun noon-3.30pm & 6-9pm**

Monty's of Kathmandu (5, D3) $$
Nepalese
A varied menu of Nepalese staples, including lamb done every which way, chicken and the odd prawn curry, served with rotis, parathas and fluffy rice.
✉ **28 Eustace St** ☎ **670 4911** 🚌 **all cross-city** 🕐 **Mon-Sat noon-2.30pm & 6-11.30pm, Sun 6-11.30pm** ♿ **V**

Queen of Tarts (6, A2) $
Cafe
A relaxed, homey cafe that specialises in cakes and pastries. At breakfast there's muffins, scones, muesli, bagels and cooked dishes, while lunch is salads and sandwiches. But don't leave without trying the chocolate pecan tart.
✉ **Cork Hill** ☎ **670 7499** 🚌 **all cross-city** 🕐 **Mon-Fri 7.30am-7pm, Sat 9am-6pm, Sun 10am-6pm** ♿ **V**

The Tea Rooms (5, C2) $$$
Modern Irish
The Tea Rooms were designed to resemble a church, and the food is indeed worthy of a few hymns. Expect Rossmore oysters baked with black pudding and Cashel blue, vegetable risotto drizzled with truffle oil, beer-battered salmon, roast quail and sculptural desserts. The wine list is excellent.
✉ **Clarence Hotel, 6-8 Wellington Quay** ☎ **670 7766** 🚌 **all cross-city** 🕐 **Mon-Fri 12.30-2.45pm & 6.30-10.30pm, Sat 6.30-10.30pm, Sun 11am-2.45pm & 6.30-10.30pm** ♿

WEST OF GRAFTON ST

Avoca Café
(6, A7) $$
Modern Irish Cafe
On the top floor of Avoca Handweavers (p. 69), this light-filled cafe serves modern Irish food with an emphasis on organics and wholefoods. Bangers and mash and sweet corn fritters compete with salads (smoked tuna, Greek, Tuscan vegie), tarts, farmhouse cheeses and panini. There are red and white wines too.
✉ 11-13 Suffolk St ☎ 672 6019 🚌 all cross-city ⏱ Mon-Sat 9am-5.30pm ⚹ V

Aya (6, B6) $$$
Sushi Bar
Hidden behind Brown Thomas, Aya does the best Japanese in the city. There's a revolving sushi bar where, Sunday to Tuesday 6-8pm, you can eat your fill for €25. You can also choose hot dishes from the menu or pick up takeaway or specialist products at the Japanese minimart next door.
✉ 49-52 Clarendon St ☎ 677 1544 🚌 all cross-city ⏱ Mon-Sat noon-4pm & 5.30-11pm, Sun noon-4pm & 5.30-10pm ⚹ V

Cooke's Cafe
(6, C5) $$$$
Californian-Mediterranean
Seafood is a speciality at this gourmet eatery, frequented by business folk and lithe ladies who lunch. Lobster salad, Galway oysters and Russian caviar are teamed with organic vegetables and salads on the light, California-meets-Mediterranean menu.
✉ 14 William St S ☎ 679 0536 🚌 all

cross-city ⏱ Tues-Sat 12.30-3pm & 6-11pm

Cornucopia (6, B6) $
Vegetarian
Hearty vegetarian and vegan dishes that change daily, served in a relaxed, country-kitchen atmosphere. Hot meals include soups, casseroles and quiches, all served with salad. There's a vegetarian cooked breakfast as an alternative to porridge, muesli and French toast.
✉ 19 Wicklow St ☎ 677 7583 🚌 all cross-city ⏱ Mon-Wed & Fri-Sat 9am-8pm, Thurs 9am-9pm ⚹ V

Gallic Kitchen
(4, L2) $
French Cafe
A sign on the wall of this small, unassuming bakery shopfront says 'Our food is so fucking good you won't believe it'. Standing at a bench, devouring a melt-in-your-mouth goat's cheese brioche, salmon roulade, smoked haddock quiche and chocolate pecan tart, we'd have to agree.
✉ 49 Francis St ☎ 454 4912 🚌 49, 50, 51b, 77, 78, 123 ⏱ Mon-Sat 9am-5pm ⚹

Good World
(6, B4) $$
Chinese
Dim sum is a must here on Sunday afternoon, but get there early. Choose from the huge selection of bite-sized treats, sip soothing tea and sink back into the buzz of it all. It's open late.
✉ 18 Great George's St S ☎ 677 5373 🚌 all cross-city ⏱ 12.30pm-3am; dim sum Sun 12.30-6pm ⚹

Juice (6, B4) $$
Vegetarian
This hip and healthy restaurant offers smart Pacific Rim–style meals, as well as smoothies, juices, organic wines and vegan beers. Casseroles, stir-fries, soups and wraps can be rounded off with a tofu dessert, cheese platter or delicious apple crumble.
✉ 73-83 Great George's St S ☎ 475 7856 🚌 all cross-city ⏱ 11.30am-midnight; brunch Sat-Sun noon-4.30pm; early bird dinners Mon-Fri 5-7pm ⚹ V

Lemon (6, B5) $
Creperie
Lemon doesn't look like much from the street – until you catch a whiff of those crepes. Then it's straight inside where, within minutes, a sweet or savoury crepe or waffle can be yours. Get it smothered in maple syrup, ice cream, coconut or Grand Marnier.
✉ 66 William St S ☎ 672 9044 🚌 all cross-city ⏱ Mon-Wed & Fri 8am-7.30pm, Thurs 8am-9.30pm, Sat 9am-7.30pm, Sun 10am-6.30pm ⚹ V

Café Mao (6, D5) $$
Asian
Café Mao attracts a chatty young crowd. The theme is Chairman Mao and it serves a mad mix of Oriental dishes, from nasi goreng to bulkoko. Anything goes, so eat your tempura with a side of garlic naan, and finish with tarte tatin.
✉ 2-3 Chatham St ☎ 670 4899 🚌 all cross-city ⏱ Mon-Thurs noon-11pm, Fri-Sat noon-

11.30pm, Sun noon-10pm ♿ until 7pm **V**

Metro Cafe (6, D5) **$**
Cafe
A loyal clientele fills Metro's relaxed, well-worn rooms, where mellow music, excellent coffee and simple cafe fare are the main draw. In summer the outdoor tables are the perfect spot for reading the paper.
✉ **43 William St S**
☎ **679 4515**
🚌 **all cross-city**
🕐 **Mon, Tues & Fri 8am-8pm, Wed 8am-9pm, Thurs 8am-10pm, Sat 9am-7pm, Sun 10.30am-6pm** ♿ **V**

Nude (6, A7) **$**
Cafe
Hyper-modern Nude looks like the juice bar at the end of the universe. The massive kitchen is fronted by a space-age, fast-food counter. Sit at a long communal bench with your hot wrap and spirulina-spiked juice and ponder Nude's slogan: 'You are Where You Eat'.
✉ **21 Suffolk St**
☎ **675 5577** 🚌 **all cross-city** 🕐 **Mon-Sat 8am-9.30pm, Sun 11am-8pm** ♿ **V**

Odessa (6, A4) **$$$**
Mediterranean
A stylish and fashionable place where you can eat surprisingly well, in comfort and style, without too crippling a strain on the back pocket. Sunday brunch is a favourite with the city's hip young things, as are the legendary Bloody Marys.
✉ **13-14 Dame Court**
☎ **670 7634** 🚌 **all cross-city** 🕐 **Mon-Fri 6-**

11.30pm, Sat-Sun noon-4.30pm & 6-11pm ♿ **V**

Peacock Alley (4, M6) **$$$$**
Modern European
Super-chef bad boy Conrad Gallagher runs this super-posh operation in the modernist Fitzwilliam Hotel. Original and wildly energetic, Gallagher puts an innovative spin on traditional French cuisine, but his burgeoning restaurant empire means he's not always in the kitchen.
✉ **Fitzwilliam Hotel, 109 St Stephen's Green W** ☎ **478 7015** 🚌 **all cross-city** 🕐 **Mon-Sat 12.30-2.30pm & 6.30-10.30pm**

QV2 (6, A5) **$$$**
Modern European
A relaxed but stylish bistro with a good value lunch and early-bird dinner menu, QV2 does Med-Asian dishes with flair. Pasta, risotto, steak, steamed mussels and sesame crab cakes are typical.
✉ **14-15 St Andrew's St** ☎ **677 3363** 🚌 **all cross-city** 🕐 **Mon-Wed noon-3pm & 6-11pm, Thurs-Sat noon-3pm & 6pm-midnight** ♿

Shanahan's on the Green (4, M6) **$$$$**
American Steakhouse
Dublin's first fine dining steakhouse is set over three floors of a beautiful Georgian town house. Its 'Oval Office' bar contains memorabilia from US presidents. The menu has lamb, pork, chicken and seafood, but pride of place goes to beefsteaks, which can set you back as much as €30

(they're worth every cent).
✉ **119 St Stephen's Green W** ☎ **407 0939**
🚌 **all cross-city** 🕐 **Mon-Fri noon-2.30pm & 6-11pm, Sat 6-11pm** ♿

Simon's Place (6, B4) **$**
Cafe
Holding a prime corner spot on George's St Arcade, Simon's is the perfect spot to nurse a cuppa and the paper. Come at lunchtime and you'll have to line up with the loyal clientele for chunky soups, big sandwiches and good coffee.
✉ **George's St Arcade, Great George's St S**
☎ **679 7821** 🚌 **all cross-city** 🕐 **Mon-Sat 8.30am-6pm** ♿ **V**

Kid Friendly
Kids are welcome at most restaurants but some places will only take child diners during the day or early evening. We've indicated the restaurants which are particularly family-friendly with the ♿ symbol. High chairs, booster seats and child servings are very rarely available – but many kitchens will cook up something appropriate if asked.

Oliver Strewe

Table for One

Eating alone in Dublin is rarely a problem, and you're unlikely to feel uncomfortable or a nuisance. Some places have a cosy atmosphere that makes you feel right at home, especially as they tend to attract other single diners with their books all day long. Here's a few:

Cafe Gertrude (p.78)
Cornucopia (p.80)
Dunne & Crescenzi (below)
Simon's Place (p.81)
Winding Stair (p.77)
Metro Cafe (p.81)

Doug McKinlay

Steps of Rome
(6, D6)   **$**
Italian
The pizza is not the best you'll ever try but eating here, with the checked plastic tablecloths, tiled floor and posters of Rome is the real charm. The potato and rosemary pizza – sold by the slice – is best. There's also pasta, salads and heart-starting espressos.
✉ **Unit 1, Chatham Court, Chatham St**
☎ **670 5630** 🚌 **all cross-city** ⏰ **Mon-Sat 10am-midnight, Sun noon-11pm ♿ V**

Trocadero (6, A6) **$$$**
Traditional Irish
Seedy burlesque venue from the street and flamboyant Belle Epoque bar inside, the Troc is a favourite of thespians, media types and the odd drag queen. Meals, served in large portions, are

supremely unfashionable but that somehow adds to the charm. The pre-theatre menu is popular, but stick around late to see the real action.
✉ **3 St Andrew's St**
☎ **677 5545**
🚌 **all cross-city**
⏰ **Mon-Sat 6pm-12.15am ♿ until 8pm**

Velure (6, D5) **$$$**
Modern European
Partly owned by local DJ Fergus Murphy, Velure offers contemporary cuisine in a funky, sophisticated setting. The red velvet booths, low lighting and gurgling fish tank set the scene for well-conceived meat and fish dishes with a twist.
✉ **47 William St S**
☎ **670 5585** 🚌 **all cross-city** ⏰ **Tues-Sat 6pm-midnight, Sun noon-6pm**

EAST OF GRAFTON ST

Cafe Java (6, D7)   **$**
Cafe
Friendly, American-style Cafe Java packs in a young, boisterous crowd who have heart-to-hearts over giant slices of apple pie and cappuccinos spiked with orange juice. The cooked breakfasts, bagels, soups and salads are big, simple and filling.
✉ **5 Anne St S** ☎ **670 7239** 🚌 **all cross-city** ⏰ **Mon-Wed & Fri 7am-7pm, Thurs 7am-9pm, Sat 8am-6.30pm, Sun 9am-6.30pm ♿ V**

The Chili Club
(6, D7) **$$**
Thai
Just visible from Anne St S, the Chili Club is one of Dublin's longest-serving

Thai restaurants. Cosy and comfortable, it serves up spicy curries, satays, meat and seafood dishes.
✉ **1 Anne's La** ☎ **677 3721** 🚌 **all cross-city** ⏰ **lunch: Mon-Sat 12.30-2.30pm; dinner: 6-11pm ♿**

Dail Bia (6, C10) **$**
Traditional Irish
The staff here speak Irish and the menu's bilingual. Everyone's welcome to sample the good, sturdy traditional fare. Stodge up at breakfast with porridge, scones or a bacon bap; for lunch there's leek soup, cockles and mussels, gammon steak or Irish salmon.
✉ **46 Kildare St** ☎ **670 6079** 🚌 **11, 11a, 14,**

14a, 15a ⏰ **Mon-Fri 8am-7pm, Sat 9.30am-5pm ♿**

Dunne & Crescenzi
(6, C9) **$**
Italian Wine Bar
Italian wines by the glass, imported Italian goods on the shelves, a simple deli menu that changes daily and one of the best coffees in town make D&C a must. Nibble on panini, antipasto, cheese or choose from the salad bar, grab a glass of red and chill out for the afternoon.
✉ **4 Frederick St S**
☎ **677 3815**
🚌 **all cross-city**
⏰ **Mon-Wed & Sat 9am-7pm, Thurs-Fri 9am-8pm ♿ V**

Fitzer's (6, C8) $$$
Modern European

An elegant but relaxed modern restaurant with outdoor tables during summer, Fitzer's contemporary menu fuses Mediterranean and Asian influences. Risotto, pasta, shitake-stuffed chicken, tiger prawns with lime – it's good, reliable fare.

✉ 51 Dawson St
☎ 677 1155
🚌 all cross-city
🕐 11.30am-11.30pm ♿

Gotham Cafe
(6, D7) $$
Cafe

A vibrant, youthful place decorated with framed *Rolling Stone* album covers, Gotham extends its New York theme to its delicious pizzas, which are named after districts in the Big Apple. Local favourites are the Chinatown and the Noho, or opt for pasta, crostini or Asian salads.

✉ 8 Anne St S ☎ 679 5266 🚌 all cross-city
🕐 Mon-Sat noon-midnight, Sun noon-10.30pm ♿ V

Jacob's Ladder
(6, B9) $$$
Modern Irish

One of the only city-centre restaurants with a view. And what a view it is – out over the playing fields of Trinity College. A fashionable place, the food is innovative and light, from grilled goat's cheese to roast quail. The lunch menu is good value.

✉ 4-5 Nassau St
☎ 670 3865 🚌 all cross-city 🕐 Tues-Sat 12.30-3pm & 6-10pm ♿

La Cave (6, D7) $$
French Wine Bar

From the outside, La Cave looks like it might be an adult bookshop, or a gangster pool hall. Wind your way downstairs and you'll discover a chic, Parisian-style wine bar with crimson walls, tiny tables and a packed crowd shouting over the Brazilian salsa music. The food is OK, but you're really here for the setting and the superb wine list.

✉ 28 Anne St S
☎ 679 4409 🚌 all cross-city 🕐 Mon-Sat

12.30pm-late, Sun 6pm-late ♿ until 6pm

La Stampa (6, D8) $$$
Modern European

The setting is gorgeous and dramatic – an opulent 19th-century house, draped in richly coloured fabrics and decorated with bright, modern artworks. The food ranges from upmarket fish and chips to organic lamb with Moroccan spices.

✉ 35 Dawson St
☎ 677 8611 🚌 all cross-city 🕐 lunch: Mon-Fri 12.30-2.30pm, dinner: 5.30-midnight ♿

Rooms with Views

Dublin is not big on views – but the following places have something special to gaze at over lunch:

Jacob's Ladder (p. 83)
Winding Stair (p. 77)
Ocean (p. 84)
Eden (p. 79)

MERRION & FITZWILLIAM SQUARES

Bang Cafe
(4, M9) $$$
Danish

Owned by the handsome Stokes twins, whose father owns Unicorn around the corner, Bang offers modern Danish cuisine in suitably minimalist, hip surrounds. The menu is interesting and heavy on seafood – dishes like chilli salt squid salad, cumin-roasted salmon salad, cauliflower fritters, and iced Scandinavian berries with white chocolate sauce.

✉ 11 Merrion Row
☎ 676 0898

🚌 10, 11, 13b, 51x
🕐 lunch: Mon-Sat 12.30-3pm, dinner: Mon-Wed 6-10.30pm, Thurs-Sat 6-11pm ♿ V

Café Boulevard
(4, N9) $
Cafe

A small, friendly cafe in the heart of the business district, this place serves hearty meals in a modern room oddly glitzed-up with a small chandelier. Breakfasts range from French toast to baps stuffed with bacon and fried egg, while lunch

includes big salads, wraps and hot dishes.

✉ 132 Baggot St Lwr
☎ 678 7054 🚌 10, 11, 13b, 51x 🕐 Mon-Fri 7am-6pm, Sat 9am-5pm ♿ V

Diep Le Shaker
(4, N9) $$$
Asian

Tucked down an alley off Pembroke St, this place is popular with the nearby business crowd, as well as media and arts mavens. The modern, light-filled restaurant on two levels serves up

Business Dining

If you need somewhere suitable to charge up your expense account, the following places offer excellent food, service and atmosphere:

Cooke's Cafe (p. 80)
Dobbins Wine Bar (below)
L'Ecrivain (at right)
Peacock Alley (p. 81)
Restaurant Patrick Guilbaud (at right)
Thornton's (p. 85)
Unicorn (at right)

top-end Chinese and Thai dishes which can be mixed and matched as you please.
✉ **55 Pembroke La** ☎ **661 1829** 🚌 **all cross-city** 🕐 **Mon-Wed 12.30-2.15pm & 6.30-10.30pm, Thurs-Fri 12.30-2.15pm & 6.30-11.15pm, Sat 6.30-11.15pm** ⚘ **until 8pm** **V**

Dobbins Wine Bar
(3, G12)   **$$$**
Traditional French
Dobbins sits opposite a row of council houses, and offers old-fashioned meals in a rather homey setting, but somehow it has remained a high-society favourite for more than 20 years. Of course, it's that *je ne sais quoi* that keeps them coming back – the conviviality, the service, the buzz and the self-perpetuating legend.
✉ **15 Stephen's La** ☎ **676 4679** 🚌 **5, 7, 7a, 8, 45, 46** 🕐 **Mon-Fri 12.30-2.30pm, Tues-Sat 7-10pm** ⚘

Ely (4, N8)   **$$**
wine bar
Just off Merrion Row, Ely combines sophisticated wine bar with tapas, mainly modern Irish food, and live jazz on Saturday nights. There are more than 70 wines available by the glass, and dishes include oysters, fish cakes, stews, bangers and mash and homemade desserts.
✉ **22 Ely Pl** ☎ **676 8986** 🚌 **all cross-city** 🕐 **Mon-Wed noon-midnight, Thurs-Sat noon-2am (drinks only 3-6pm)** ⚘ **until 7pm**

L'Ecrivain
(4, N10)   **$$$$**
French
Many foodies consider this the best restaurant in town, where sophisticated French cooking meets quality Irish ingredients in a surprisingly laid-back setting. Expect lots of seafood – wild Irish salmon, Dublin Bay prawns – cooked innovatively and beautifully presented. Booking essential.
✉ **112 Baggot St Lwr** ☎ **661 1919** 🚌 **10, 11, 13b, 51x** 🕐 **Mon-Fri 12.30-2pm & 7-10.30pm, Sat 7-11pm** ⚘ **until 8pm** **V**

Ocean
(3, F13)   **$$**
Seafood
Once the redevelopment of the Grand Canal Docks area is complete, Ocean will have one of the best views in town. Overlooking the water, this trendy, minimalist eatery sensibly specialises in fresh seafood, cooked simply and cleanly.
✉ **Charlotte Quay Dock, Ringsend** ☎ **668 8862** 🚌 **all cross-city** 🕐 **Mon-Fri noon-11pm, Sat noon-1.30am, Sun 12.30pm-11pm (kitchen closes 10pm)** ⚘ **V**

Restaurant Patrick Guilbaud
(4, M9)   **$$$$**
French
With two Michelin stars tucked under its belt, this elegant restaurant is set in luxurious surrounds. The service is formal, the food proudly French and the wine list extensive. Surprisingly, the dishes are not overly fiddled with; it's just excellent produce, beautifully cooked and elegantly presented. Bookings essential.
✉ **Merrion Hotel, 21 Merrion St Upper** ☎ **676 4192** 🚌 **all cross-city** 🕐 **Tues-Sat 12.30-2.15pm & 7.30-10.15pm** ⚘

Unicorn (4, N9)   **$$$**
Italian
Saturday lunch at the Unicorn is a Dublin tradition, as media types, socialites, politicos and legal eagles gossip, guffaw and clink glasses in conspiratorial rapture. At lunch many opt for the extensive antipasto bar, while the bistro-style evening menu features Italian classics, done well and priced to match the fashionable surrounds. Booking advised.
✉ **12b Merrion Court, Merrion Row** ☎ **676 2182** 🚌 **10, 11, 13b, 51x** 🕐 **Mon-Sat 12.30-3.30pm & 6-11.30pm** ⚘ **lunch only**

Bar Italia: bragging baristas

AROUND CAMDEN ST

Havana (4, P5) $
Tapas Bar
Bustling and bursting with energy, this Cuban-Spanish eaterie in a former poultry shop is a great spot to be on a Friday or Saturday night. Wines, beers and cocktails lubricate the mixed crowd, who munch endlessly on the tasty tapas. Every Saturday from 11.30pm there's salsa music and dancing.
✉ **3 Camden Market, Grantham St** ☎ **476 0046** 🚌 **14, 15, 65, 83** ⏱ **Mon-Wed noon-10.30pm, Thurs noon-11.30pm, Fri noon-midnight, Sat noon-2am ♿**

Pad Thai (3, H10) $$
Thai
A large restaurant spread over two floors, Pad Thai is comfortable and colourful with an extensive menu that includes spicy soups, Thai salads, noodles and various meat and vegetarian dishes. The finger food is great to share.
✉ **30 Richmond St S** ☎ **475 5551** 🚌 **14, 14a, 15, 83** ⏱ **lunch: Mon-Fri 12.30-3pm; dinner: Sun-Thurs 5-10pm, Fri-Sat 5-11pm ♿ highchairs available** V

Pig & Heifer (4, P5) $
Cafe
A simple, modern cafe that does a good line in cholesterol-building cooked breakfasts and New York–style hot sandwiches. There are 30 different breads to choose from, the cheeses come from the owner's farm, and there's plenty of horseradish and sauerkraut to dollop on your pastrami.
✉ **2 Charlotte Way** ☎ **478 3182** 🚌 **all cross-city** ⏱ **Mon-Fri 7.30am-6pm, Sat 10am-4pm ♿**

Thornton's (3, H9) $$$$
Modern Irish-French
Kevin Thornton's two-Michelin-star canalside restaurant delivers Irish produce cooked with Gallic flair: poached salmon with beluga caviar and cucumber jelly, bacon and cabbage terrine with leek sauce, pigeon with cep consomme.
✉ **1 Portobello Rd** ☎ **454 9067** 🚌 **14, 15, 65, 83** ⏱ **lunch: Fri 12.30-2pm; dinner: Tues-Sat: 7-11.30pm**

BALLSBRIDGE

Bella Cuba (3, J13) $$$
Cuban
A romantic little place with great daiquiris, salsa music on Friday and Saturday nights, and offbeat dishes like Havana meat pies, black bean soup, fried yucca fingers and chicken stuffed with chorizo. There's also a host of seafood options.
✉ **11 Ballsbridge Tce** ☎ **660 5539** 🚌 **5, 7, 7a, 8, 45, 46** ⏱ **5.30-11pm ♿ V**

Kites (3, J13) $$$
Cantonese
This is an upmarket Chinese restaurant with Cantonese, Peking and Sichuan dishes on the extensive menu. Apart from chicken, beef, pork, lamb and seafood done zillions of ways, it has curries, soups and noodles but few vegetarian options.
✉ **17 Ballsbridge Tce** ☎ **660 7415** 🚌 **5, 7, 7a, 8, 45, 46** ⏱ **Mon-Fri 12.30-2pm & 6.30-11.30pm, Sat 6.30-11.30pm, Sun 6.30-11pm**

Lobster Pot (3, J13) $$$
French Seafood
The cosy dining room at this top-end seafood specialist is subtly decorated with nautical paraphernalia, including the odd plastic lobster. The food is traditional French – moules marinière, fish provençale, mornay or meunière sauces and seafood chowder. Book ahead.
✉ **9 Ballsbridge Tce** ☎ **668 0025** 🚌 **5, 7, 7a, 8, 45, 46** ⏱ **Mon-Fri 12.30-2pm & 7-10.30pm, Sat 7-10.30pm ♿**

Roly's Bistro (3, J13) $$$
Traditional Irish
Roly's is a Dublin institution – always packed and with reliably good food. There are basics (leek and potato soup) and more adventurous fare (Gorgonzola and asparagus tart) but most people come back for the Kerry lamb, the pork stuffed with rhubarb and apple or the Irish beef. Book ahead.
✉ **7 Ballsbridge Tce** ☎ **668 2611** 🚌 **5, 7, 7a, 8, 45, 46** ⏱ **noon-3pm & 6-10pm ♿ V**

RANELAGH

Er Buchetto
(3, K12) $
Italian Cafe
This small cafe could be in Rome – and not just because of the opera on the stereo and the football trinkets. The menu has pasta, panini and bruschetta as well as a cooked breakfast with Italian sausage, tomato and basil on toasted ciabatta. Amoretti tart, tiramisu, peach nectar and rich, creamy coffee round it all off.
✉ 71 Ranelagh Rd
☎ 496 8885 🚌 11, 11a, 13b, 44, 86 ⏰ Mon-Sat 9am-6.30pm, Sun 11am-4pm ♿ V

Gammell's Deli
(3, J11) $
Deli Cafe
After you've snared a table out front, join the queue and choose from the deli counter laden with gourmet pies, pastries, quiches, salads and cakes. A full breakfast can also be had, as well as a range of breads, cheeses and olives to take away.
✉ 33 Ranelagh Rd
☎ 496 2311 🚌 11, 11a, 13b, 44, 86 ⏰ 8.30am-8.30pm ♿ V

Nectar (3, J11) $
Cafe
The staff can be a bit off-hand, but the food is good – an interesting range of wraps, pasta, salads and smoothies, as well as full breakfast, brunch and daily specials. Wines are available and after 5pm you can only have drinks with meals.
✉ 53 Ranelagh Rd
☎ 491 0934

🚌 11, 11a, 13b, 44, 86 ⏰ Mon-Sat 10am-11pm, Sun 10am-5pm ♿ V

Tribeca (3, K12) $$
American Brasserie
This New York–style brasserie has been packed since the day it opened and runs a waiting list from 5pm nightly. So what's the big deal? Beef and salmon burgers, rib eye with blue cheese, spicy rare beef salad and prosciutto and goat's cheese omelettes. Eaten in a funky, wooden interior adorned with photos of yellow cabs, politicians and rabbis.
✉ 65 Ranelagh Rd
☎ 4974174 🚌 11, 11a, 13b, 44, 86 ⏰ noon-11pm ♿

WORTH THE TRIP

Caviston's (1, B5) $$$
Traditional Seafood
Caviston's is considered by many to be the best seafood restaurant in Dublin. The small, unassuming room is packed for each of the three daily sittings, while in the deli next door locals buy fresh seafood and gourmet items to whip up at home. Booking essential.
✉ 59 Glasthule Rd, Sandycove ☎ 280 9120 🚌 Glasthule & Sandycove
⏰ restaurant sittings: noon-1.30pm, 1.30-3pm, 3-5pm ♿

Johnnie Fox's
(1, B5) $$
Seafood Pub
Ireland's highest pub, Johnnie Fox's is about 45 minutes from the city in the Wicklow Mountains. Some people find it kitsch and overdone – and the pub does go in for a lot of self-promotion – but it's actually an authentic old place full of bric-a-brac, gnarled benches, sawdust floors and crackling open fires. The fabulous (but pricey) seafood and nightly Irish music are another draw, as is the rolling country scenery en route.
✉ Glencullen, Co. Wicklow ☎ 295 5647 🚌 44b from Hawkins St ⏰ Mon-Sat noon-10.15pm, Sun 4-10pm ♿

Late-night Eats
Most kitchens shut around 10pm, but there are some places where you can feed the beast a little later. **Eddie Rocket's** (7 Anne St S; 6, D7; ☎ 679 7340; Sun-Thurs 7.30am-1am, Fri-Sat 7.30am-4.30am) is a saviour for many a hungry Dub. This cheap and cheerful 1950s-style US diner dishes out anything from breakfast to burgers and fries. Other options are more upmarket, such as **Trocadero** (p. 82) which jumps till late, and **Juice** (p. 80), where hip young things suck down organic juices to stave off that inevitable hangover.

entertainment

Gone are the days when all you could hope for in Dublin was a drink in a grimy pub and a dance at a seedy basement disco. Dublin is now one of Europe's most energetic cities, rejuvenated by wealth, optimism and a predominantly young population out to have a good time, seven days a week.

From Thursday to Sunday, the capital's 700-odd pubs and dozens of clubs are packed to the hilt with locals, as well as tourists on a wild weekend away. Its reputation for fun has made the city one of the most popular short-break destinations in Europe, and stag and hen parties from the UK arrive in their hundreds every weekend. For tips on pub culture, see the rounds system in Dos & Don'ts, p. 12.

The capacity of Dubliners to booze and party is legendary. But if that's not your scene, don't fret – there are plenty of options, from theatre, comedy and film to folk, rock, jazz, blues and classical music.

Listings

Entertainment listings can be found in the weekly *Hot Press* magazine (€2.50), the fortnightly *In Dublin* magazine (€2.50), or the free *Event Guide*, available at many bars and cafes. Wednesday's *Irish Times* (€1.25) has a pull-out section called *The Ticket*, and the *Evening Herald* (€0.85) offers the same on Thursdays. For listings and a laugh get *The Slate*, a free mag that sticks a pin in Dublin's buoyant ego. Check out **e** www.mcd.ie, www.ireland .com/dublin, www.entertainment.ie and www.timeout.com/dublin for electronic listings.

Top Spots

The most obvious and popular entertainment area is **Temple Bar**, which transforms itself nightly into a party district crawling with fun-seekers. Despite a ban on stags and hens at many pubs here, you'll still see gaggles of very drunk people wearing penises on their heads, tripping on the cobblestones and vomiting outside the few pubs that accept them. Locals tend to avoid Temple Bar on weekends.

The area immediately south of Temple Bar, and **west of Grafton St**, is packed with excellent pubs and clubs and attracts a more discerning crowd. Great George's St S especially is lined with places to drink and dance. **East of Grafton St** are more pubs and bars, though these are more upmarket and tend to attract an older, more groomed crowd.

While much of the nightlife is concentrated on the southside, the north is slowly taking off: **Capel St** (4, G4) is showing signs of life, and the stretch of riverfront from **Ormond Quay Upper** (4, J3) to **Bachelor's Walk** (4, H6) is already home to some fashionable bars.

Doug McKinlay

Flauting his talent.

Bookings

Theatre, comedy and classical concert tickets are usually booked through the venue, while tickets for touring international bands or big-name local talent are either sold at the venue or through a number of booking agencies. These include HMV on Grafton St (6, D6; ☎ 679 5334, 24hr credit-card bookings ☎ 456 9569) and Ticketmaster (☎ 1890 925 100). HMV has another branch at 18 Henry St (4, F6; ☎ 873 2899).

SPECIAL EVENTS

March *St Patrick's Day* – held on the 17th, with street parties, green beer, fireworks and a spectacular parade
Dublin Film Festival – various cinemas host big- and small-budget films from Ireland and around the world. For details ☎ 679 2937; e www.iol.ie/dff

March-April *Howth Jazz Festival* – held on the Easter Bank Holiday in this pretty seaside suburb; most gigs are free

late April–early May *Heineken Green Energy Festival* – one of the city's prime pop and rock festivals, with local and international bands at various venues

late May *Mardi Gras* – the last weekend of the month sees in Dublin's gay pride celebration, with a parade and other festivities

June *Women's Mini-Marathon* – 10km charity run on the second Sunday of the month, attracting up to 35,000 participants (see picture, right)
Dublin Writers Festival – four-day literature festival attracting Irish and international writers to its readings, performances and talks

June-July *Music in the Park* – free music festival at parks around the city

July *Guinness Blues Festival* – gigs at various venues, culminating in a show outside the Bank of Ireland on College Green (5, D7)

August *Dublin Horse Show* – Royal Dublin Society Showgrounds (see p.102) hosts an international showjumping competition

September *All-Ireland Finals* – Croke Park (see p.102) goes wild with the hurling finals (second Sunday of the month) and Gaelic football finals (fourth Sunday)

October *Dublin Theatre Festival* – two-week festival of theatre, Europe's biggest (e www.eircomtheatrefestival.com)
Dublin City Marathon – last Monday of the month

November *French Film Festival* – organised by the French embassy's cultural department

December-January *Funderland* – two-week traditional funfair at the Royal Dublin Society Showground (see p.102)

Eoin Clarke

PUBS & BARS

Despite a recent relaxation of licensing laws, Ireland still has some of the most conservative drinking legislation in Europe. On Monday to Wednesday pubs generally close at 11.30pm, with half an hour's drink-up time, while Thursday to Saturday it's last drinks at 12.30am and out by 1am. On Sundays closing time is 11pm. A handful of pubs and bars have late licences. All are closed on Christmas Day and Good Friday.

TRADITIONAL PUBS

The Brazen Head
(4, J1) Reputed to be Dublin's oldest pub, the Brazen Head was founded in 1198, but the present building dates from 1668. Attracting foreign students and tourists as well as locals, the pub has traditional Irish music on Tuesday, Thursday and Friday, kicking off around 9pm.
✉ 20 Bridge St Lwr
☎ 679 5186 🚌 134
🕐 Mon-Wed 10.30am-11.30pm, Thurs-Sat 10.30am-12.30pm, Sun 12.30pm-11pm
♿ until 7pm

Doheny & Nesbitt's
(4, N9) Opened in 1867 as a grocer's shop, this pub has antique snugs, dark-wood panelling and a pressed-metal roof. It's a favourite haunt of politicians and journalists, Leinster House being only a short stroll away.
✉ 5 Baggot St Lwr
☎ 676 2945
🚌 10, 11, 13b, 51x
🕐 Mon-Fri 10.30am-11.30pm, Sat 10.30am-1am, Sun 11am-11pm
♿ until 7pm

Flowing Tide (4, G7)
Directly opposite the Abbey Theatre, this place attracts a great mix of theatregoers, northside locals and the odd thespian downing a quick one between rehearsals. It's loud, full of chat and a great place to drink.
✉ 9 Abbey St Lwr
☎ 874 0842
🚌 all cross-city
🕐 Mon-Wed 10.30am-11.30pm, Thurs-Sat 10.30am-12.30am, Sun 12.30pm-11pm
♿ until 7pm

Grogan's Castle Lounge (6, C5)
Known simply as Grogan's (after the original owner), this old place is a city-centre institution. Long patronised by writers, painters and other bohemian types, it's laid-back and contemplative much of the day. Oddly, drinks are slightly cheaper in the stone-floor bar than in the carpeted lounge.
✉ 15 William St S
☎ 677 9320
🚌 all cross-city
🕐 Mon-Wed 10.30am-11.30pm, Thurs-Sat 10.30am-12.30pm, Sun 12.30-11pm
♿ until 7pm

Horseshoe Bar (6, F9)
A joke in Dublin is that the major political decisions of the day aren't made in parliament but here, in the horseshoe-shaped bar at the Shelbourne. Politicians of every hue rub shoulders with journalists and businessfolk in a fairly relaxed atmosphere, despite the rather grand surrounds.
✉ Shelbourne Hotel, St Stephen's Green
☎ 676 6471
🚌 all cross-city
🕐 Mon-Sat 10.30am-11pm
♿ until 7pm

Doug McKinlay

Centuries of drinking

International Bar
(6, B5) A fantastic old pub adorned with stained glass and mirrors, it's famous for its comedy nights and live jazz and blues sessions on Friday and Saturday. Ardal O'Hanlon, who played Dougal in *Father Ted*, started his career here doing stand-up comedy.
✉ 23 Wicklow St
☎ 677 9250
🚌 all cross-city
🕐 pub: Mon-Wed

10.30am-11.30pm,
Thurs-Sat 10.30am-
12.30am, Sun 12.30-
11pm; comedy: Mon,
Wed & Thurs 9pm
⑤ comedy €6.40/5.10
♿ until 7pm

Kehoe's (6, D7)
This is one of the most
atmospheric pubs in the city,
with a beautiful Victorian
bar, a comfy snug and
plenty of other little nooks
and crannies. Upstairs,
drinks are served in what
was once the publican's
living room – and it looks it.
✉ 9 Anne St S
☎ 677 8312
🚌 all cross-city
🕐 Mon-Wed 10.30am-
11.30pm, Thurs-Sat
10.30am-12.30am,
Sun 10.30am-11pm
♿ until 7pm

Long Hall (6, C4)
With ornate Victorian
woodwork, mirrors and
chandeliers, the Long Hall
is one of the city's most
beautiful and best-loved
pubs. From musk-coloured
walls to mirrored columns
behind the bar, it's all
elegantly dingy. The bar-
tenders are experts at their
craft, an increasingly rare
sight in Dublin these days.
✉ 51 Great George's
St S ☎ 475 1590
🚌 16, 16a, 19, 19a,
65, 83 🕐 Mon-Wed
noon-11.30pm, Thurs-
Fri noon-12.30am,
Sat 10.30am-12.30am,
Sun 2-11pm
♿ until 6pm

Mulligans (4, H8)
Built in the 1850s,
Mulligans has changed little since then. A place for
ser-ious drinking, it is
reputed to serve the best
Guinness in Ireland and is

popular with journalists
from the nearby newspaper
offices. The pub appeared
as the local in the film
My Left Foot with Daniel
Day Lewis.
✉ 8 Poolbeg St
☎ 677 5582
🚌 14, 44, 47, 48, 62
🚊 Tara St
🕐 Mon-Wed 10.30am-
11.30pm, Thurs-Sat
10.30am-12.30am,
Sun 12.30am-11pm
♿ until 5pm

O'Neill's (6, A6)
A labyrinthine old pub near
Trinity College, O'Neill's
dates from the late 19th
century, though a tavern
has stood on this site for
more than 300 years.
The odd combination of
students and stockbrokers
lends a chaotic air. Good
food is also on offer.
✉ 2 Suffolk St
☎ 679 3671
🚌 all cross-city
🕐 Mon-Wed 10.30am-
11.30pm, Thurs-Sat
10.30am-12.30am, Sun
12.30-11pm
♿ until 6pm

The Oval (4, G6)
A few doors down from
the *Irish Independent*, the
Oval is another popular
journalists' hang-out. The
original 1820s pub, which
is mentioned in *Ulysses*,
was destroyed in the Easter
Rising – this one dates
back to the 1920s.
✉ 78 Abbey St Middle
☎ 872 1259
🚌 all cross-city
🕐 Mon-Wed 10.30am-
11.30pm, Thurs-Sat
10.30am-12.30am, Sun
noon-11pm
♿ until 7pm

Palace Bar (5, B7)
With its mirrors, etched

glass and wooden niches,
Palace Bar is often said to
be the perfect example of
an old Dublin pub. It's popular with journalists from
the nearby *Irish Times* and
was patronised by writers
Patrick Kavanagh and
Flann O'Brien last century.
✉ 21 Fleet St
☎ 677 9290
🚌 all cross-city
🕐 Mon-Wed 10.30am-
11.30pm, Thurs-Sat
10.30am-12.30am,
Sun 12.30-11pm
♿ until 6pm

Stag's Head (6, A4)
Built in 1770 but remod-
elled in 1895 at the height
of Victorian opulence, this
pub has magnificent
stained glass, chandeliers
and marble, elaborate
carved wood and, of
course, mounted stags'
heads. It can get crowded
but it's worth it – the
food's good too.
✉ 1 Dame Court
☎ 679 3701
🚌 all cross-city
🕐 Mon-Wed 10.30am-
11.30pm, Thurs-Sat
10.30am-12.30am
♿ until 6pm

Toner's (4, N9)
With its stone floor and
old grocer's shelves and
drawers, Toner's feels like a
country pub in the heart of
the city. Though Victorian,
it's not elaborately decorated and draws a mainly
business crowd. It's not
touristy but many visitors
seek out its simple charms.
✉ 139 Baggot St Lwr
☎ 676 3090
🚌 10, 11, 13b, 51x
🕐 Mon-Wed 10.30am-
11.30pm, Thurs-Sat
10.30am-12.30am,
Sun 12.30-11pm
♿ until 7pm

Brewing Up a Storm

There's no doubt about it – the pub is the heart of social life in Dublin. It is the place where generation gaps are bridged, social ranks dissolved, inhibitions lowered, tongues loosened, stories told and songs sung.

Many Dublin pubs have a proud history of rebellion, acting as bolt holes for nationalists plotting the overthrow of the British from their bar stools. Other pubs have simply provided a home away from home for generations of workers; a place to chat, drink and forget about life's worries.

Brewing in Ireland probably goes back as far as the Bronze Age, but it was between the 4th and 5th centuries AD that the techniques used for distilling whiskey and brewing beer were first perfected by monks who brought the skills back from their ecclesiastical jaunts in the Middle East. The first drinks were made as remedies but the monks soon discovered their intoxicating qualities.

By the 16th century, women in Dublin were brewing and distilling in their homes for family and friends. Those who made a superior brew soon acquired a reputation and began selling their surplus stock to outsiders. Thus, the alehouse and 'the local' were born. The industry boomed, and by the 17th and 18th centuries it was estimated that a third of the city's houses sold ale.

It wasn't long before men cottoned on to the potential for money-making and in the late 18th century professional distillers and brewers came onto the scene. Arthur Guinness (p. 19) was one of the first to emerge, setting up shop on the site of a failed brewery in St James's Gate in 1759. John Jameson joined the fray in 1780, establishing the Smithfield whiskey distillery on Bow St (p. 39) in 1792.

Today there are almost 100 brands of Irish whiskey, and most of them you will only find in Ireland. Popular brands include Power's, Paddy, Bushmills and Wise's. As for beer, home-grown talents to watch out for include: Kilkenny-brewed Smithwick's; Beamish Red Ale from Cork; Caffrey's Irish Ale from Antrim; McCardles Traditional Ale; and the growing number of beers offered by Dublin's burgeoning microbreweries (p. 93).

Doug McKinlay

Drinkers in modern Dublin are spoiled for choice with variety on tap.

MODERN BARS

The Bailey (6, C7)
You'd never know it now, but the Bailey has a long history. Once a rebel safe house, Sinn Féin founder Arthur Griffith drank here, as did Michael Collins. Today it is sleek, modern and minimalist, attracting a well-to-do crowd for lunch at the outdoor tables.
✉ 2 Duke St
☎ 670 4939
🚌 all cross-city
🕐 Mon-Wed noon-11.30pm, Thurs-Sat noon-12.30am, Sun noon-11pm
♿ until 7pm

The Front Lounge
(5, E1) The front half of this large, sophisticated bar is lined with sofas and dark nooks, while the so-called Back Lounge is mood-lit and dressed up with a grand piano and chandelier. It draws a mixed, trendy crowd and is popular with the gay community.
✉ 33-34 Parliament St
☎ 670 4112
🚌 all cross-city
🕐 Mon-Thurs noon-11.30pm, Fri-Sat noon-1.30am, Sun noon-11pm

The Globe (6, B4)
The Globe was one of the first of the new breed of fashionable pubs to open in the city. Still immensely popular, it is one of the few trendy joints that doesn't give a damn what you're wearing. Consequently, it's truly hip.
✉ 11 Great George's St S
☎ 671 1220
🚌 all cross-city
🕐 noon-11.30pm
Ⓢ free

Hogan's (6, C4)
Once a traditional pub, Hogan's is a large, fashionable bar with red leather couches, mood lighting and an Art Deco club feel. A popular hang-out for young professionals, it gets busy at weekends with folks eager to take advantage of the late licence.
✉ 35 Great George's St S ☎ 677 5904
🚌 all cross-city
🕐 Mon-Wed noon-11.30pm, Thurs noon-12.30am, Fri-Sat noon-2.30am, Sun noon-11pm
♿ until 6pm

Life (4, F7)
Cavernous, modern and spread over two levels, Life was the epitome of cool when it opened. The fickle fashion pack may have moved on, but Life is still a good place to hang out, with DJs upstairs from Thursday to Saturday and food served during the day.
✉ Irish Life Mall, Abbey St Lwr ☎ 878 1032
🚌 all cross-city
🕐 Sun-Wed noon-11.30pm, Thurs-Sat noon-2.30am
♿ until 6pm

Lobo (4, H4)
This is the northside's version of the Octagon Bar (p. 93), only far more difficult to get into if you don't look a million bucks. If dressing glam is your thing, and you manage to get in, your prize is to spend an evening in the company of Dublin's well-to-do socialites.
✉ Morrisson Hotel, Ormond Quay Lwr
☎ 878 2999
🅔 www.morrisonhotel.ie 🚌 all cross-city
🕐 Fri & Sat 9pm-3am

Modern Green Bar
(4, N5) With simple, modern decor enhanced by a series of digital photos of the Liffey on the walls, the bar combines great music (there are DJs nightly) and a convivial, friendly atmosphere that attracts students and young professionals. The all-day menu is good.
✉ 31 Wexford St
☎ 478 0583
🚌 16, 16a, 19, 19a, 65, 83 🕐 Mon-Wed noon-11.30pm, Thurs-Fri noon-12.30pm, Sat 1pm-12.30am, Sun 1-11pm
♿ until 7pm

Mono (4, N5)
This large venue is spread over two floors. The decor is made up of futuristic neon lights and metal, befitting the techno and house acts that provide the soundtrack. Downstairs is Bar Mono which is open during the day for food and drink, while upstairs transforms into Club Mono after dark for a variety of DJ gigs.
✉ 30 Wexford St
☎ 478 0391
🚌 16, 16a, 19, 19a, 65, 83 🕐 Mon-Wed noon-11.30pm, Thurs-Fri

Two pints of the dark stuff

noon-12.30pm, Sat 1pm-
12.30am, Sun 1-11pm
⑤ bar: free, club: €10-15

Octagon Bar (5, C2)

This swish bar at the
Clarence Hotel (owned by
U2) has a domed skylight
and lots of wood panelling,
but not much character. It
attracts a mixed crowd,
including the odd celebrity,
and can be a comfortable
place to drink when everything else in Temple Bar is
packed.
✉ The Clarence Hotel,
6-8 Wellington Quay
☎ 670 9000
e www.theclarence.ie
🚌 all cross-city
🕐 Mon-Thurs 11am-
11.30pm, Fri-Sat
11am-12.30am, Sun
12.30-11pm

Odeon (4, P6)

In the old Harcourt train
station, Odeon is a large,
loud, busy pub with a
50m-long bar and ample
space for the hundreds of
punters who flock here
after work during the
week, and the glamorous
crowd who strut their stuff
on weekends.
✉ 57 Harcourt St
☎ 478 2088
🚌 14, 15, 65, 83
🕐 Mon-Wed noon-
11.30pm, Thurs-Sat noon-
12.30am, Sun 1-11pm
♿ until 7pm

Peter's Pub (6, D5)

A small, quiet bar around
the corner from the Gaiety
Theatre, Peter's is comfy
and newly refurbished but
old fashioned at the same
time. Great for early
evening drinks.
✉ 1 Johnston Pl
☎ 677 8588 🚌 all
cross-city 🕐 Mon-Wed
11am-11.30pm,

Micro-Revolution

A number of microbreweries are challenging the
supremacy of Guinness for the hearts and tastebuds
of Dubliners. The best known is the Porterhouse
(below) in Temple Bar, with nine of its own beers as
well as an incredible list of international beers and
wines.

Another contender is **Messrs Maguire** (1-2
Burgh Quay; 4, H7; ☎ 670 5777), a gigantic 'über-
bar' spread across three levels that offers five of its
own brews, from a creamy Porter to the German-
style Haus beer.

Last but not least, the **Dublin Brewing
Company** (141-146 King St N; 4, F2; ☎ 872 8622;
e www.dublinbrewing.com) operates during business hours only (Mon-Fri 9am-5.30pm) selling its four
beers which include the well-loved Revolution Red.

Thurs-Sat 11am-
12.30am, Sun 12.30-
11pm
♿ until 7pm

The Porterhouse

(5, D1) This microbrewery
and pub has sensational
beers, all made in Dublin
and chemical free. From a
Pilsner-style beer to the
Oyster Stout (brewed with
real oysters), this place is
worth a prolonged sam-
pling session. There are
traditional music sessions
several nights a week and
food is served daily.
✉ 16-18 Parliament St
☎ 679 8847 e www
.porterhousebrewco.com
🚌 all cross-city
🕐 Mon-Wed noon-
11.30pm, Thurs
noon-12.30am,
Fri-Sat 12.30pm-1am,
Sun 12.30-11pm
♿ until 7pm

Pravda (5, A4)

At the northern end of
Ha'penny Bridge, Pravda is
a Russian-themed megabar
in a former lost-property
office. Apart from Cyrillic

script on the walls and the
collective-farm proportions
of the place, there's little
else Soviet about it. It's
relaxed and easy-going,
but the bouncers can get
picky on weekends.
✉ 35 Liffey St Lwr
☎ 874 0076 🚌 all
cross-city 🕐 Sun-Wed
noon-11.30pm, Thurs
noon-12.30am, Fri-Sat
noon-2.30am
♿ until 7pm

Sam Sara (6, D8)

With its cathedral-like
proportions and elaborate,
Moroccan-style decor, Sam
Sara is an impressive sight.
It's best appreciated during
the week as on weekends
it becomes a heavily per-
fumed crush of air-kissing,
designer-clad fashionistas
(and older, less fashionable
men ogling them).
✉ 36 Dawson St
☎ 671 7723 🚌 10,
14, 14a, 15 🕐 Mon-
Wed noon-midnight,
Thurs noon-1am, Fri-Sat
noon-2.30am, Sun
noon-11pm
♿ until 7pm

Slattery's (4, G4)
Once a down-and-dirty dive renowned as the home of Dublin pub rock, Slattery's has been majorly refurbished and now boasts brown leather banquettes, a central bar, '60s-style fittings and chart CDs on the stereo. It's popular with students and young tourists at

Pulling pints at the friendly Stag's Head.

Going Solo
Dublin is one city where being alone never has to mean being lonely. Some of the most welcoming bars and pubs for solo travellers include:

International Bar (p.89)

Kehoe's (p. 90)

The Oval (p. 90)

Stag's Head (p. 90)

The Globe (p. 92)

Peter's Pub (p. 93)

Thomas Read (p. 94)

night, and locals during the day.
- ⊠ **129 Capel St**
- ☎ 872 7971
- 🚌 37, 70, 134, 172
- 🕐 Mon-Wed 11am-12.30am, Thurs 11am-1.30am, Fri-Sat 11am-2am, Sun 11am-11.30pm
- ♿ until 7pm

Thomas Read (5, E2)
The clientele at this spacious, airy bar, spread across two levels, seems to favour a selection of wine and coffee over beer. During the day it's a great place to relax and read the newspaper. For a more traditional setting its annexe, the Oak, is a great place for a pint.
- ⊠ **1 Parliament St**
- ☎ 670 7220
- 🚌 all cross-city
- 🕐 Mon-Wed 11.30am-11.30pm, Thurs-Sat 11.30am-midnight, Sun 11.30am-11pm
- ♿ until 7pm

CINEMAS

Irish Film Centre
(5, D3) The IFC shows classics and new independent films, including some yet-to-be-classified flicks. You have to be a member to see a movie here, but you can buy just a one-week membership when you buy your ticket. It's only €1.30 per group of any size. The complex also has a bar, cafe and excellent bookshop.
- ⊠ **6 Eustace St** ☎ 679 5744 **e** www.fii.ie
- 🚌 all cross-city
- 🕐 centre: 10am-11.30pm; films 2-11pm
- 💲 matinees €5.10/4.45, evenings €5.70/5.10

Savoy (4, F6)
A four-screen, first-run cinema with late-night shows at weekends.
- ⊠ **O'Connell St Upper**
- ☎ 874 6000
- 🚌 all cross-city
- 🕐 2-11pm 💲 before 6pm: €5.60/4.60; after 6pm: €7.50/4.60 ♿ yes

Screen (5, B10)
Between Trinity College and O'Connell Bridge, Screen shows fairly good art-house films on its three screens.
- ⊠ **2 Townsend St**
- ☎ 672 5500 🚌 5, 7, 7a, 8, 14 🚉 Tara St

🕐 2-10.30pm
💲 before 6pm: €5.60/4.60; after 6pm: €7.50/4.60 ♿ yes

UGC Multiplex (4, F4)
This seven-screen cinema has replaced many smaller cinemas. There are late shows Friday and Saturday night, starting around 11.30pm.
- ⊠ **Parnell Centre, Parnell St**
- ☎ 872 8400
- 🚌 all cross-city
- 🕐 Sun-Thurs 11.30am-11.30pm, Fri-Sat 11.30am-1.30am
- 💲 €7.50/4.70-5.50
- ♿ yes

TRADITIONAL IRISH MUSIC

The Brazen Head
See p. 89.

Chief O'Neill's (4, G1)
A big, new bar in the Smithfield Village complex, the Chief has traditional music sessions on Thursday nights, starting around 8pm. There's food daily until 10pm.
✉ Smithfield Village
☎ 817 3860 🚌 134
🕐 Mon-Wed 10.30am-11.30pm, Thurs-Sat 10.30am-12.30am, Sun 12.30pm-11pm
⑤ free ♿ yes until 7pm

Cobblestone (4, F1)
Bordering Smithfield Square, this great old bar features traditional musicians, who usually play until after closing time. The quality of the music is excellent.
✉ 77 King St N
☎ 872 1799 🚌 134
🕐 Mon-Wed 3-11.30pm, Thurs-Sat noon-12.30am, Sun noon-11pm
⑤ €8-10

Harcourt Hotel (4, O6)
This is one of Dublin's long-running traditional music venues, with lively sessions from class acts in the residents' bar most Friday to Monday nights.
✉ 60-61 Harcourt St
☎ 478 3677 🚌 15, 15a, 20, 61, 86
🕐 music: 9.30pm-late
⑤ free

Hughes' Bar (4, H2)
By day this pub is popular with barristers and their clients from the nearby Four Courts, and the early opening hours cater for the workers from the market

across the street. But by night the place transforms into a traditional music venue, where you might also see some line-dancing.
✉ 19 Chancery St
☎ 872 6540 🚌 all cross-city 🕐 Mon-Wed 7am-11.30pm, Thurs-Sat 7am-12.30am, Sun 7-11pm ⑤ free
♿ until 7pm

O'Donoghue's (4, M8)
O'Donoghue's is the most renowned traditional music bar in Dublin, where well-known folk group the Dubliners started out in the 1960s. On warm summer evenings a young, international crowd spills into the courtyard beside the pub.
✉ 15 Merrion Row
☎ 676 2807
🚌 10, 11, 13b, 51x
🕐 Mon-Wed 10.30am-11.30pm, Thurs-Sat 10.30am-12.30am, Sun 12.30-11pm
⑤ free
♿ until 7pm

The Norseman (5, C3)
This refurbished watering hole in the heart of Temple Bar has live traditional music several times a week. Popular with an eclectic crowd, from tourists to theatre folk, it's

Second fiddle to none

warm and welcoming.
✉ 27-29 Essex St E
☎ 671 5135 🚌 all cross-city 🕐 music starts 9.30pm ⑤ free

Oliver St John Gogarty's (5, C6)
The traditional music sessions at this always jumping Temple Bar pub are extremely popular with tourists, most of whom don't mind that the music is less than authentic.
✉ 58-59 Fleet St
☎ 671 1822 📧 www .olivergogartys.com
🚌 all cross-city
🕐 sessions Mon-Sat 2.30-7pm & 9pm-2am, Sun noon-2pm, 5-7pm & 8.30pm-1am
⑤ free ♿ yes

The Porterhouse
See p. 93.

Traditional Irish drinking, er, music session

CK, JAZZ & BLUES

bassador Theatre
E6) Recently re-opened
the top of O'Connell St,
this former cinema has
already established its
street cred by snaring
some interesting inter-
national acts. There's a
spacious downstairs
auditorium, while upstairs
it's seating only in old-
cinema seats complete
with drinks holders.
⌂ O'Connell St
e www.mcd.ie 🚌 all
cross-city ⌚ varies;
doors open 7.30pm
⑤ most gigs €17-27

Bruxelles (6, D6)
See live rock and blues
bands a couple of nights a
week, perhaps the only
link the now-trendy pub
has to its heavy metal
past. A swirl of authentic
Art Nouveau design, it's
worth popping your head

in for a look.
✉ 7-8 Harry St
☎ 677 5362
🚌 all cross-city
⌚ Sun-Wed noon-
1.30am, Thurs-Sat
noon-2.30am
⑤ free ♿ until 5pm

**Eamonn Doran's
Imbibing Emporium**
(5, C5) A sprawling pub
and club, Doran's is dark
and dingy downstairs, but
that suits the various rock
acts that play there.
Upstairs in the pub proper
there's often traditional
music sessions.
✉ 3a Crown Alley
☎ 679 9114
🚌 all cross-city
⌚ Mon-Sat 11am-
2.30am, Sun 12.30pm-
2.30am ⑤ €5-12

JJ Smyth's (6, E3)
Jazz and blues nightly at

this friendly pub draw a
regular crowd of dedicated
music lovers. The Irish Blues
Club plays on Tuesdays and
long-standing resident
bands on other nights.
✉ 12 Aungier St
☎ 475 2565
🚌 16, 16a, 19, 19a,
65, 83 ⌚ most shows
start 8.30-9.30pm
⑤ €5-7

Olympia Theatre
See p. 99.

Vicar St (4, K1)
There's a varied program
of acts, with a strong emphasis on folk and jazz, at
this purpose-built, seated
music venue. Though the
sound system is good, the
auditorium itself is a little
lacking in atmosphere.
✉ 58-59 Thomas St
☎ 454 5533
e www.vicarstreet
.com 🚌 51b, 78a, 123,
206 ⌚ Mon-Sat 11am-
11pm ⑤ varies

Whelan's (4, N5)
A good gig here can be
quite magical. The crowd
gathers round the elevated
central stage and more
peer down from the circular
balcony – everyone
mouthing the words to
their favourite songs and
ballads. Whelan's has an
interesting parade of
Dublin's finest singer-
songwriters – well worth
a look.
✉ 26 Wexford St
(enter venue via
Camden Row)
☎ 478 0766 **e** www
.whelanslive.com
🚌 14, 15, 65, 83
⌚ doors open 8pm
⑤ most shows €6-12

The Big Gigs

Big international acts increasingly include Dublin on
their tour circuits. Here's where they usually play:

Point Depot (East Link Bridge, North Wall Quay;
3, E14; ☎ 836 3633) – originally a rail terminus and
quite soulless, but with a capacity of 6000

Lansdowne Rd Stadium (Ballsbridge, Dublin 4;
3, G14; ☎ 668 9300) – normally a rugby and football ground, it's also used for the occasional rock
concert

Croke Park (Clonliffe Rd; 3, B11; ☎ 855 8176) –
65,000-capacity GAA stadium that hosts the odd
concert

RDS Showgrounds (Ballsbridge, Dublin 4; 3, J14;
☎ 668 0866) – open-air show-jumping arena that
holds 40,000

Slane Castle (Slane, County Meath; ☎ 041-982
4207) – 46km north-west of Dublin, home to the
annual Slane Festival and the odd special gig, like a
U2 concert

CLASSICAL MUSIC & OPERA

Classical music in Dublin has had a hard time of it, plagued by inadequate funding and questionable repertoires. Things are improving though, and the scene is regularly enhanced by visiting performers and orchestras.

Bank of Ireland Arts Centre (5, C6)
Apart from art exhibitions and the banking museum, the arts centre hosts free lunchtime recitals every two weeks or so, as well as an evening program of concerts. Call for details.
✉ Foster Pl
☎ 671 1488 e www .bankofireland.ie
🚌 all cross-city
🕐 box office: Tues-Fri 11am-4pm ⑤ evening concerts €8.90 ♿

Hugh Lane Gallery
See p. 20.

National Concert Hall (4, O7) Ireland's premier classical concert venue, the National Concert Hall is host to weekly performances by the National Symphony Orchestra and a varied program of visiting international artists. There's also jazz, traditional Irish and other contemporary concerts. From June to September it puts on inexpensive lunchtime concerts on Tuesdays from 1.05-2pm.
✉ Earlsfort Tce
☎ booking 417 0000; info 417 0077
e www.nch.ie
🚌 10, 11, 13, 14, 15, 44, 86 🕐 booking office: Mon-Sat 10am-7pm ⑤ varies
♿ special summer concerts & programs

National Gallery of Ireland
See p. 25.

RDS Concert Hall (3, J14) The huge concert hall at the Royal Dublin Society Showgrounds hosts a rich program of classical

St Pat's hosts angelic voices

music and opera throughout the year.
✉ Ballsbridge
☎ 668 0866
🚌 5, 7, 7a, 8, 45
🚉 Sandymount
🕐 varies ⑤ varies ♿

Music of the Gods

Many of Dublin's churches have accomplished choirs which make full use of the heavenly acoustics, including:

Christ Church Cathedral
(p. 15) – come to hear choral evensong four times a week (call for more information)

St Stephen's Church
(p. 43) – the acoustics in the 'Peppercanister Church' are superb and it hosts concerts on an ad hoc basis

St Ann's Church (Dawson St; 6, D8; ☎ 676 7727; e www.connect.ie/ccp; 🚌 10, 11, 13b, 14, 14a, 20b) – free lunchtime organ recitals in July and August on Thursdays at 1.15pm (call for details)

St Patrick's Cathedral
(p. 29; see picture, left) – hear the choir sing evensong at 5.35pm Monday to Friday, and try to book tickets for the carols performed around Christmas

THEATRE & COMEDY

Theatre bookings can usually be made by quoting a credit-card number over the phone; you can collect your tickets just before the performance. Most plays begin between 8 and 8.30pm.

Abbey Theatre (4, G7)

Together with the more experimental Peacock Theatre on the same premises, The Abbey is Ireland's national theatre. The Abbey shows work by established contemporary Irish writers as well as classics by WB Yeats, JM Synge, Sean O'Casey and Samuel Beckett. At the Peacock works tend to be by young writers and performed by less established actors.
✉ Abbey St Lwr
☎ 878 7222
e www.abbeytheatre
.ie 🚌 all cross-city
🕐 box office: Mon-Sat 10.30am-7pm
💲 Peacock: €10-15; Abbey: €12-25 ♿ yes

Andrew's Lane Theatre (6, A5)

This is a well-established, commercial fringe theatre that shows work by touring local companies and overseas productions, often comedy or light drama.
✉ 9-17 St Andrews La
☎ 679 5720 e www
.andrewslane.com
🚌 all cross-city
🕐 box office: Mon-Sat 10.30am-7pm
💲 free-€17 ♿ yes

Crypt Arts Centre

(6, B2) An atmospheric and intimate space housed in the crypt of the Chapel Royal, this venue serves many of Dublin's young, up-and-coming companies, as well as the odd live music performance. Tragedies and philosophical

Behan there, done that

Novelist, playwright and journalist Brendan Behan was a legendary Dublin hell raiser and drinker whose antics regularly landed him in prison and hospital, and had him barred from dozens of pubs. In his short but eventful life he did time for IRA activities and the attempted murder of a policeman, was a columnist for *The Irish Press*, and then turned to literature. His books include *Borstal Boy* and *The Scarperer* and a celebrated play *The Hostage*. Sadly, his lifestyle got the better of him and he died of cirrhosis of the liver in 1964, aged 40.

works are often attempted.
✉ Dublin Castle, Dame St ☎ 671 3387
🚌 all cross-city
🕐 box office: Mon-Fri 10am-6pm, Sat 1-5pm
💲 €10-12/7.50

All smiles at the Gaiety Theatre

Emma Miller

Gaiety Theatre (6, E6)

Opened in 1871, this Victorian theatre was recently restored to its former glory. Its repertoire is diverse, from modern plays, musicals, comedies and revues to Shakespeare. Opera Ireland have a season here and on Friday and Saturday nights the venue is taken over by salsa and soul clubs until 4am.
✉ King St S
☎ 677 1717 e www
.gaietytheatre.com
🚌 all cross-city 🕐 box office: Mon-Sat 10am-7pm 💲 €12-25 ♿

The Gate (4, E6)

International classics from the likes of Harold Pinter and Noel Coward, and older Irish works by playwrights such as Oscar Wilde, George Bernard Shaw and Oliver Goldsmith are performed here, although newer plays are staged too.
✉ Parnell Sq ☎ 874 4045 🚌 all cross-city
🕐 box office: Mon-Sat 10am-7pm 💲 €15-20

Ha'penny Bridge Inn
(5, B5) From Tuesday to Thursday you can hear some pretty funny comedians (as well as some truly awful ones) do their schtick in the upstairs room of this Temple Bar pub. Tuesday night's Battle of the Axe, an improv night that features a lot of crowd participation is the best of them.
- ✉ **42 Wellington Quay, Temple Bar**
- ☎ **677 0616**
- 🚌 **all cross-city**
- ⏰ Tues-Thurs 9pm
- ⑤ €6.40/5.10

Lambert Puppet Theatre
See p. 49.

Laughter Lounge
(4, G7) Dublin's only purpose-built comedy venue can squeeze in 400 punters for live shows which feature four high-quality Irish and international acts each night.
- ✉ **Eden Quay**
- ☎ **1800 266 339**
- 🚌 **all cross-city**
- ⏰ show starts 9pm most nights ⑤ €15

Olympia Theatre
(5, E2) Ornate, old, Victorian music hall that specialises in light plays, comedy and, at Christmas time, panto. In recent years though, this pleasantly tatty place has gained more of a reputation for its live gigs, including performances by some ɪ international acts.
- ✉ **72 Dame St**
- ☎ **677 7744**
- 🚌 **all cross-city** ⏰ box office: Mon-Sat 10am-6.30pm ⑤ €15-20
- ♿ yes

Project Arts Centre
(5, E3) Experimental plays from up-and-coming Irish and foreign writers, some brilliant, others execrable.
- ✉ **39 Essex St E**
- ☎ **1850 260027**
- 🅴 **www.project.ie**
- 🚌 **all cross-city**
- ⏰ box office: Mon-Sat 11am-7pm
- ⑤ €12-15/10

DANCE CLUBS

Most clubs open just before the pubs close – between 11pm and midnight – and close at 2.30 or 3am. Entry to most is between €5 and €8 on weekdays, and up to €13 at weekends. Clubs transform themselves every night of the week, catering to diverse musical (and sexual) orientations. To find what suits you pick up a listings guide (p. 87).

Gaiety Theatre
See p. 98.

The Kitchen (5, C2)
Considering its widespread fame, U2's Kitchen nightclub is surprisingly laid back. The music is hard and fast on a fairly small dance floor, while the back bar is usually patronised by celebrities and wannabes.
- ✉ **The Clarence Hotel, 6-8 Wellington Quay**
- ☎ **677 6635** 🅴 **www .theclarence.ie** 🚌 **all cross-city** ⏰ 11pm-2.30am ⑤ €6-13

Lillie's Bordello (6, B7)
Lillie's is strictly for the well-heeled – the favourite nightclub of local and visiting celebrities. As you might expect, the music is mostly safe and commercial.
- ✉ **Adam Court, off Grafton St** ☎ **679 9204** 🚌 **all cross-city** ⏰ 11pm-3am ⑤ €5-13

PoD (4, P6)
The PoD, 'Place of Dance', is Dublin's most renowned nightclub. A futuristic, metal-gothic cathedral of dance, it attracts a large weekend crowd of twenty-somethings. To get past the notoriously difficult bouncers you'll need to look the part.
- ✉ **35 Harcourt St**
- ☎ **478 0166**
- 🅴 **www.pod.ie**
- 🚌 **14, 15, 65, 83**
- ⏰ Tues-Sun 11pm-3am
- ⑤ €5-10

Red Box (4, P6)
Upstairs from PoD and owned by the same entrepreneur, Red Box is the best venue for dance gigs, with top European dance bands and DJs strutting their stuff to crowds of groovy movers. The dance floor is enormous and the willing crowds really fill it up.
- ✉ **35 Harcourt St**
- ☎ **478 0225**
- 🅴 **www.pod.ie**
- 🚌 **14, 15, 65, 83**
- ⏰ Tues-Sun 11pm-3am
- ⑤ €6-13

...ard's (6, C9)

...ard's is not quite as ...oty as Lillie's but it tries be. An intimate club, it ...kes its patrons to dress up and has a strict door policy when busy. Music is mainly house, with soul, funk and jazz making the odd appearance.
✉ Frederick St S
☎ 677 5876 🚊 all cross-city ⏰ Mon-Fri 10.30pm-2.30am, Sat 2pm-2.30am, Sun 6pm-2.30am ⑤ free

RíRá (6, B4)

One of the friendlier clubs in the city centre, this place is full nearly seven nights a week. Refreshingly, the bouncers here are friendly, funny and very fair. The emphasis is on funk, both old and new, with ne'er a house beat to be heard.
✉ Dame Court ☎ 677 4835 🚊 all cross-city ⏰ 11.30pm-3am ⑤ €6-10

The Shelter (4, K1)

A 300-capacity theatre attached to the Vicar St venue (p. 96), Shelter hosts a variety of gigs and club nights. The best is 'Velure' on Saturdays, with its mix of funky soul, latin and percussive house that has a die-hard following.
✉ Vicar St, 58-59 Thomas St ☎ 454 5533 e www.vicarstreet .com 🚊 51b, 78a, 123, 206 ⏰ 10.30pm-3am ⑤ €5-15

Switch (5, D3)

Small, sweaty and seriously hip, Switch has a terrific selection of different dance beats mixed by excellent local DJs, helped along by international guests. Regular nights include drum and bass on Friday, techno on Saturday and deep and funky house on Sunday.
✉ 11 Eustace St ☎ 670 7655 🚊 all cross-city ⏰ 11pm-2.30am ⑤ €6-10

Temple Bar Music Centre (5, D4)

TBMC combines a live venue, club, bar and cafe with rehearsal rooms, music classes and recording studios. Music-wise, there's something on every night to suit every taste, from funk and disco to guitar-driven indie rock. A popular salsa class is held on Tuesday at 7.30pm, with a salsa club following at 10.30pm.
✉ Curved St ☎ 670 9202 e www.tbmc.ie 🚊 all cross-city ⏰ 9.30am-2am ⑤ club: €6-8; gigs: €6-18 ♿ 'Blast' all-ages gig Sat noon: €7.50/6.50/5

Bright lights at TBMC

GAY & LESBIAN DUBLIN

The fabulous Mardi Gras takes place over the last weekend in May, while the annual Alternative Miss Ireland pageant usually runs during the third weekend in March. For details of both festivals call ☎ 873 4932.

The Boilerhouse Sauna (5, D2)

This is a popular late-night destination for people looking to sweat it out after partying at the George, just around the corner. It's big and very clean, and is reputed to be the best-run of Dublin's saunas.
✉ 12 Crane La ☎ 677 3130 🚊 all cross-city ⏰ Sun-Thurs 1pm-5am, Fri-Sat 24hrs ⑤ €13

The Front Lounge

see p. 92.

The George (6, A4)

You can't miss the bright purple George, Temple Bar's only overtly gay bar, which has a reputation for becoming ever more wild and wacky as the night progresses. At 6.30pm on Sunday it is packed for an enormously popular Bingo night, while Thursday night is the Missing Link game-show hosted by Annie Balls.
✉ 89 Great George's St S ☎ 478 2983 🚊 all cross-city ⏰ Mon-Tue 12.30-11pm, Wed-Sun 12.30pm-2.30am ⑤ most nights €4-8 after 10pm

Gubu (5, B1)
Run by the owners of the Globe and the Front Lounge, 'Gaybu', as it has been dubbed, is a stylish bar on up-and-coming Capel St. Saturday's 'Groove On', with DJ Dandelion of 'Strictly Handbag' fame, is popular.
✉ Capel St ☎ 874 0710 🚌 37, 70, 134, 172 🕐 Sun-Wed 4-11.30pm, Thurs-Sat 4pm-12.30am 💲 free

Stonewallz (4, K2)
Molloy's Bar hosts Dublin's only women-only night, with DJs playing to three floors and a chill-out zone.
✉ Molloy's Bar, 13 High St Christchurch ☎ 677 3207 🚌 all cross-city 🕐 Sat 8.30pm -12.30am 💲 €5.10, €7.60 after 10pm

Out on the Liffey
(4, J3) The northside's gay and lesbian stronghold for many years, this pub has developed a bit of a rough reputation, mostly due to party drugs. Even so, it's still a great bar, despite the

Gay Club Nights

Plenty of clubs in Dublin run gay and lesbian nig. Though the scene is constantly changing, the follow. nights have built up a steady following in recent time.

HAM – Friday night at PoD (p. 99) is 'Homo Action Movies', one of Dublin's most enduring gay nights, with uplifting and progressive House. Every second week the 'Gristle Cabaret' precedes 'HAM'.

Strictly Handbag – Monday night club at RíRá (p. 100) attracts a mixed, but heavily gay, crowd for cheesy and sleazy '80s hits downstairs and '60s and '70s pop upstairs. Pre-club knees-up at the Front Lounge (p. 92) from 9pm.

Hilton Edwards – one of the hardest places to get into unless you're dripping with glamour, this Sunday night club at Spy (Powerscourt Townhouse, William St S; 6, C6; ☎ 677 0014; 9pm-3am) is run by the folks from 'HAM'.

presence of ever-watchful bouncers. Wednesday is the popular karaoke night, open to both men and women.
✉ 27 Ormond Quay Upper ☎ 872 2480 🚌 all cross-city 🕐 Mon-Sat 11am-11.30pm, Sun 11am-11pm 💲 free

Vortex Spa (5, B2)
The most luxurious of

Dublin's saunas, with excellent facilities; large steam rooms, comfortable saunas, plus plenty of other nooks, crannies and cubicles.
✉ 1 Great Strand St, Dublin 1 ☎ 878 0898 🚌 all cross-city 🕐 Sun-Thurs 1pm-5am, non-stop Fri 1pm-Mon 5am 💲 €11.50 before 6pm, €13 after 6pm

SPECTATOR SPORT

Hurling

For the uninitiated, hurling is a fascinating game to watch. It has elements of hockey and lacrosse – players hit the ball along the ground or through the air or even carry it on the end of their hurley or *camán*. Fast-paced and furious, the skills displayed are astounding. Dublin isn't a great hurling power – the best teams come from Kilkenny and Cork. The All Ireland Hurling Final at Croke Park takes place in September attracting crowds of more than 80,000.

Football

Along with hurling, **Gaelic football** is Ireland's major Gaelic Athletics Association sport. Like hurling, it's a high-speed, aggressive game. Ireland's most popular sport, Gaelic football uses a round ball that is kicked along the ground soccer-style, or passed between players as in rugby. It's not dissimilar to Australian Rules football and some Gaelic stars have gone on to make it big in Oz. The All Ireland final takes place in September, at Croke Park.

hile hurling and Gaelic football have their greatest following in rural
....nd, **football (soccer)** and **rugby** are probably more popular in
....blin. Support for British soccer teams, especially Manchester United,
....verpool and Glasgow Celtic, is high, though the Irish national team also
attracts a full house when it plays. For details of international matches contact the Football Association of Ireland (☎ 676 6864).

Ireland is also a power in world rugby and great attention is paid to the annual Six Nations Championship, which pits Ireland against England, Wales, Scotland, France and Italy. Even more passion is likely to be roused when the national team plays Australia. International soccer and rugby matches take place at Lansdowne Rd Stadium (3, G14) in Ballsbridge.

Racing

The Irish love horse racing, a fact that can be easily witnessed at racetracks on the outskirts of Dublin. Leopardstown in south Dublin is the home of the prestigious Hennessey Gold Cup, which runs in February. The Irish Grand National is held on Easter Monday at Fairyhouse (1, A3), 19km north-west of Dublin in County Meath.

Greyhound racing takes place at Harold's Cross Park (3, K8), a short hop from the city centre, and the more comfortable Shelbourne Greyhound Stadium (3, F14) in Ringsend, only 10 minutes from the centre. Races are held two or three times a week from February to early December; call to check days and starting times (they usually begin around 7.30pm).

Golf

The popularity of Ireland's fastest-growing sport is due in part to the success of Irish golfers such as Darren Clarke, Padraig Harrington and Paul McGinley. The Smurfit European Open takes place in late July/early August at the K Club (1, B3) in County Kildare, which was designed by Arnold Palmer.

Major Sporting Venues
Croke Park (Dublin 3; 3, B11; ☎ 836 3222; 🚌 3, 11, 11a, 16, 16a, 51a from O'Connell St; 🚊 Connolly)
Lansdowne Rd Stadium (Ballsbridge; 3, G14; ☎ 668 4601; 🚊 Lansdowne Rd)
RDS Showgrounds (Ballsbridge; 3, J14; ☎ 668 0866; 🚌 5, 7, 7a, 8, 45; 🚊 Sandymount)
Leopardstown (Foxrock, Dublin 18; 1, B5; ☎ 289 3607; e www.leopardstown.com; 🚌 special services run from Eden Quay on race days)
Fairyhouse Racecourse (1, A3; ☎ 825 6167)
Harold's Cross Park (151 Harold's Cross Rd; 3, K8; ☎ 497 1081; 🚌 16, 16a, 19a, 49)
Shelbourne Greyhound Stadium (Ringsend; 3, F14; ☎ 668 3502; 🚌 3 from O'Connell St)
K Club (Straffan, Co. Kildare; 1, B3; ☎ 676 6650)

Hannah Levy

places to stay

Dublin is one of Europe's more expensive cities to sleep in, and u...
reach the upper price brackets, you're not always getting great...
for money. Dublin's tourism boom also means that in high season – ...
around May to September – getting the room you want, at a reasona...
price, can be a challenge. New
hotels are opening all the time but
it's still wise to book well ahead.

If you're only in Dublin for the
weekend, it's unwise to stay anywhere but the city centre or a short
stroll away, as you can waste precious
time getting around by bus, train or
taxi. Not surprisingly, accommodation south of the Liffey is pricier than
that on the northside. While some
good deals can be found in the
north, most bargains are in less than

Room Rates

The categories used in this chapter indicate the cost per night of a stan-dard double room in high season.

Deluxe	€250-350
Top End	€150-249
Mid-Range	€80-149
Budget	under €79

Richard Cummins

salubrious areas, where drugs and crime are a problem. If you stay there, keep a close watch on your bags and wallets and take care when walking at night.

Most budget to mid-range places charge low and high season rates, and priced are bumped up during holidays, festivals or sporting events. At top-end hotels, always check what discounts are available on the published rack rates. Top-end and deluxe hotels fall into two categories – period Georgian ele-gance and cool, minimalist chic. No matter what the decor, you can expect luxurious surrounds, king-size beds, satellite TV, in-room videos, full room service, PC/fax connections and discreet, professional pampering. Most also have gyms and business centres.

Dublin's mid-range accommodation is more of a mixed bag, ranging from no-nonsense but soulless chains to small B&Bs in old Georgian town houses. The pricier B&Bs in this category are beautifully decked out and extremely comfortable, while at the lower end rooms are simple, a little worn and often rather overbearingly decorated. Here you can look forward to kitsch knick-knacks, chintzy curtains, lace doilies and clashing floral

fabrics so loud they'll burn your
retinas. Your B&B hosts could be
gracious and discreet, indifferent,
rude or just plain mad. As for
breakfast, it can range from home-
baked breads, fruit and farmhouse
cheeses to a traditional, fat-laden
fry-up.

Cheaper B&Bs and hostels
make up the budget end, and while
they can sometimes be grim, the
ones listed here are clean, bright
and good value.

Bookings

If you arrive without accommodation, staff at Dublin Tourism's walk-in book-ing offices will find you a room for €2.50 plus a 10% deposit.

If you want to book a hotel over the phone, either from elsewhere in Ireland or abroad, you'll need to con-tact Gulliver Info Res, Dublin Tourism's computerised reservations service. See p. 114 for a list of Dublin Tourism offices and Gulliver contact numbers.

XE

...ey Court

...3) In the quiet, leafy ...s of upmarket ...sbridge, this spacious, ...mptuous hotel is favoured ...y visiting dignitaries and rock stars playing at the nearby RDS Showgrounds. Though situated south-east of the centre, it is one minute from the DART and a short stroll from the restaurants of Pembroke Rd or Ballsbridge Terrace.

✉ Lansdowne Rd, Ballsbridge, Dublin 4 ☎ 660 1711; fax 661 7238 e berkeley_court@jurysdoyle.com 🚌 7, 8, 45 🚉 Lansdowne Rd ✕ Palm Court Cafe; Berkeley Room

The Clarence (5, C2)

Owned by Bono and The Edge of U2, the Clarence is so hyped it disappoints some visitors. To set the record straight – the hotel is down-to-earth, elegant and understated. There's plenty of oak panelling, leather, stonework and plush carpets. The service is excellent, the Octagon Bar is convivial and in the basement is the hip Kitchen nightclub.

✉ 6-8 Wellington Quay, Dublin 2 ☎ 670 9000; fax 670 7800 e reservations@theclarence.ie; www.theclarence.ie 🚌 all cross-city ✕ The Tea Rooms (p. 79)

Fitzwilliam (6, E5)

Modernist but luxurious, with wood, marble and leather throughout, this Terence Conran Group designed hotel is one for the style buffs. The design harks back to the 1920s and '30s,

but with sharper edges. The rooms are elegant if a little small. A Michelin-starred restaurant, bar and roof garden add to the appeal.

✉ St Stephen's Green, Dublin 2 ☎ 478 7000; fax 478 7878 e enq@fitzwilliam-hotel.com; www.fitzwilliam-hotel.com 🚌 all cross-city ✕ Peacock Alley (p. 81)

The Gresham (4, E6)

Old-world ambience in an 1817 landmark building overlooking O'Connell St: Waterford chandeliers, a sweeping staircase and an elegant bar set the scene for discreet, formal service and an upmarket clientele. Rooms are large, comfortable and traditional.

✉ 20-22 O'Connell St Upper, Dublin 1 ☎ 874 6881; fax 878 7175 e gresham@indigo.ie; www.gresham-hotels.com 🚌 all cross-city ✕ Aberdeen Restaurant; Toddy's Bar

The Merrion (4, M9)

Quite possibly the city's best hotel, the Merrion combines exquisite period detailing, a spectacular garden and the largest private art collection in the city. Afternoon tea can be taken in the expansive drawing rooms, the pool is modelled on Roman baths and there's an atmospheric bar in the old wine cellars. Oh, and a Michelin-starred restaurant.

✉ Merrion St Upper, Dublin 2 ☎ 603 0600; fax 603 0700 e info@merrionhotel.ie; www.merrionhotel.com 🚌 5, 7, 8, 10, 11, 45 🚉 Pearse ✕ Restaurant Patrick Guilbaud (p. 84); Mornington Brasserie ⚕

The Morrison (4, H4)

Set on the northern quays, this cutting-edge hotel was partly styled by fashion designer John Rocha. With a stark, vaguely Oriental tone, it's all sleek black wood, white leather couches and splashes of red and gold. The downstairs Lobo bar is one of the hippest spots in town for Dublin's new rich.

✉ Ormond Quay, Dublin 1 ☎ 887 2400; fax 878 3185 e info@morrisonhotel.ie; www.morrisonhotel.ie 🚌 all cross-city ✕ Halo (p. 77), Cafe Bar

The Shelbourne
(4, M8) The grand dame of Dublin hotels, this place has been the hub of high society for more than 170 years. From a drink in the Horseshoe Bar, favoured by

The elegant Shelbourne Hotel

politicians, to afternoon tea in the Lord Mayor's Lounge, it's old-fashioned style and service at its best. Now owned by Le Meridien, the rooms don't quite match the elegance of the foyer, but that's not really what you're here for. Dog owners can bring their pooches.
✉ **27 St Stephen's Green, Dublin 2** ☎ **676 6471; fax 661 6006** ⓔ **shelbournein fo@forte-hotels.com; www.shelbourne.ie** 🚌 all cross-city ✕ The Side Door; No. 27

Stephen's Green Hotel (4, N5)

A sleek, modern place fronted by an arched glass atrium, the hotel occupies a prime position on the south-western corner of St Stephen's Green. Rich fabrics in red, black and neutrals adorn the comfy rooms.
✉ **St Stephen's Green, Dublin 2** ☎ **607 3600; fax 661 5663** ⓔ **stephensgreenres @ocallaghanhotels.ie; www.ocallaghanhotels.ie** 🚌 all cross-city ✕ The Pie Dish ♿

Westbury (6, C6)

Along with the Clarence, this is *the* celebrity hotel; a grand, classic but modern place just off Grafton St in the heart of the main shopping district. Rooms on the upper floors offer views of the Dublin Hills and the large lounge areas are popular for afternoon teas.
✉ **Grafton St, Dublin 2** ☎ **679 1122; fax 679 7078** ⓔ **westbury_ hotel @jurysdoyle.com** ✕ The Russell Room; Sandbank Bistro ♿

TOP END

Brooks Hotel (6, C4)

Tucked away on a quiet lane just east of Grafton St, the Brooks has a 19th-century club atmosphere, with dark wood repro-Georgian furnishings, shelves lined with old books and plump, patterned sofas. It's a little contrived, but sumptuous nonetheless and the service is extremely professional.
✉ **59-62 Drury St, Dublin 2** ☎ **670 4000; fax 670 4455** ⓔ **reservations @brookshotel.ie; www.sinnotthotels.com** 🚌 all cross-city ✕ Francesca's Restaurant

Longfield's (4, N10)

This 26-room hotel between Merrion and Fitzwilliam Squares is in two Georgian terraces. The period decor shows attention to detail – from reproduction patterned wallpaper to fringed lamps. Some rooms are a little small, but plush.
✉ **Fitzwilliam St Lwr, Dublin 2** ☎ **676 1367; fax 676 1542**

ⓔ **info@longfields.ie; www.longfields.ie** 🚌 **10, 11, 13b, 51x** 🚆 Pearse ✕ Number 10

Mercer Hotel (6, E4)

The bland exterior doesn't do justice to the hotel's large, pleasantly decorated rooms, with their sizeable modern bathrooms. Not heavily traditional, nor cutting edge, it's comfortably in-between. Its position near St Stephen's Green and Grafton St is a bonus.
✉ **Mercer St Lwr, Dublin 2** ☎ **478 2179; fax 478 0328** ⓔ **stay@mercerhotel .ie; www.mercerhotel .ie** 🚌 all cross-city ✕ Cusak's ♿

Morgan (5, B6)

At the Morgan you get crisp, white, minimalist style in a boutique atmosphere, but few hotel facilities. There's no restaurant or gym, but its Temple Bar location means that everything is on your doorstep. Front rooms can get noisy, so light sleepers should

request one at the back.
✉ **10 Fleet St, Temple Bar, Dublin 2** ☎ **679 3939; fax 679 3946** ⓔ **sales@themorgan .com; www.themorgan .com** 🚌 all cross-city

Number 31 (4, P8)

Architect Sam Stephenson designed and lived in this mews house near the Grand Canal. Now his groovy sunken lounge and mirrored bar are the public areas of a lovely guesthouse with individually furnished rooms. Note that only six rooms are in the original house; another 15 are across the garden in a restored town house.
✉ **31 Leeson Close, Dublin 2** ☎ **676 5011; fax 676 2929** ⓔ **number31@iol.ie; www.number31.ie** 🚌 **11, 11a, 13b, 46, 58, 58c**

The Schoolhouse (3, G13)

Housed in a listed 1916 former school on a pretty stretch of the Grand Canal, this small four-star hotel has 31 plushly furnished traditional-style

rooms that are labelled as if they were classrooms. A little twee, but all is forgiven when you see the restaurant and bar with their soaring roofs.
✉ 2-8 Northumberland Rd, Ballsbridge, Dublin 4
☎ 667 5014; fax 667 5015 e school@school househotel.iol.ie; www .schoolhousehotel.com

🚌 5, 7, 7a, 8, 45, 46
🚉 Grand Canal Dock
🍴 Satchels Restaurant; Inkwell Bar ♿

Trinity Capital Hotel (2, A4) Part of the local Capital chain, this contemporary hotel on the north side of Trinity College has large, well-designed rooms with natural wood and Art

Deco–style furnishings. There are triples and, for true indulgence, oval-shaped minisuites with spas.
✉ Pearse St, Dublin 2
☎ 648 1000; fax 648 1010 e info@trinity capital-hotel.com; www.capital-hotels.com
🚌 1, 2, 3
🚉 Pearse
🍴 restaurant ♿

MID-RANGE

Albany House (4, N6) Stained glass, elegant furnishings and original plasterwork make Albany House a little Georgian gem. If you can snare one of the bigger rooms, with their lofty ceilings, you'll be doing better than at some of the top-end hotels. An abundant spread greets you at breakfast.
✉ 84 Harcourt St, Dublin 2 ☎ 475 1092; fax 475 1093
e albany@indigo.ie; www.byrne-hotels-ireland .com 🚌 15, 16, 19, 122

Earl of Kildare Hotel (6, C10) Above a large, sprawling bar and nightclub, the hotel's 33 good-sized rooms have recently been revamped in bright furnishings. Most rooms are en suite, and there are a number of triples.
✉ Kildare St, Dublin 2
☎ 679 4388; fax 679 4914 e eok@iol.ie
🚌 all cross-city
🍴 restaurant

Fitzwilliam Guesthouse (4, N10) Just south of Merrion Square, this pleasant B&B in a Georgian town house offers old-fashioned homey comforts. Rooms are quite sizeable and en suite, with

high ceilings and obligatory floral furnishings.
✉ 41 Fitzwilliam St Upper, Dublin 2 ☎ 660 5155; fax 676 7488
🚌 10, 11, 13b, 51x
🍴 Moe's Restaurant

Harvey's Guesthouse (4, B6) Run by mother and son team Eilish and Robert Flood, this exceptionally friendly B&B, in two adjoining 250-year-old Georgian buildings, has been lovingly restored with

period furniture and features. All rooms are en suite and non-smoking.
✉ 11 Gardiner St Upper, Dublin 1 ☎ 874 8384; fax 874 5510
e harveysguesthse@ iol.ie; www.harveys guesthouse.com
🚌 11, 16, 41

Hotel Saint George (4, D6) Located at the top of O'Connell St, this B&B is friendly and comfortable. Though the front lounge has

Home Away From Home
Self-catering apartments are a good option for visitors staying a few days, for groups of friends, or families with kids. Apartments range from one-room studios to two-bed flats with lounge areas, and include bathrooms and kitchenettes. Good, central places include:

Oliver St John Gogarty's Penthouse Apartments (5, C6; p. 108) – perched high atop the pub, these one to three bedroom places have views of Temple Bar
Litton Lane Apartments (4, H6) – basic and modern two-bedroom flats in a secure riverside complex
Clarion Stephen's Hall (14-17 Leeson St Lwr; 4, O8; ☎ 638 1111; e stephens@premgroup.ie, www .premgroup.ie) – deluxe studios and suites, with in-room safe, fax and modem facilities and CD players
Latchfords (99-100 Baggot St Lwr; 4, O10; ☎ 676 0784; e latchfords@eircom.net, www.latchfords -accomm.com) – studios and two-bedroom flats in a Georgian town house

some stylish Georgian features and antiques, the fresh, bright rooms are done up in simple new furnishings of the loud floral variety. All rooms are en suite.

✉ 7 Parnell Sq E, Dublin 1 ☎ 874 5611; fax 874 5582
📧 hotels@indigo.ie
🚌 all cross-city
🍴 Georgian Brasserie

Jurys Inn Christchurch (4, K3)
This big chain hotel directly opposite Christ Church Cathedral is big (182 rooms), basic and bland, but it's clean, safe and an absolute bargain for the location. Rooms are charged at a flat rate.

✉ Christchurch Pl, Dublin 8 ☎ 454 0000; fax 454 0012 📧 christchurch_inn @jurysdoyle .com; www.jurys.com
🚌 50, 54a, 56a, 150
🍴 Arches Restaurant; The Inn Pub 🚼

Leeson Inn (4, P8)
Moving from the glitzy foyer to the small, simple rooms is a bit jarring, but the rooms are clean, modern, have modem points and are refreshingly free of the granny-like furnishings which blight many places.

✉ 24 Leeson St Lwr, Dublin 2 ☎ 662 2002; fax 662 1567 📧 leesonin@iol.ie /leesoninn 🚌 11, 11a, 13b, 46, 58, 58c

Merrion Square Manor (4, L10)
One of the nicest central B&Bs, with period antiques and chandeliers in a Georgian town house. The 18 bedrooms are decorated with stylish furniture, including padded armchairs and

Travelling with Children
Finding accommodation for a young family can be difficult in Dublin. While almost all deluxe and top-end hotels offer 24-hour babysitting services and extra beds or cots if pressed, generally they are not keen to encourage or promote child visitors. Boutique-style hotels or B&Bs will not usually accept children, and mid-range and even cheap B&Bs also tend to discourage young guests. Your best bet is a larger chain hotel, a friendly, relaxed B&B, a serviced apartment, or a hostel where you can house the whole family in one room, usually with en suite. In this guide, we have denoted places that are particularly child-friendly with a 🚼.

Finding a nesting place for the little duckies isn't easy.

wooden beds with crisp white linen.

✉ 31 Merrion Sq N, Dublin 2 ☎ 662 8551; fax 662 8556 📧 merrionmanor@eircom.net; www.merrionsquare manor.com 🚌 5, 7, 7a, 8, 45, 46 🚉 Pearse

Othello (4, F8)
One of several B&Bs along Gardiner St, Othello is a family-run venture that's friendlier than some of the others. The rooms out back have small bathrooms, but get a room in the old section and you'll have high ceilings, period touches and sizeable wash facilities.

✉ 74 Gardiner St Lwr, Dublin 1 ☎ 855 4271; fax 855 7460
🚌 11, 16, 41

The Townhouse
(4, F8) Get a room here and you'll be staying in one of the city's most interesting and good-value hotels. Each of the rooms is

decorated differently – contemporary and minimalist in the new wing, velvety and whimsical in the Georgian part. The colourful dining room leads out to a Japanese garden.

✉ 47-48 Gardiner St Lwr, Dublin 1 ☎ 878 8808; fax 878 8787
📧 gtrotter@indigo.ie; www.townhouseof dublin.com 🚉 Connolly

Wynn's Hotel (4, G7)
Just off O'Connell St and steps away from the Abbey Theatre, this refurbished 19th-century hotel is excellent value. Its 70 en suite rooms are large and comfortable, with simple, neutral decor.

✉ 35-36 Abbey St Lwr, Dublin 1 ☎ 874 5131; fax 874 1556
📧 info@wynnshotel.ie; www.wynnshotel.ie
🚌 all cross-city
🍴 Peacock Restaurant; Saints & Scholars Bar

BUDGET

Abbey Court Hostel
(4, G6) In a great location on the Liffey, just west of O'Connell Bridge, this hostel is clean, well secured and friendly. Facilities include a dining hall, conservatory and barbecue area, and many of the pleasantly decorated rooms and dorms are en suite with hot power showers.
✉ 29 Bachelor's Walk, Dublin 1 ☎ 878 0700; fax 878 0719 e info@abbey-court .com; www.abbey-court .com 🚌 all cross-city

Barnacles Temple Bar House (5, C4)
A good choice if you don't mind being in the thick of it, this hostel has bright, clean dorms and rooms – all en suite. There's a TV room with an open fireplace.
✉ 1 Cecilia St, Temple Bar, Dublin 2 ☎ 671 6277; fax 671 6591 e tbh@barnacles.ie 🚌 all cross-city ♿

Carmel House (4, B6)
This family-run B&B has a period lounge and nine comfortable and clean rooms with bathroom, TV, central heating and car parking.
✉ 16 Gardiner St Upper, Dublin 1 ☎ 874 1639; fax 878 6903 🚌 11, 16, 41

Clifden Guesthouse
(4, C6) Between Mountjoy and Parnell Squares in north Dublin, this B&B is in a beautifully refurbished Georgian house with fine old rooms and plenty of amenities, including free car parking. Good value.
✉ 32 Gardiner Pl, Dublin 1 ☎ 874 6364 fax 874 6122 e bnb@ indigo.ie; www.clifden house.com 🚌 11, 16, 41

Globetrotters Hostel
(4, F8) Sharing a breakfast room and Japanese-style garden with the Townhouse Hotel (p. 107), this well-kept hostel has 6-bed and 12-bed dorms, all en suite. Brightly painted and with full Irish breakfast included, it's better than your average backpackers.
✉ 46-48 Gardiner St Lwr, Dublin 1 ☎ 873 5893; fax 878 8787 e gtrotter@indigo.ie; www.iol.ie/globetrotters 🚉 Connolly

Litton Lane Hostel
(4, H6) In a converted recording studio once used by Van Morrison and Sinead O'Connor, this hostel is central, convenient and extremely comfortable. The public spaces are brightly decorated and all of the rooms have been painted with music-related murals. The rate includes breakfast.
✉ 2-4 Litton La, Dublin 1 ☎ 872 8389; fax 872 0039 e litton@indigo.ie 🚌 all cross-city ♿

Mount Eccles Court Budget Accommodation
(4, D6) Well-priced doubles as well as beds in 4-16 person dorms in a sprawling renovated Georgian town house. Clean, bright and with comfortable bedding, it's on one of the northside's most beautiful streets.
✉ 42 Great George's St N, Dublin 1 ☎ 873 0826; fax 878 3554 e info@eccles hostel .com; www.eccles hostel.com 🚌 11, 16, 41

Oliver St John Gogarty's Hostel
(5, C6) Next door to the popular Temple Bar pub of the same name, this hostel has basic, clean dorm rooms with comfortable bunks and a number of high-quality twins, triples and quads. It can be very noisy.
✉ 18-21 Anglesea St, Temple Bar, Dublin 2 ☎ 671 1822; fax 671 7637 e olivergogartys @hotmail.com; www.olivergogartys .com 🚌 all cross-city ✕ restaurant & pub

Gay Stays
Most of the city's hotels wouldn't bat an eyelid if same-sex couples checked in, but the same can't be said of many of the city's B&Bs. Exclusively gay places include:

Frankie's Guesthouse (8 Camden Pl; 4, O5; ☎/fax 478 3087; e www.frankiesguesthouse.com) – 12 homey rooms in an old mews house, with cable TV, full Irish breakfast and a plant-filled roof terrace
Inn on the Liffey (21 Ormond Quay Upper; 4, H3; ☎ 677 0828, fax 872 4165, e innontheliffey@hot mail.com) – clean and neat rooms on the northside quays, and guests have free access to the Dock sauna

facts for the visitor

Doug McKinlay

Four Courts and the O'Donovan Rossa Bridge

VAL & DEPARTURE

is accessible by air and sea,
direct flights from Europe and
USA, ferry links to the UK and
nce, as well as bus-ferry combin-
ions to/from the UK. The prolifer-
ation of low-cost airlines mean
discounted tickets to/from Europe
are often available. However, from
the US it is usually cheaper to fly to
London and connect to Dublin.

Air

Dublin airport (1, A4) is 13km north
of the city centre. It has an exchange
bureau and a Bank of Ireland offering currency exchange. There's a
post office, a Dublin Tourism office,
a transport desk with train and bus
details, plus a choice of shops and
car-hire counters.

Left Luggage
The Greencaps Left Luggage &
Porterage office (☎ 814 4633), in
the car park atrium, is open daily
6am-11pm. It charges €3.20-4.45
per item for 24 hours.

Information

General Inquiries
☎ 814 1111

Flight Information
Aer Lingus ☎ 886 6705; British Midland
☎ 814 4259; City Jet ☎ 844 5577;
Ryanair ☎ 1550 200 200

Car park Information
☎ 814 4328

Online airport information
e www.dublin-airport.com

Airport Access
Three different bus services as well as
taxis connect the airport to the city.

Airlink Express Operated by
Dublin Bus (☎ 872 0000, 873 4222),
Airlink Express runs two buses at a
flat rate of €4.50: No 747, to/from
the central bus station (Busáras,

4, F9) and Dublin Bus offices on
O'Connell St (4, F6); and No 748,
to/from Heuston (3, E6) and
Connolly (4, E10) stations. The trip
takes 30-40 minutes or more.

Aircoach With luxury air-con
buses, Aircoach (☎ 844 7118,
e www.aircoach.ie) operates between the airport and 15 locations
in Dublin 5am-11.30pm daily. Stops
include: Gresham Hotel (4, E6), cnr
Trinity College and Grafton St
(2, D1), Merrion Square (4, L9),
Dawson St (6, E8) and Leeson St.
Another service goes to the International Financial Services Centre
(4, G9) and Connolly station (4, E10)
before going north to Malahide.
One-way trips cost €5.10.

Public Bus The much slower public
bus service is a less attractive option.
Nos 41, 41a and 41c go to Eden
Quay near O'Connell St (4, G7). The
often crowded journey can take
over an hour, but at €1.40 it's cheap.

Taxi A taxi to the centre takes
about half an hour and costs around
€16.50. There's a supplementary
charge of €1 from the airport and
additional charges for baggage.

Bus

Busáras (4, F9), on Store St, is
Dublin's central bus station and
home to Bus Éireann (☎ 836 6111,
e www.buseireann.ie), the Republic's national bus line. There's
also a Bus Éireann desk in the
Dublin Bus information office
(4, F6) on O'Connell St. Private bus
companies that run services around
the country include Nestor Coaches
(☎ 832 0094) to Galway, and
JJ Kavanagh Rapid Express (☎ 679
1549) to Waterford and Limerick.
   Bus Éireann and, from the UK,
National Express (☎ 0870 5808080,

[e] www.gobycoach.com) also operate Eurolines services ([e] www.eurolines.com) direct from London and other UK centres to Dublin. Slattery's of London (UK ☎ 020-7730 3666, 7482 1604) has routes from/to the UK, but journeys can be cramped and delays common.

Irish Rambler tickets (€41 for three days, €92 for eight days and €133 for 15 days) are available from Bus Éireann and allow unlimited bus travel within the Republic.

Train

The train network is improving but is still slow, poorly maintained and expensive. Iarnród Éireann (Irish Rail; 35 Abbey St Lwr, Dublin 1; 4, G7; ☎ 836 6222; [e] www.irishrail.ie) operates the Republic's trains on routes that fan out from Dublin.

Connolly station (☎ 836 3333) has trains to Belfast, Derry and other points in the north. Heuston station (☎ 836 5421) has services to Cork, Galway, Limerick and other points throughout the Republic.

The Emerald Card (€157.50 for eight days' travel over 15 days, or €272 for 15 days in 30) gives you unlimited travel throughout the Republic and Northern Ireland on several carriers.

Ferry

Ferry services from Britain sail to two ports in Dublin. The Dublin city ferry terminal (☎ 855 2222) is 3km from the centre and public transport is linked to departures and arrivals. Dun Laoghaire's Carlisle ferry terminal (☎ 280 1905), on the southern side of Dublin Bay, is easily accessible by DART or public bus.

From the UK, Stena Line (☎ 0990 707070, [e] www.stenaline.co.uk) operates speedy passenger and car services from Holyhead in Wales to Dun Laoghaire (1½ hrs) and a car-only ferry Holyhead-Dublin (3½ hrs). Irish Ferries (UK ☎ 0990 171717;

[e] www.irishferries.com) operates passenger and car ferries from Holyhead to Dublin. Stena Line has an office at Dun Laoghaire (☎ 204 7600) while Irish Ferries has a city office at 2-4 Merrion Row (4, M8; ☎ 1890 313131).

Travel Documents

Passport
Passports are not required by UK-born British citizens travelling from Britain, but bring some ID. EU citizens may use a passport or national ID card. All other nationalities must carry a valid passport.

Visa
EU citizens can stay indefinitely and nationals of Australia, Canada, Japan, New Zealand, South Africa and the USA need no visa if entering as a tourist for up to three months.

Return/Onward Ticket
A return or onward ticket may be required if there's any doubt that you have sufficient funds to support yourself in Ireland.

Customs

The import and export of currency is unrestricted. Goods brought in and exported within the EU incur no additional taxes, provided duty has been paid in the EU and goods are for personal consumption.

Duty Free

Duty-free sales within the EU no longer exist. For those travelling between Ireland and a non-EU country, duty-free limits are: 200 cigarettes, 2L of wine, 1L of spirits or strong liquor (over 22% alcohol), 60mL of perfume, and 250mL of eau de toilette.

Departure Tax

Airport taxes are always prepaid with your air ticket.

GETTING AROUND

Dublin's buses and train service do little to ease the appalling street congestion. Getting around the centre is best done on foot or bicycle and trips further out should be timed to avoid rush hours. Thankfully the Luas light rail service is under construction.

Travel Passes

Rambler bus passes are available for 1/3/5/7 days for €4.40/8.25/12.70/15.87. A one-day family Rambler is excellent value.

Rail-only passes, for DART and suburban train services, cost €15.87/57.50 for a week/month. An adult pass combining rail and bus costs €6.60/12.70/21.59 for 1/4/7 days (ID photo required).

Bus passes should be bought in advance from Dublin Bus (see below) or from the many ticket agents around the city (look for signs in shop windows). Buy rail passes from any DART or suburban rail stations, or the Irish Railways Office (35 Abbey St Lwr; 4, G7; ☎ 836 6222).

Bus

Dublin Bus (4, F6; ☎ 873 4222, e www.dublinbus.ie), at 59 O'Connell St Upper, is open Mon 8.30am-5.30pm, Tues-Fri 9am-5.30pm and Sat 9am-1pm. The office provides free maps, timetables and advice.

Dublin buses are usually green double-deckers or small, red-and-yellow 'Imps'. They run 6am-11.30pm, less frequently on Sundays. Fares are calculated on stages travelled, from €0.85 for up to three stages to €1.50 for up to 23. Tender exact change when boarding; if you pay too much a receipt is issued, which is reimbursed at the Dublin Bus office.

Nitelink buses run on 22 routes Mon-Sat nights. Buses depart from College St, Westmoreland St and D'Olier St (4, J7). Tues-Thurs, there are two departures, (12.30am and 2am). Fri-Sun departures are at 12.30am, 2am and every 20 minutes until 3.30am or 4.30am. Most journeys cost €3.80.

Train

Dublin Area Rapid Transport (DART) runs along the coast as far north as Howth and Malahide and as far south as Bray. Services depart every 10-20 minutes, 6.30am-midnight, less frequently on Sundays. One-way tickets from central Dublin to Dun Laoghaire/Howth cost €1.50; to Bray it's €1.70. A one-day unlimited DART ticket costs €5.10.

Taxi

Taxis can be hailed on the street or found at ranks, including O'Connell St, College Green and St Stephen's Green near Grafton St. It can be difficult to get a cab, especially Thurs to Sat after pubs close. Many companies dispatch taxis by radio but run out of cars at peak times; be sure to book as early as you can. Try City Cabs (☎ 872 7272) or National Radio Cabs (☎ 677 2222).

Flagfall is €2.40 , then €0.15 for every 1/9 mile (or 40 seconds); supplements include phone bookings (€2.50), night travel (€1) and luggage (€0.50 per item).

Bicycle

Exploring Dublin by bike can be convenient, quick and fun – but the traffic, aggressive drivers, lack of lock-up facilities and the high rate of theft are undeniable downsides.

Dublin Bike Tours & Rental (☎ 679 0899; e www.dublinbike tours.com; open Apr-Oct), based in the Harding Hotel on Fishamble St (4, K3), rents Raleigh Pioneers and Tourers for €12.70/50 a day/week. Panniers, helmets, baby seats and rain gear are available.

Car & Motorcycle

With severe congestion, scarce parking, diligent traffic wardens and even more committed car thieves, it's hardly worth driving in central Dublin. Secure car parks are recommended by police – but they can be expensive. Leaded petrol costs about €1 a litre with unleaded a bit less.

Road Rules

Driving is on the left. It's obligatory to wear a seatbelt and children under 12 are not allowed in front seats. Motorcyclists must wear helmets. Speed limits are 70mph (112km/h) on motorways, 60mph (96km/h) on other roads and 30mph (48km/h) in towns. The blood-alcohol limit is 80mg of alcohol per 100mL of blood – or 0.08%.

Rental

Dublin's international car rental firms include Avis (☎ 605 7555 e www.avis.com), Budget (☎ 9802, e www.budgetcarrenta and Hertz (☎ 660 2255, e w .hertz.com). Local compani include Argus (☎ 490 4444 e www.argus-rentacar.com) and Murrays Europcar (☎ 614 2800, e www.europcar.com). Typical high season rates start at €45/240 a day/week.

Driving Licence & Permit

To drive in Ireland pack your home-country licence or an International Driving Permit.

Motoring Organisations

The Automobile Association of Ireland (AA; ☎ 617 9950) is at 23 Suffolk St (6, A6) and their breakdown number is ☎ 1800 667 788. Similar organisations in other countries have reciprocal arrangements with the AA but services usually only extend to a free tow.

PRACTICAL INFORMATION

Climate & When to Go

The peak period is July-August when the weather is warmest and days longest, but expect big crowds at sights, higher costs and scarce accommodation. In quieter winter months weather is usually miserable, days shorter and some tourist facilities shut. June or September are best: weather is pleasant, it's less crowded and everything is open. Visiting around St Patrick's Day (March 17) is recommended as the city celebrates with a parade, fireworks, street dancing and other events.

Tourist Information

Tourist Information Abroad

Information on Dublin and all of Ireland is available from the national tourist office, Bord Fáilte (e www.ireland.travel.ie), whose overseas offices include:

Australia
   5th fl, 36 Carrington St, Sydney 2000 (☎ 02-9299 6177)

Canada
   Suite 934, 160 Bloor St East, Toronto M4W 1B9 (☎ 416-929 2777)

Dublin
Elevation 47m/-154ft

Rainfall (mm): 100, 75, 50, 25, 0

Temperature (°C): 30, 20, 10, 0, -10 — (°F): 86, 68, 50, 32, 14

J F M A M J J A S O N D

...rue de Miromesnil, 75008 Paris
(☎ 01-7020 0020)

...w Zealand
2nd fl, Dingwall Building, 87 Queen St, Auckland 1 (☎ 09-379 8720)

Northern Ireland
53 Castle St, Belfast, BT1 1GH (☎ 028-9032 7888)

UK
Ireland House, 150 New Bond St, London W1S 2AQ (☎ 0800 039 7000)

USA
345 Park Ave, New York, NY 10154 (☎ 212-418 0800 or 1 800 223 6470)

Local Tourist Information

The main tourist authority is Dublin Tourism, with three city-centre offices. The Dublin Tourism Centre (☎ 605 7700, e information@ dublintourism.ie; www.visitdublin .ie), at 2 Suffolk St (6, A6), is by far the biggest. In July and August it's open Mon-Sat 8.30am-6.30pm and Sun 10.30am-3.30pm; the rest of the year it's Mon-Sat 9am-5.30pm and bank holidays 10.30am-3pm. As well as being a great source of information, the centre can book accommodation and tours.

The other Dublin Tourism branches are at 14 O'Connell St (4, F6; Mon-Sat 9am-5pm) and Baggot St Bridge (3, G12; Mon-Fri 9.30am-5pm), in the foyer of the Bord Fáilte office (☎ 1 850 230 330), which provides information on the rest of the country.

All the Dublin Tourism offices are walk-in services only. Phone bookings and reservations are provided by Gulliver Info Res, a computerised service that is available through Dublin Tourism offices and worldwide. It provides up-to-date information on events, attractions and transport as well as booking accommodation. In Ireland call ☎ 1 800 668 668; in Britain ☎ 0800 668 668 66; from the rest of the world ☎ +353 669 792 083.

Embassies

Australia
2nd fl, Fitzwilton House, Wilton Terrace, Dublin 2 (4, P9; ☎ 676 1517)

Canada
4th fl, 65-68 St Stephen's Green, Dublin 2 (4, N7; ☎ 478 1988)

New Zealand
Closest embassy is London: New Zealand House, Haymarket, London SW1 4QT (☎ +44-20-7930 8422)

South Africa
Earlsfort Centre, Earlsfort Tce, Dublin 2 (4, O7; ☎ 661 5553)

UK
29 Merrion Rd, Dublin 4 (3, J14; ☎ 205 3700)

USA
42 Elgin Rd, Dublin 4 (3, H13; ☎ 668 8777)

Money

Currency

On 1 January, 2002, Ireland adopted the European single currency, the euro (€). Ireland's old currency, the punt (£), was to be withdrawn and the changeover complete by July 1, 2002. For more information, visit the European Union's website (e www.europa.eu.int/euro/html/ entry.html) or Euro Changeover Board of Ireland (e www.irlgov .ie/ecbi-euro).

The euro (€) is divided into 100 cents (c). Coins come in 1c, 2c, 5c, 10c, 20c and 50c, as well as €1 and €2. Note denominations are: €5, €10, €20, €50, €100, €200 and €500.

The punt is converted at a set rate of £0.787564 to €1. In this book, where new euro prices were not available at the time of research we have made a direct conversion based on the official rate.

Travellers Cheques

Most major brands of travellers cheques are accepted in Ireland

and can be cashed at banks, exchange offices and some post offices. American Express (☎ 679 9000) is at 41 Nassau St (6, B7), while Thomas Cook (☎ 677 1721) is at 118 Grafton St (6, E6). Travellers cheques are rarely accepted for everyday transactions so cash them beforehand.

Credit Cards
Major credit cards, especially American Express, MasterCard and Visa, are widely accepted, though some B&Bs only take cash. For 24hr card cancellations or assistance call:

American Express	☎ 1800 282 728
Diners Club	☎ 1800 409 204
MasterCard	☎ 1800 557 378
Visa	☎ 1800 558 002

ATMs
Irish ATMs are linked up to international systems such as Cirrus, Maestro or Plus. The Allied Irish Bank (AIB) and Bank of Ireland have many centrally located ATMs.

Changing Money
Banks usually have the best exchange rates and lowest commission charges, though moneychangers open later and have shorter queues. Many post offices have currency exchange counters. There's a cluster of banks in College Green, opposite Trinity College, all with exchange facilities. The bureau de change at the Bank of Ireland headquarters, Westmoreland St (5, C8), is open Mon-Fri 8am-10pm, Sat 9am-10pm and Sun 10am-10pm in high season.

Tipping

Tipping is becoming more common, but is still not as prevalent as in the USA or the rest of Europe. If a restaurant adds a service charge (usually 10%) no tip is required. If not, most people tip 10% and round up taxi fares. For hotel porters €1 per bag is acceptable.

Discounts

Most of Dublin's attractions offer discounts to children under 16, students and OAPs (old age pensioners). Family tickets usually give entry to two adults and two children, although public transport passes for families allow up to four children.

Heritage Cards (see p. 13) give unlimited admission for one year to sites managed by Dúchas in Dublin and Ireland.

Student & Youth Cards
The International Student Identity Card (ISIC) is accepted at sights and on public transport. The An Óige (Irish Youth Hostel Association; 61 Mountjoy St; 4, C4; ☎ 830 4555) sells a card for €15.25 that offers discounts at hostels.

Seniors' Cards
Senior citizens usually need only show proof of age to receive discounts, including government and privately run sights and on public transport.

Travel Insurance

A policy covering theft, loss, medical expenses and compensation for cancellation or delays is highly recommended. If items are lost or stolen, make sure you get a police report straight away or your insurer might not pay up.

Opening Hours

Banks
    Mon-Wed & Fri 10am-4pm, Thurs 10am-5pm

Offices
    Mon-Fri 9am-5pm

Shops
    Most open Mon-Sat 9am or 10am-6pm, Sun noon-6pm. On Thurs many shops stay open later (around 8pm), while some are closed on Sun.

Public Holidays

Jan 1	New Year's Day
Mar 17	St Patrick's Day
Mar/Apr	Good Friday
Mar/Apr	Easter Monday
May 1	May Day
June	June Holiday (1st Mon)
Aug	August Holiday (1st Mon)
Oct	October Holiday (last Mon)
Dec 25	Christmas Day
Dec 26	St Stephen's Day

Time

Dublin Standard Time is on GMT/UTC. Daylight-saving time is practised mid-March–late October. At noon in Dublin it's:

7am in New York
3am in Los Angeles
noon in London
2pm in Johannesburg
midnight in Auckland
10pm in Sydney

Electricity

Electricity is 220V, 50Hz AC. Plugs and sockets are the flat three-pin type, as in Britain. Adaptors are widely available. Travellers from North America will need a voltage converter for 110V appliances.

Weights & Measures

Ireland is slowly moving towards the metric system but imperial measurements are still common. All green roadsigns and newer white ones give distances in kilometres, older white ones use miles. Speed limits are in miles, food is priced and weighed in kilos or pounds (depending on where it's being sold), beer comes in pints and half pints. See the conversion table on p. 122.

Post

An Post (the Irish Postal Service) is reliable, efficient and usually on time. Aside from the GPO (4, G6) on O'Connell St, the post offices on Anne St S (6, D7) and St Andrew's St (6, A6) are close to the centre. Some newsagents operate as sub-post offices, and most sell stamps. All mail to Britain and Europe goes by air so there's no need to use airmail envelopes or stickers.

Postal Rates

Within Ireland and to Britain, all letters up to 25g cost 38c; to the rest of the EU 41c, and the rest of the world 57c. Anything heavier than 25g is more expensive: a first class (priority) 50g letter, for instance, will cost 44c within Ireland, 51c to Britain, 83c to Europe and 95c elsewhere. Second class (economy) rates are cheaper but delivery is much slower.

Opening Hours

The GPO is open Mon-Sat 8am-8pm, Sun 10am-6.30pm. Regular branches are open Mon-Fri 8.30am-5.30pm or 6pm, Sat 9am-1pm.

Telephone

Local calls from a public phone cost €0.25 for three minutes. Eircom is Ireland's largest service provider, and all of Dublin's public phones bear its name. Public phones accept coins, phonecards and/or credit cards or reverse charges.

The cheapest place for international calls in Dublin is at Talk Shop (www.talkshop.ie), with several branches across the city centre, including The Granary, 20 Temple Lane (5, D4; ☎ 672 7212; 9am-11pm) and 5 O'Connell St Upper (4, F6; ☎ 872 0200; 9am-11pm).

Phonecards

Prepaid phonecards (known as callcards) are widely available from newsagents, post offices and convenience stores. They come in units of 10 (€2.55), 20 (€4.45) and 50 (€10.15). One unit equals a local phone call. Lonely Planet's eKno Communication Card, specifically aimed at travellers, provides competitive international calls (avoid using it for local calls), messaging services and free email. Logon to **e** www.ekno.lonelyplanet.com for information on joining and accessing the service.

Mobile Phones

Ireland uses the GSM 900/1800 cellular phone system, which is compatible with European and Australian but not North American or Japanese phones. There are three Irish service providers: Eircell (087), ESAT Digifone (086) and Meteor (085). All have links with most international GSM providers, which allow you to 'roam' onto a local service on arrival. You can also purchase a pay-as-you-go package with a local provider as long as you have your own mobile phone.

Country & City Codes

Ireland	☎ 353
Dublin	☎ 01

To ring Dublin from abroad, drop the 0 from the city code before dialing the local number (eg, ☎ +353 1-444 4444). From within Ireland, dial the 01 Dublin code before the local number (eg, ☎ 01-444 4444). The same goes for mobile phones – if calling a mobile from abroad, drop the 0 at the start, and keep the 0 if you're calling locally.

Useful Numbers

Directory Inquiries	☎ 11811
International Directory Inquiries	☎ 11818
International Operator	☎ 114
Ireland/Great Britain Operator	☎ 10
Time	☎ 1191
Weather	☎ 1550 123822

International Direct Dial Codes

Dial ☎ 00 followed by:

Australia	☎ 61
Canada	☎ 1
Japan	☎ 81
New Zealand	☎ 64
South Africa	☎ 27
UK	☎ 44
USA	☎ 1

Email/www

Internet cafes are dotted all over and many open late. If you've packed your laptop, note that the Republic uses square-pinned, three-pronged power plug (like the UK) and most hotels take RJ-11 phone jacks.

Internet Service Providers

Most major global ISPs have dial-in nodes in Ireland; it's best to download lists of dial-in numbers before you leave home. If you access the Internet through a smaller ISP, your best option is to open an account with a global ISP or sign on to a local provider while in Ireland. In Dublin, local ISPs include Eircom.net, Oceanfree and IOL, who offer a non-subscription-based service with timed usage charged on a metered phone line.

Internet Cafes

If you can't access the Internet from your hotel, try a cybercafe:

Central Cyber Cafe
1st fl, 6 Grafton St (6, B7; ☎ 677 8298; **e** www.centralcafe.ie; €1.60/15mins, 20% student discount). Open Mon-Fri 8am-11pm, Sat 9am-11pm, Sun 10am-10pm.

Global Internet Café
Basement, 8 O'Connell St Lower, Dublin 1 (4, G7; ☎ 878 0295; **e** www.global cafe.ie). Prices and opening hours as for Central Cyber Cafe (above).

Internet Exchange
3 Cecilia St, Dublin 2 (5, C4; ☎ 670 3000; **e** www.internet-exchange.co.uk; from €2.50/hr off-peak). Open 9am-11pm.

Does Not Compute

Unit 2, Pudding Row, Essex St West, Temple Bar (4, J4; ☎ 670 4464; **e** www.doesnotcompute.ie; from €2.50/hr off-peak). Open Sun-Thurs 24hrs, Fri-Sat 10am-11pm. Also at Bleeding Horse pub, 25 Camden St Upper (4, P5; ☎ 4766 4928). Open Mon-Fri 10am-11pm, Sat-Sun 12pm-11pm.

Useful Sites

The Lonely Planet website (**e** www.lonelyplanet.com) offers a speedy link to many of Dublin's websites. Others to try include:

Bord Fáilte
e www.ireland.travel.ie

Dublin Tourism
e www.visitdublin.com

Irish Times
e www.ireland.com

Indigo (Internet Service Provider)
e www.indigo.ie

The Real Dublin Pub Guide
e www.dublinpubs.net

Doing Business

The Industrial Development Authority (IDA; **e** www.idaireland.com) is a state-run organisation responsible for attracting new business to Ireland and encouraging those already there to expand. The Dublin Chamber of Commerce (7 Clare St, Dublin 2; ☎ 661 4111) and Chamber of Commerce of Ireland (22 Merrion Sq, Dublin 2; ☎ 661 2888; **e** www.chambersireland.ie) are also useful contacts.

Premier Business Centres (☎ 639 1218; **e** www.premgroup.com) have several serviced offices in Dublin with boardrooms, secretarial services, voice mailboxes, ISDN lines, teleconferencing and full office facilities. Words Language Services (70 Baggot St Lwr, Dublin 2; ☎ 661 0240) do translations for corporate needs.

Newspapers & Magazines

The main Irish dailies are the *Irish Times* (**e** www.ireland.com), *Irish Independent* (**e** www.independ ent ie) and *Irish Examiner* (**e** www .irishexaminer.ie). The *Evening Herald* is an evening tabloid, while Sunday papers include the *Sunday Tribune* and the *Sunday Business Post*, the best financial newspaper in the country. *In Dublin* is the main entertainment listings magazine.

British papers and magazines are available on the day of issue and are cheaper than Irish papers. Eason's on O'Connell St (4, G6; ☎ 837 3811) and other large newsagents sell wide selections of foreign and regional Irish papers.

Radio

Radio na Telefís Éireann (RTE) is Ireland's government-sponsored national broadcasting body. There are three state-controlled radio stations. Two – RTE Radio 1 (89.6FM) and RTE's 2FM (91.8FM) – are broadcast in English, and Radio na Gaeltachta in Irish. Commercial stations include: 98FM, 104FM and Today FM (100 to 102 on the dial) for classic rock. Also worth checking out are some of the unlicensed 'pirate' stations, including Power FM (97.2FM) which offers a mix of dance music; XFM (107.1FM), an alternative station; and Trinity FM (96.7FM), the city's only college radio.

TV

Ireland has three state-controlled TV channels: RTE 1, Network 2 and the Irish-language TnaG. There's also an independent station, TV3. British BBC1 and BBC2, ITV and Channel 4 programs can also be picked up. Satellite TV channels include Sky, MTV and UK Gold.

Photography & Video

Print and slide film, camera gear and repairs are readily available from the many camera shops in the centre. Developing and printing a 24-exposure print film typically costs around €10.50 at a one-hour service or from €6.50 for a slower turnaround. Slide processing costs about €9 a roll.

Ireland uses the VHF PAL system for video, which is incompatible with NTSC or SECAM.

Health

Immunisations
No vaccinations are required enter Ireland.

Precautions
Dublin has no serious health problems. Although Ireland is still a largely rural country, there is no risk of rabies due to stringent laws that banning importation of any animal products. Dublin's tap water is safe to drink and food preparation is hygienic. Be prepared for lots of rain, even in summer.

Insurance & Medical Treatment
Travel insurance is advisable to cover medical treatment you may need while in Dublin. The Eastern Regional Health Authority (☎ 679 0700, 1800 520 520; e www.erha.ie), Dr Steevens' Hospital, Dublin 8 (3, E6), has a Choice of Doctor Scheme, which can advise on suitable doctors 9am-5pm, Mon-Fri. Your hotel or embassy can also suggest a doctor.

Several countries have reciprocal agreements with Ireland for treatment of visitors. EU Citizens are entitled to free hospital treatment and should obtain an E111 form prior to departure. The system does not cover US or Canadian visitors. Ask your insurance agent or broker before you travel if your health plan is valid in Ireland.

Medical Services
Hospitals with 24hr accident and emergency departments include:

Mater Misericordiae Hospital
    Eccles St, Dublin 7 (4, A4; ☎ 803 2000)
St James's Hospital
    James St, Dublin 8 (3, F6; ☎ 453 7941)

Dental Services
If you chip a tooth or require emergency treatment, head to the Dental Hospital, 20 Lincoln Pl (2, E5; ☎ 612 7200). Be there at 8am to secure a consultation ticket for morning sessions, or at midday for afternoon sessions.

Pharmacies
The following pharmacies are open late:

O'Connell's Late Night Pharmacy
    55 O'Connell St (4, G7; ☎ 873 0427; 7.30am-10pm)
Dame St Pharmacy
    16 Dame St (5, E3; ☎ 670 4523; 8am-10pm)

Toilets

Dublin has virtually no public toilets in the city centre. If you need to go, try a bar; if it is empty and you're not buying a drink, it's best to ask the bartender for permission to use the toilet first. All big shopping complexes, like St Stephen's Green (4, E5) and the Jervis Centre (4, G5), have toilets, as do some department stores.

Safety Concerns

Dublin is one of Europe's safest capitals, but recently its good reputation has been marred by increasing petty crime and racism. Pickpocketing, bag-snatching and car break-ins are on the rise, so don't show off valuables, keep wallets tucked away and never leave anything in vehicles. Pushbikes are top targets and locals recommend using two locks to secure both wheels and taking your seat with you!

Certain parts of Dublin are unsafe and visitors should avoid run-down, deserted-looking and poorly lit areas. Phoenix Park is not safe at night, and Dolphin's Barn in the inner south-west is best avoided any time of day. Unfortunately, many cheap traveller hostels are in the rougher parts of north Dublin, where heroin is a big problem.

Drink induced violence can sometimes erupt as drunk youths spill onto the streets at pub closing time. Increased immigration has stirred racism and many black or Asian people in Dublin have experienced forms of racial harassment. Thankfully, violence is infrequent. If you are taunted on the street, keep calm and don't engage abusers in conversation. Report serious incidents to police.

Lost Property
Report all lost property to police to validate insurance claims. To retrieve lost items call: Dublin Bus ☎ 703 1321; Bus Éireann ☎ 703 2489; Dublin airport ☎ 814 4483; Connolly station ☎ 703 2363; Heuston station ☎ 703 2102; Taxis Carriage Office (☎ 475 5888); Ferry Services ☎ 855 2296.

Keeping Copies
Make photocopies of all your important documents, keep some with you, separate from the originals, and leave a copy at home. You can also store details of documents in Lonely Planet's free online Travel Vault, password-protected and accessible worldwide. See ⓔ www.ekno.lonelyplanet.com.

Emergency Numbers

Ambulance, Fire, Police	☎ 999 or 112
Police (non-emergency)	☎ 666 6666
Rape Crisis Line	☎ 1800 778 888

Women Travellers

In Dublin women are treated in the same way as they are in any other cosmopolitan city, but outside the city old-fashioned attitudes prevail. As in every other city, lone women should exercise caution when walking at night or in dodgy areas.

Tampons are widely available at chemists or supermarkets, and oral contraceptives are available with a doctor's prescription. The Well Woman Centre (67 Pembroke Rd; 3, H12; ☎ 660 9860) advises on women's health issues and can prescribe the morning-after pill.

Gay & Lesbian Travellers

For such an overwhelmingly Catholic country, Irish laws on homosexuality are surprisingly liberal and progressive. Despite its dogma on the matter, the Catholic Church has maintained a silent neutrality on the issue. In Dublin the gay and lesbian scene is loud, proud and very vibrant. It is most obvious in the city centre, with several gay bars and clubs around Temple Bar and another batch of bars and saunas on the northside around Ormond Quay (see p. 101). There are even a couple of specialist gay B&Bs (p. 108). Ireland's gay and lesbian orientated websites have all kinds of information and include Gay Ireland (ⓔ www.gay-ireland.com) and Channel Queer (ⓔ www.channelqueer.com).

Information & Organisations
The magazine *In Dublin* has a gay and lesbian section. The free monthly *Gay Community News* (ⓔ www.gcn.ie) is available at Temple Bar Information Centre on Eustace St (5, C3; ☎ 671 5717) and various cafes and bars.

Outhouse (☎ 873 4932, ⓔ www.outhouse.ie) is the national Lesbian & Gay federation. The Gay Switchboard (☎ 872 1055) takes calls Sun-Fri 8-10pm and Sat 3.30-6pm, while the Lesbian Line (☎ 872 9911) is open Thurs 7-9pm.

Senior Travellers

Dublin's manageable size and the proximity of major sights make it a highly accessible destination for seniors. Almost all sights offer senior discounts on production of relevant identification.

Bus drivers are usually friendly and patient with seniors who need extra time getting on and off, and most buses have designated seats for older travellers.

Disabled Travellers

Guesthouses, hotels and sights in Ireland are slowly being adapted for people with disabilities though there is still a long way to go. A great deal of sights, hotels and shops are in historic buildings which have no disabled access and cannot have lifts or ramps installed because of preservation orders.

Public transport is also problematic; some very new buses have low floors and designated wheelchair spots, many do not. For train travel, call ahead for an employee of Iarnród Éireann (Irish Rail) to accompany you to the train and arrange for someone to help you off at your destination.

For venues listed in this book, a wheelchair icon and the description 'excellent' indicate that access is available throughout the venue. A 'good' rating means that there are some facilities and 'poor' means that there are few available. If in doubt, call ahead to check.

Information & Organisations

Bord Fáilte's annual accommodation guide, *Be Our Guest*, gives places that are accessible by wheelchair. You can obtain general information on ☎ 1800 350 150, a free hotline, or from Comhairle (☎ 874 7503).

Other useful organisations include: The Catholic Institute for the Deaf (☎ 830 0522); Cerebral Palsy Ireland (☎ 269 5355); Cystic Fibrosis Association of Ireland (☎ 496 2433); Irish Wheelchair Association (☎ 661 6183).

Language

English is spoken in Dublin. Although Irish (a Gaelic language) is spoken in parts of rural Ireland, most Dubliners speak a pidgin version of the language, if at all. Still, Irish is considered the official language of Ireland, and all official documents and street signs are in Irish or bilingual.

Dubliners' command of English – particularly the inventive use of vocabulary – has been lauded throughout the English-speaking world. The syntax used by Dubliners – and the Irish in general – involves a unique word order that is usually related to the Irish language. One linguistic peculiarity is the use of 'after' in such constructions as 'I'm just after my dinner', which is a way of saying 'I have just had my dinner'.

But it is in the art of word choice that Dubliners truly excel. Dubliners never get drunk – they get stewed, stocious, hammered, locked, mouldy, fluthered, creased, elephants – or a dozen other words that describe their various states of inebriation.

When 'dare's drink taken', Dubliners are pretty adept at trading insults. If you are intent on causing trouble you'll be dismissed as a 'gouger' or a 'scut', while if you're prone to saying the wrong thing at the wrong time you'll have to live with being described as a 'gobdaw'.

In a more docile mood, Dubliners refer to each other in a unique way. 'Me old segosha' (ostensibly derived from the sequoia tree, inferring solid and sturdy) is a longtime friend; a nice person is described as being a 'good head' or a 'decent oul' skin'; while someone who's the life and soul of the party is 'a panic'.

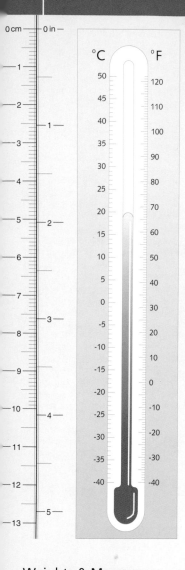

Conversion Table

Clothing Sizes
Measurements approximate only; try before you buy.

Women's Clothing
Aust/NZ	8	10	12	14	16	18
Europe	36	38	40	42	44	46
Japan	5	7	9	11	13	15
UK	8	10	12	14	16	18
USA	6	8	10	12	14	16

Women's Shoes
Aust/NZ	5	6	7	8	9	10
Europe	35	36	37	38	39	40
France only	35	36	38	39	40	42
Japan	22	23	24	25	26	27
UK	3½	4½	5½	6½	7½	8½
USA	5	6	7	8	9	10

Men's Clothing
Aust/NZ	92	96	100	104	108	112
Europe	46	48	50	52	54	56
Japan	S		M	M		L
UK	35	36	37	38	39	40
USA	35	36	37	38	39	40

Men's Shirts (Collar Sizes)
Aust/NZ	38	39	40	41	42	43
Europe	38	39	40	41	42	43
Japan	38	39	40	41	42	43
UK	15	15½	16	16½	17	17½
USA	15	15½	16	16½	17	17½

Men's Shoes
Aust/NZ	7	8	9	10	11	12
Europe	41	42	43	44½	46	47
Japan	26	27	27.5	28	29	30
UK	7	8	9	10	11	12
USA	7½	8½	9½	10½	11½	12½

Weights & Measures

Weight
1kg = 2.2lb
1lb = 0.45kg
1g = 0.04oz
1oz = 28g

Volume
1 litre = 0.26 US gallons
1 US gallon = 3.8 litres
1 litre = 0.22 imperial gallons
1 imperial gallon = 4.55 litres

Length & Distance
1 inch = 2.54cm
1cm = 0.39 inches
1m = 3.3ft = 1.1yds
1ft = 0.3m
1km = 0.62 miles
1 mile = 1.6km

lonely planet

Lonely Planet is the world's most successful independent travel information company with offices in Australia, the US, UK and France. With a reputation for comprehensive, reliable travel information, Lonely Planet is a print and electronic publishing leader, with over 650 titles and 22 series catering for travellers' individual needs.

At Lonely Planet we believe that travellers can make a positive contribution to the countries they visit – if they respect their host communities and spend their money wisely. Since 1986 a percentage of the income from books has been donated to aid and human rights projects.

www.lonelyplanet.com

For news, views and free subscriptions to print and email newsletters, and a full list of LP titles, click on Lonely Planet's award-winning website.

On the Town

A romantic escape to Paris or a mad shopping dash through New York City, the locals' secret bars or a city's top attractions – whether you have 24 hours to kill or months to explore, Lonely Planet's On the Town products will give you the low-down.

Condensed guides are ideal pocket guides for when time is tight. Their quick-view maps, full-colour layout and opinionated reviews help short-term visitors target the top sights and discover the very best eating, shopping and entertainment options a city has to offer.

For more indepth coverage, **City guides** offer insights into a city's character and cultural background as well as providing broad coverage of where to eat, stay and play. **CitySync**, a digital guide for your handheld unit, allows you to reference stacks of opinionated, well-researched travel information. Portable and durable **City Maps** are perfect for locating those back-street bars or hard-to-find local haunts.

'Ideal for a generation of fast movers.'

– Gourmet Traveller on Condensed guides

Condensed Guides

- Amsterdam
- Athens (May 2002)
- Barcelona (May 2002)
- Boston
- California
- Chicago
- Crete
- Dublin
- Frankfurt
- Hong Kong
- London
- New York City
- Paris
- Prague (May 2002)
- Rome .
- Sydney
- Tokyo
- Venice (June 2002)
- Washington, DC (May 2002)

index

See also separate indexes for Places to Eat (p. 126), Places to Stay (p. 127), Shops (p. 127) and Sights with map references (p. 128).

PLACES TO EAT

PLACES TO STAY

SHOPS

sights – quick index